— As.

— Metaxological

— The Gift of Being (97)
  & INDIFFERENCE on God.

THE WILLIAM DESMOND READER

conatus essendi — the striving, struggle
for living

passio essendi — the pure giftedness
of our being which is the prior
foundation on which the later is
built.

The Buffered self
→ Porous self
  & the End of Metaphysics

Aft replaces th pirous selfs
need for transcendence.
↳ music as the
  new T₃

— The Buffered self, the pirous self,
  and the relation to transcendence
  (or & the new transcendence)

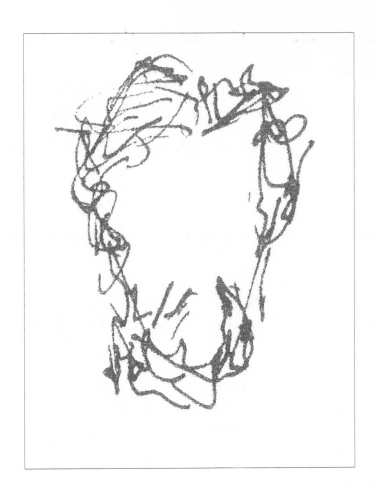

Sketch of William Desmond by Christopher Ben Simpson

THE WILLIAM DESMOND READER

EDITED AND WITH AN INTRODUCTION BY

CHRISTOPHER BEN SIMPSON

FOREWORD BY
JOHN D. CAPUTO

STATE UNIVERSITY OF NEW YORK PRESS

Frontispiece and cover illustrations of William Desmond by Christopher Ben Simpson

Published by
STATE UNIVERSITY OF NEW YORK PRESS, ALBANY

© 2012 State University of New York

All rights reserved

Printed in the United States of America

For information, contact
State University of New York Press, Albany, NY
www.sunypress.edu

Production, Laurie D. Searl
Marketing, Kate McDonnell

Library of Congress Cataloging-in-Publication Data

Desmond, William, 1951–
    [Selections. 2012]
    The William Desmond reader / edited and with an introduction by Christopher Ben Simpson.
        p. cm.
    Includes bibliographical references and index.
    ISBN 978-1-4384-4292-1 (pbk. : alk. paper)
    ISBN 978-1-4384-4291-4 (hardcover : alk. paper)
    I. Simpson, Christopher Ben, 1973–   II. Title.

B1626.D471 2012
192—dc23   2011035850

10 9 8 7 6 5 4 3 2 1

CONTENTS

PART IV

AESTHETICS AND PHILOSOPHY OF ART

PART V

RETROSPECTIONS AND REFLECTIONS

FOREWORD

William Desmond is one of the leading voices in contemporary philosophy in the continentalist tradition. Although Desmond is a skillful reader of philosophical texts and a renowned interpreter of the work of Hegel in particular, he is best known as an original philosopher in his own right, having been at the forefront over the years in cultivating a singularly contemporary style of metaphysics. Metaphysics in the grand style has gone out of fashion among philosophers in the postmodern and resolutely postmetaphysical tradition. But Desmond proposes an approach to metaphysics that avoids the extreme of a priori arguments, like the ontological proof, and adheres more closely to an experiential base.

The theoretical core and signature idea of Desmond's thought is the "between," which leads him to describe his work as a "metaxology" (from the Greek *metaxu*). The metaxological can be thought of as a different way to relate the same and the different, in contrast to the Hegelian way of "dialectical" mediation, which unites them in a higher unity. For the upshot of Hegelian mediation, he argues, is to close the circle between the same and the different and thereby to subordinate everything to the rule of a higher integration and sameness. The "between" means to keep this circle open and in that way to preserve difference. Never attaining the ground of a higher totalizing and integrating unity, the "between" occupies the open space that preserves the distance of the same from the different. The same does not return to itself through the different; rather the space of play between the same and the different is sustained, allowing for relations of otherness, difference, and plurality to obtain along several orders—between mind and being, immanence and transcendence, finite and infinite, and singular and universal. Desmond thus is able to orchestrate his leitmotif across several philosophical domains—including art, ethics, and religion—but the guiding insight is at root metaphysical.

Viewed in the light of postmetaphysical critiques of Hegel, Desmond's work invites three questions having to do in turn with classical metaphysics, contemporary phenomenological ontology, and the postmetaphysical.

First, how does the metaxological differ from the analogical? Is Desmond proposing a contemporary version of the classical theory of the analogy of being, which seems to be how he is taken by John Milbank.[1] In the analogy of being, being is everywhere itself yet everywhere diversified; the analogical does not fall into sheer equivocity, on the one side, even as, on the other side, the diversity of being is grounded in unity but without embracing a totalizing unity. There is a unity to the analogy of being in Aquinas, but not the totalizing and systematic one we find in early modern rationalists or in Hegel. What separates Desmond's thinking of the between from the metaphysics of analogy in Aquinas? Is it the role of the between to convey this venerable classical metaphysical motif in a contemporary setting?

Second, let us suppose, as I am inclined to suppose, that metaxology differs from a classical metaphysics of analogy because it emphasizes the concrete and experiential and eschews abstract a priori arguments and formal schemata such as "proportionality," which typify the classical style of metaphysics. If so, then we are led to ask the question that is put to him by Richard Kearney in the interview: how is metaxology related to contemporary phenomenology? How is metaxological metaphysics different from a contemporary phenomenological ontology? If, as Desmond says, he is inclined next to write a book of "songs," how different is this from Merleau-Ponty's conception of language as a song to the world? Is metaxology an exploration of the fundamental characteristics of being (classical metaphysics) but one that is precisely anchored by the experience of being (phenomenology), calling for a return to metaphysics but one that in fact sails the ship of metaphysics closer to the shores of experience than classical metaphysics? Are we to think it differs from classical metaphysics not in terms of substance but in terms of its *via*, of a style and approach more deeply experiential, and that it differs from phenomenology only in its Husserlian mode while extending the reach of phenomenology to the ontological?

Third, if the advantage of the metaxological schema is that it preserves difference, distance, concreteness, and the singular in a way that is lost in Hegel, then we are led to ask, at the other extreme, how it differs from the poststructuralist figures who make the same criticism of Hegel and strike out in the same direction of difference. The latter are faulted by Desmond for breaking the bonds of the between by overemphasizing difference and "equivocity" (in just the way monists break these bonds by overemphasizing sameness and univocity). What difference, we might ask, does the difference between poststructuralist difference and metaxological difference make?

Perhaps we are being asked by Desmond to think that the "between" is precisely between classical metaphysical analogy, phenomenological ontology and postmetaphysical difference. It is a tribute to Desmond's work that he provokes questions like this, which forces us to reconsider a wide-ranging and weighty series of issues that lie at the heart of the debates that take place in contemporary continental thought. His metaxological thinking is a unique and creative voice in the contemporary dialogue. But the "contemporary dialogue" in continental thought is changing, and this change bears directly on the place of Desmond's work today.

I would like to conclude with a remark on the timeliness of publishing this volume of Desmond's writings at the present moment, after the death of Derrida and his generation, which some see as a turning point in continental philosophy. For a long time now Desmond's fidelity to metaphysical thinking has been a minority view among continentalists, who have been variously shooting for something beyond, without or otherwise than being. Throughout Desmond remained undaunted and bravely took a stand with being and the goodness of being, sometimes feeling, I am sure, like the sole soldier still standing at his post. But we are at present witnessing a resurgence of interest in metaphysics, a resurrection of the question of the "real," and a reassessment of the philosophical tradition before Kant in which speculative thinking flourished.[2] For a new generation, the philosophical tradition from Kant on is dead—not only from Kant to Heidegger to Derrida, but also from Kant to Wittgenstein and contemporary analytic philosophy. Kant and the post-Kantians, the Kantian version of the "Copernican Revolution," are criticized for a subjectivism that has reduced the world to a construction of thought, language, or culture, for having reduced reality to its "correlation" with the mind. Accordingly, the renewal of realism advocated by the new generation means to replace mind with matter. The return of realism represents a return of a militant atheistic materialism for which the "absolute" means matter measured mercilessly by its mathematical properties. Any such realism would vigorously contest the metaphysical metaxological "agapeics" of Desmond as another round of nostalgia, another attempt to reenchant the real with religion, with the Good, or with the good old God, another round of putting a shine on being, or giving it a bit of a buzz, by way of a metaphysics that is more religious piety than real philosophy. The new realism is a ruthless repetition of rationalism, an attempt to disenchant the world anew, this time pulling up religion by the roots. It would no doubt criticize Desmond's "between" as a religiously inspired humanism in which the absoluteness of being is displaced by the experiential relation between thinking and the absolute. The new realism insists that "being" as "absolute" be taken alone, absolved, as being, as the real, and not as between.

Desmond thus represents a different voice. Like continentalists from Kierkegaard to Derrida, he stands for loyalty to the concrete and experiential, but unlike them he is a realist and a metaphysician. Like the new realists, he takes his stand with metaphysics, but unlike them he is not a materialist. The absolute for him is not matter, his metaphysics is not atheistic, and his interest in the tradition before Kant extends beyond the speculative rationalisms of the seventeenth and eighteenth centuries, who are held captive by mathematics, and reaches back to the more ample view of the great medieval masters. The challenge that Desmond faces, and the challenge that he himself in turn poses to contemporary thinking, lies—and what could be more fitting than this?—in his being between this new militant mathematico-metaphysical atheism and the postmetaphysical continentalist traditions that have descended from Kierkegaard and phenomenology and have always left room for God and a religious relationship with the world.

We are very much indebted to Christopher Simpson for skillfully crafting a nicely articulated and integrated collection of the most crucial texts of one of the most important voices in Anglophone philosophy today, a thinker of singular relevance for contemporary times.

John D. Caputo
Thomas J. Watson Professor of Religion, Emeritus
Syracuse University

David R. Cook Professor of Philosophy, Emeritus
Villanova University

NOTES

1. John Milbank, "The Double Glory," in Slavoj Žižek and John Milbank, *The Monstrosity of Christ: Paradox or Dialectic*, ed. Creston Davis (Cambridge: MIT Press, 2009), 110–233.

2. Quentin Meillassoux, *After Finitude: An Essay on the Necessity of Contingency*, trans. Ray Brassier (London: Continuum, 2008), is at the center of this movement. He is a student of Badiou. While there is some debate about how to describe it, the term "speculative realism" is taking root. For commentary on the movement as a whole, see *The Speculative Turn: Continental Materialism and Realism*, ed. Levi Bryant, Nick Srnicek, and Graham Harman (Melbourne: re.press, 2011). To be precise, Meillassoux rejects "metaphysics," which he describes as the view that there is a necessary being, God, who is exactly what he rejects, while his own view, which is that the only necessity is contingency itself, is described as a "speculative philosophy" of the "absolute."

ACKNOWLEDGMENTS

I would like to thank Creston Davis for the initial impetus and inspiration for this volume and Jack Caputo and Richard Kearney for their fine contributions to it. I am grateful to Michael Robinson for his invaluable assistance in compiling the texts and index. The Institute of Philosophy at Katholeike Universiteit Leuven provided needed assistance that enabled this project to come to completion. Finally, I thank William Desmond for his wise help and kind generosity throughout the process.

The editor and publisher gratefully acknowledge the permission granted to reproduce the copyrighted material by William Desmond in this book:

PART I: METAPHYSICS AND PHILOSOPHY

"The Fourfold Way": "Being, Determination, and Dialectic," *Review of Metaphysics*, 48 (June 1995), 762–64.

"Transcendences": *God and the Between* (Oxford: Blackwell, 2008), 22–23.

"The Truth of Metaphysics": *Being and the Between* (Albany: State University of New York Press, 1995), xi–xvii.

"What Is Metaphysical Thinking?" *Being and the Between* (Albany: State University of New York Press, 1995), 3–7, 44–46.

"Metaphysics and Dialectic": "Being, Determination, and Dialectic," *Review of Metaphysics* 48 (June 1995), 731–40, 758–60.

"The Metaxological": *Being and the Between* (Albany: State University of New York Press, 1995), 177–82, 194–200.

"The Idiocy of Being": *Perplexity and Ultimacy* (Albany: State University of New York Press, 1995), 55, 61–63, 98–101.

"Agapeic Mind": *Perplexity and Ultimacy* (Albany: State University of New York Press, 1995), 103–05, 118–23.

PART II: ETHICS AND ETHOS

"Autonomy and Freedom": "Autonomia Turannos," *Ethical Perspectives* 5, no. 4 (1998), 233–37.

"The Potencies of the Ethical": *Ethics and the Between* (Albany: State University of New York Press, 2001), 10–13.

"Metaxological Ethics": *Ethics and the Between* (Albany: State University of New York Press, 2001), 163–70, 217–20.

PART III: RELIGION AND THE PHILOSOPHY OF GOD

"Agapeic Origin": *Perplexity and Ultimacy* (Albany: State University of New York Press, 1995), 229–32.

"Breaking the Silence": *God and the Between* (Oxford: Blackwell, 2008).

"Godlessness": *God and the Between* (Oxford: Blackwell, 2008), 17–19.

"Beyond Godlessness": *God and the Between* (Oxford: Blackwell, 2008), 31–32, 33–35, 43–45.

"Hegel's Counterfeit Double": *Hegel's God: A Counterfeit Double?* (Aldershot: Ashgate, 2003), 8–11, 111–13.

"God and the Metaxological Way": *God and the Between* (Oxford: Blackwell, 2008), 116–17.

"God and Hyperbole": *God and the Between* (Oxford: Blackwell, 2008), 126–56 (selected portions).

"God beyond the Whole": *God and the Between* (Oxford: Blackwell, 2008).

"God Being Over-Being": *God and the Between* (Oxford: Blackwell, 2008), 282–87.

PART IV: AESTHETICS

"Being Aesthetic": *Philosophy and Its Others* (Albany: State University of New York Press, 1990), 63–64, 87–88, 90–93, 102–09.

"Being at a Loss": On Philosophy and the Tragic: *Perplexity and Ultimacy* (Albany: State University of New York Press, 1995), 27-44.

"Art and Transcendence": *Art, Origins, Otherness: Between Philosophy and Art* (Albany: State University of New York Press, 2003), 265–67, 271–73, 290–94.

INTRODUCTION

God saw everything that he had made, and indeed, it was very good. And there was evening and there was morning, the sixth day.

—Genesis 1:31 (NRSV)

"So correct opinion is the kind of thing we are looking for, between understanding and ignorance."

"What can Eros be, then? A mortal?"

"Far from it."

"What, then?"

"As in the other examples, something between a mortal and an immortal . . ."

"What power does such a spirit possess?"

"He acts as an interpreter and means of communication between gods and men . . . Occupying this middle position he plays a vital role holding the world together."

—Plato[1]

The True is the whole.

—Hegel[2]

Untimely—that is to say, acting counter to our time and thereby acting on our time and, let us hope, for the benefit of a time to come.

Untimely men: their home is not in this age but elsewhere, and it is elsewhere too that their explanation and justification is to be found.

—Nietzsche[3]

William Desmond was born and grew up in Cork city in southern Ireland. As a young man, he was briefly a Dominican novice. While he developed an early interest in the poetry of the English romantics, Desmond eventually committed to the study of philosophy at University College Cork. He then earned his doctorate at Penn State where he studied with Carl Vaught and Paul Weiss. Afterward, he taught at Loyola College in Baltimore for twelve years. (While at Loyola, Desmond came to know Weiss as a friend and fellow metaphysician.) Since 1994 he has been a professor of philosophy at the Higher Institute of Philosophy at Katholieke Universiteit Leuven. In this time he has held several honorary and visiting chairs including the David Cook Visiting Chair at Villanova University (since 2005).

In numerous essays and in a dozen books—from his sustained meditations upon and engagement with Hegel to his original and magisterial trilogy (*Being and the Between*, *Ethics and the Between*, and *God and the Between*)— William Desmond has been a consistently *untimely* thinker, addressing the times from a position of a certain outside. Sensitized to the other, Desmond calls attention to a "between," a community, a relation to the other. Desmond addresses the question of relation after the moment of difference—seeing that relation without otherness negates relation, collapses into oneness (what relation?) and that otherness without relation is a negated, absent other (what other?). In doing so, Desmond returns to classical and yet persistent, undying questions of being, of the good, of God—a different, affirmative saying of and returning to traditional themes (untimely if not unwelcome for the pathologically novel modern) after the ascetic severity of the turning-from and not-saying of difference in the present age.

To such an end, Desmond's work evinces an attentive reading of key figures in the Western philosophical tradition. We note the three most prominent. From Plato, Desmond gleans the *eros* of thought, of our being self-transcending toward ultimacy, an immanent orientation and exigency directing and propelling us toward the transcendent; the *metaxu* of being, of our between-being, between being and nothing, between the self-same and the other; the plurivocity of philosophy, the fruitful if less-than-fully-determinate excess of a poetic philosophy speaking in many voices. From Hegel he gleans the dynamic resources of dialectic, the unfolding play of determinacy and indeterminacy; the persistent attentiveness to the question of intelligibility in the progression of thought; the sense of a complex whole even opening beyond dialectic. From Nietzsche he gleans the recognition of becoming and the equivocal; the yea-saying, affirmative, Dionysian celebration of the finite and the earth; the critique of rational reductionisms, the nihilism of our merely human valuations; the poetic mode of philosophy (like Plato).

In regard to a reliance on the resources of a broadly Christian theology, Desmond can be seen as a thinker between theology and philosophy, between Jerusalem and Athens, not merely a philosopher who has religious insights, who has philosophical ways of thinking about God, but as a part of the great tradition of Christian philosophical theologians drawing on the philosophical font of Neoplatonism extending from Pseudo-Dionysius and Augustine to Bonaventure and Aquinas and beyond. Desmond, as with these earlier figures, thinks that philosophy and theology can relate to each other intimately, constructively—complementing and completing each other—that indeed theology and philosophy are better off for their interrelation. Desmond can be seen as taking up this tradition (in spirit if not in the letter) that went into recess with the rise of modernity.[4]

Desmond's philosophy is both metaphysical and continental. In this he has been on the vanguard of metaphysics' surprising return around the turn of the century under the influence of figures such as Gilles Deleuze, Alain Badiou, Slavoj Žižek, and John Milbank. In the 1980s and 1990s, however, Desmond spoke of metaphysics (and God) when it was decidedly not fashionable to do so—in the midst of a "postmodern" continental philosophy committed to the critique of ontotheology and the overcoming of metaphysics. Instead of seeing metaphysics as an imperial and misguided option that should be avoided, inoculated against, its influence extracted, Desmond sees metaphysics as, at once, unavoidable and unending (without closure). Metaphysics arises from an urgent need to be mindful of, to interpret, to grasp the "plenitude" of the "intimate strangeness" of the enigmatic happening of being in the world around us.[5] This task is an infinite one—with no completion or realization or consummation or end of metaphysics that brings it to a close and to an end.

Likewise, Desmond's work was and is untimely in his speaking explicitly of God—not just human religiosity or transcendence generally (though he does certainly address these), but God—in a milieu in which atheism is de rigueur. Desmond characterizes the modern ethos up into the present as displaying a certain "allergy to transcendence"—an indifference about the question of God, if not an irritation or hostility toward the question.[6] Our once "porous" ways to God have become "clogged."[7] The modern picture of the world that is still very much with us is a godless one—a world of inherently worthless, neutral being where humanity's valueless valuations are little more than fictive whistlings in the dark. In this milieu, God has become problematic, needing to be justified on secular terms, in terms of an immanent already deracinated ethos. In this context, Desmond's work calls our attention to the *hyperbolic* and excessive givens within finitude that call, carry, "throw" us, beyond the immanent frame toward the transcendent. Even after the modern death of God we are always already *with* God—bearing a *porosity* that is a primal and intimate being-open-to and being-with God; we are always already *unto* God—bearing an *urgency of ultimacy* in which we are oriented, driven, propelled in our own exceeding of ourselves beyond ourselves, toward God.

The aim of this reader is to provide a needed way into William Desmond's important and yet often difficult body of work—to enable one to gain an understanding of Desmond's philosophy in his own words in a single relatively brief volume. This book consists of selections from Desmond's works, carefully chosen to best represent and to clearly introduce the key ideas, perspectives, and contributions of his philosophy as a whole. The selections are intentionally laid out so that one can gain an understanding of Desmond's thought in his own words—with later selections often building on earlier ones. Indeed, many of Desmond's key ideas are introduced in the first part on metaphysics. On the rare occasion that an unfamiliar term is used that is not more or less immediately explained, the reader should refer to the index. The readings are organized into four parts representing the major topoi of Desmond's work: metaphysics, ethics, religion, and art. Following the readings is an original essay by Desmond reflecting on these topoi in his thought. The volume concludes with an interview with Desmond conducted by Richard Kearney.[8]

NOTES

1. Plato, Symposium in *Symposium and Phaedrus*, tr. Tom Griffith (Everyman's Library, 2001), 202a, 202d–e.

2. G. W. F. Hegel, *Phenomenology of Spirit*, tr. A. V. Miller (Oxford: Oxford University Press, 1977), 11.

3. Friedrich Nietzsche, *Untimely Meditations*, tr. R. J. Hollingdale, ed. Daniel Breazeale (Cambridge: Cambridge University Press, 1997), 60, 198.

4. Further, in his work as a post-Hegelian, protopostmodern, yet metaphysical, theist (indeed, robustly Christian) thinker—sometimes poetic, sometimes systematic—Desmond stands in striking proximity to Kierkegaard. For more on this resonance, see my *The Truth Is the Way: Kierkegaard's* Theologia Viatorum (London: SCM Press, 2010).

5. William Desmond, "Neither Deconstruction nor Reconstruction," *International Philosophical Quarterly* 40, no. 1 (March 2000): 157; *Being and the Between* (New York: State University of New York Press, 1995), xiii. A revised version of this essay will be included in Desmond's forthcoming *The Intimate Strangeness of Being: Metaphysics after Dialectic* (Washington, DC: Catholic University of America Press).

6. William Desmond, *Hegel's God* (Aldershot: Ashgate, 2003), 4.

7. William Desmond, *God and the Between* (Oxford: Blackwell, 2008), 25–27.

8. For a secondary work that gives a systematic introduction to Desmond's thought, see my *Religion, Metaphysics, and the Postmodern: William Desmond and John D. Caputo* (Bloomington: Indiana University Press, 2009). For a collection of essays on aspects of Desmond's thought in dialogue with other thinkers and disciplines, see Thomas A. F. Kelly, ed., *Between System and Poetics: William Desmond and Philosophy after Dialectic* (Aldershot: Ashgate, 2007).

WILLIAM DESMOND'S WORKS

(IN ORDER OF PUBLICATION)

Art and the Absolute. State University of New York Press, 1986.
Desire, Dialectic and Otherness. Yale University Press, 1987.
Philosophy and Its Others. State University of New York Press, 1990.
Beyond Hegel and Dialectic. State University of New York Press, 1992.
Being and the Between. State University of New York Press, 1995.
Perplexity and Ultimacy. State University of New York Press, 1995.
Ethics and the Between. State University of New York Press, 2001.
Hegel's God: A Counterfeit Double? Ashgate, 2003.
Art, Origins, Otherness: Between Philosophy and Art. State University of New York Press, 2003.
Is There a Sabbath for Thought? Fordham University Press, 2005.
God and the Between. Blackwell, 2008.
Being Between: Conditions of Irish Thought. Leabhar Breac and Centre for Irish Studies, NUI Galway, 2008.
The Intimate Strangeness of Being: Metaphysics after Dialectic. Catholic University Press, 2012.

Selected Articles

"Being, Determination, and Dialectic." *Review of Metaphysics* 48 (June 1995).
"Autonomia Turannos." *Ethical Perspectives* 5, no. 4 (1998).

PART I

METAPHYSICS AND PHILOSOPHY

univocal - having only one possible meaning

equivocal - open to more than one interpretation

dialectical - relating to logical discussion of ideas
concerned with or acting through opposing forces

metaxological - between

THE FOURFOLD WAY

From "Being, Determination, and Dialectic"

WHAT IT MEANS to BE

I suggest a fourfold way to rethink the perplexities of metaphysics. This four-fold way is not at all indefinite but complexly defined by the univocal, the equivocal, the dialectical, and the metaxological understandings of being.

Our understanding of what it means to be comes to definition in a complex interplay between indetermination and determination, transcen-dence and immanence, otherness and sameness, difference and identity. Very broadly and first, the *univocal* sense of being stresses the notion of sameness, *univocal* or unity, sometimes even immediate sameness, of mind and being. Correla- *m, hd/being* tive to the univocal sense of being is the search for determinate solutions to determinate problems, impelled by specific curiosity. Second, the *equivocal* *equivocal* sense accentuates diversity, the unmediated difference of being and mind, sometimes to the point of setting them into oppositional otherness. Perplex-ity in its restless encounter with troubling ambiguities can be correlated with this sense of the equivocal. Third, the *dialectical* sense emphasizes the mediation of the different, the reintegration of the diverse, the mediated *Dialectical* conjunction of mind and being. Its mediation is primarily self-mediation, hence the side of the same is privileged in this conjunction. In the above we have seen how this leads to a strong stress on self-determination. Fourth, the *metaxological* sense gives a *logos* of the *metaxu*, the between. It puts *Metaxological* stress on the mediated community of mind and being, but not in terms of the self-mediation of the same. It calls attention to a pluralized mediation, beyond closed self-mediation from the side of the same, and hospitable to the mediation of the other, or transcendent, out of its own otherness. It puts the emphasis on an intermediation, not a self-mediation, however dialectically qualified. Moreover, the *inter* is shaped plurally by different mediations of mind and being, same and other, mediations not subsumable into one total self-mediation. The metaxological sense keeps open the spaces of otherness in the between, and it does not domesticate the ruptures that shake the complacencies of our mediations of being. Moreover, it tries to deal with the limitations of dialectical determination, especially so with respect to the excess of the overdetermined givenness of being.

3

There is an immediacy to the metaxological, in the sense that it is at work before we articulate it reflectively in our categories. It is shown in what we might call the preobjective community of mindfulness and being that is inarticulately given in the original astonishment. It is at work in the univocal, the equivocal, the dialectical, but not known explicitly as such, and when stated exclusively in their terms it is distorted, because it is truncated. The metaxological is the truth of the univocal, the equivocal, and the dialectical. When we try to articulate it, we are trying to find the right words for what is given in the overdeterminacy of the original astonishment. The other three senses help to articulate the truth of the metaxological, but we risk error when they are absolutized and claimed to cover the entire milieu of being. Our sense of metaphysical thinking must try to be true to the being of the between. Also, it must not falsely claim to have the categories that finally determine what itself is not exhausted by any determination.

Does this fourfold sense of being mean we conceive of metaphysics simply as a science of categories? There is a categorial side to this fourfold, but this side does not exhaust the matter. While we require systematic categorial thinking, we also require a dynamic hermeneutics of being; and, as I have suggested, there are perplexities at the edge of systematic categorial determination. They trouble the self-confidence of systematic categorial thinking and call for a different ruminative mindfulness. Metaphysics must find room for the thought of such limit perplexities, as well as the originating sources of astonishment that, in the first instance, precede yet precipitate determinate mindfulness through which we become provisionally at home with the more familiar world. The fourfold sense of being offers an interlocking set of articulations of transcendence—both the transcending of mind and the transcendence of being, and without the closure of either to ultimate transcendence.

What I call metaxological metaphysics offers itself as an unfolding interpretation, both systematic and hermeneutic, of the many sides of the plenitude of the happening of being, as manifest to mindfulness in the between. It is all but impossible for us to be absolutely true to the plenitude of this happening. Failure of some sort is inevitable. This impossible truthfulness is asked of us, however, even if inevitable failure brings us back to the truth of our finitude. This failure may itself become another success of sorts, if it renews metaphysical astonishment before the enigma of being that was, and is, and always will be too much for us, in excess of our best efforts at conceptualization.

— Metaxological metaphysics —

TRANSCENDENCES

From *God and the Between*

We can better find our bearings if we distinguish the following senses of transcendence. In broad strokes, they correspond to the other-being of nature, of the self-being of the human, and the difference of the divine. It is not only their character but their interrelations that are important. How we understand them is rooted in our attunement to the primal ethos and reflected in the reconfigured ethos.

First transcendence (T¹): The transcendence of beings as other in exteriority. The transcendence of such beings consists in their not being the product of our process of thinking; their otherness to us resists complete reduction to our categories, especially insofar as they simply are at all. Their otherness as being at all gives rise to the question, what makes possible both their possibility, as well as their actuality? What makes possible the possibility of their being at all? This is a metaphysical question not about the "what" of their being but the "that" of their being there at all: why beings and not nothing? The possibility of a further transcendence as other to their transcendence is opened by such questions.

Second transcendence (T²): The transcendence of *self-being*, self-transcendence. The meaning of possibility is here realized in interiority rather than determined externally. Human self-transcendence is of special moment here. There is possibility as freedom, as the promise of self-determination. We are impelled to the further question, is this self-transcendence, in relation to the first transcendence (T¹), an anomalous overreaching into emptiness, or a genuine self-surpassing toward an even further transcendence as other? Is our self-surpassing driven by a lack to fulfill only itself, or to seeking fulfillment in what is other to itself? Is it more than lacking and seeking what is infinitely more than itself, whether lacking or not? An important question here: does our understanding of our own self-transcending rely too much on the *conatus essendi* and not enough on the *passio essendi*?

Third transcendence (T³): original transcendence as still *other—transcendence* itself, not as the exterior, not as the interior, but as the superior. This would be a *hyperbolic* sense of transcendence, bringing to mind the

5

question of God beyond the immanence of transcendence in nature and human being. If we were to call this third hyperbolic form "Transcendence itself," it would be in excess of determinate beings, as their original ground; it would be beyond human self-transcendence, as its most ultimate possibilizing source. It would also be beyond the ordinary doublet of possibility/ reality, as their most ultimate possibilizing source. It would not be just a possibility, nor indeed a determinate realization of possibility. It would have to be "real" possibilizing power, in a manner more original and other than immanent possibility and realization. It would have to be original, creative possibilizing beyond determinate possibility, and "real" beyond all determinate realization, beyond all self-determining self-realization.

If such third transcendence were in excess of determinacy and our self-determining, would it be but a merely *indefinite beyond* to finite being? If so, would not its participation in the happening of the between be feeble? Is there rather a third transcendence that is not such an empty indefinite but excessive: overdetermined in a surplus sense, hyperbolic, not indefinite? If so, it would not be comprehended under any finite category of the possible or real. It would be above, *huper, über* them, and yet most intimate to finite being as enabling it to be at all, and to be free. What must this possibilizing power be, such as to give rise to finite being as *other* to itself, and hence as possibilizing the finite space, or middle, for first and second transcendence? Such a third transcendence could not be identified with any projection onto some ultimate other of the first two senses. There could be no objectification (T^1) or subjectification (T^2) of third transcendence (T^3). Rather it would seem that second transcendence (T^2), in its ineradicable recalcitrance to complete objectification, is pointed beyond both objectness and subjectness to transobjective and transsubjective transcendence (T^3). And perhaps first transcendence (T^1) is not also devoid of its own ambiguous signs of this hyperbolic transcendence.

Much more must be said, but for now this is the relevant point. Third transcendence (T^3) has been made problematic in modernity, both by a univocalizing objectification of first transcendence (T^1) and by developments of second transcendence (T^2), especially when this last defines itself hugely in terms of its own autonomy. Then a logic of *self-determination* stands guard over all our thinking and the thinking of what is other to our self-determination. Inevitably, third transcendence (T^3) becomes endowed with an equivocal position. There is a tension, indeed an antinomy, between autonomy and transcendence. This is not just a mere contradiction, but a tension wherein different possibilities for human thought and life take shape. In this equivocal space the traditional respect accorded to third transcendence (T^3) from an essentially religious point of view comes under onslaught. Into that space of equivocality, our "creativity," our "poetry," so to speak, inserts itself, as somehow answering the tension of autonomy and transcendence. Human "art" comes to assume roles previously accorded to religion. Is the antinomy resolved? Or does third transcendence still remain mockingly "beyond"—or welcoming?

Art becomes only acceptable transcendence

THE TRUTH OF METAPHYSICS

From *Being and the Between*

Long, long ago, Plato told us that the human being is neither a god nor a beast, but someone in between. Philosophy too is in between, neither completely wise nor entirely ignorant. What then would it mean to philosophize in between? What is the being of the between?

Metaphysics will not be the deduction of a system of categories from an irrefrangible logical principle. As both systematic and hermeneutic, it offers itself as an unfolding interpretation of the many sides of the plenitude of the happening of being, as manifest to mindfulness in the between. To be absolutely true to the plenitude of this happening is all but impossible for us, and indeed failure of some sort is inevitable. But this impossible truthfulness is asked of us, even if inevitable failure brings us back to the truth of our finitude. This failure may itself be a success of sorts, in renewing metaphysical astonishment before the enigma of being that was, and is, and always will be too much for us, in excess of our groping efforts.

I do not subscribe to the view, fashionable in some quarters, that philosophy does not deal with truth, or that it must give up this, its ancient and noble calling. I want to state some considerations that bear on the truth of the following. These remarks make most sense after the fact, that is, subsequent to the effort to understand the meaning of this work as a whole. First, since we are in the middle, the truth of metaphysics is not deductive from some abstract first principle, more geometrico. Nor is it a matter of inductive generalization. Inductive generalization takes its sights from the particularities of determinate beings and processes; but our consideration is not only on the level of determinations, but also on the happening of determinate being, the coming to be of determination. Being is manifesting itself; we require an interpretive fidelity to this happening of manifestation in the middle. The meaning of that manifestness is not itself initially manifest. We have to become mindful of its full riches, of its overt concretions, its secret latencies, its potential for deformation and dissimulation.

Second, if we cannot renege on the systematic side of philosophy, we can rightly ask: What are the essential relations between mind and being, between self and other, same and different, identity and difference? What

9

do we make of the perennial perplexities about origin, creation, things, intelligibilities, selves, communities, truth and the good? My claim is that the fourfold sense of being offers a flexible systematic framework that allows us complexly and very comprehensively to interpret the variety of possible relations, and the very ontological richness of what is at stake in each of the perplexities.

Third, does this mean that we could calculate all the possibilities? I reject this way of putting the issue, since some of the essential possibilities are open. They are defined relative to the creative coming to be of beings, out of an overdetermined source of origination; or they define the very opening of freedom in the beings in relation. Our understanding of being in the between calls for the acknowledgment of indeterminacy—and this not in the sense of the merely indefinite. The point about systematic categories is not to impose a skeletal structure on being, and so to bind it up in conceptual domestication. It is to think through the happening of being to the utmost extent of its intelligibility, but not in this to claim to have mastered conceptually its still overdetermined otherness. We might say that categorial understanding is most genuine when it opens beyond categorial immanence, participating in the very transcending of mindfulness towards the dynamic happening of being in the between.

Fourth, this means that the truth of what is at stake has a certain openness to it. If we seek to be true to the concrete manifestness of the happening of being, and if there is a certain latent promise in this happening, the very openness of our "being true" is implied. I will more fully address the notion of "being true" in a later chapter. But I am here saying that there is no absolute certitude, no master category, no absolute knowing in the Hegelian manner. Why? Because all these sacrifice the otherness of the happening of being to the immanence of categorial rationality at home in its own conceptual immanence.

If there is no Hegelian master category, I do not deny that the metaxological seeks the best understanding possible. How is this measured? There are notions of truth consonant with univocity, equivocity, and dialectic, and this too will occupy us more fully. I now call notice to a double unfolding that causes us to move from one sense to the next, as a more adequate effort to think through the truth of the happening of being. The double unfolding has to do, first with the self-coherence of the specific mode of being and mind, and second with its truthfulness to what is other to thought. Let me say something on this.

Thus univocity tries to fix the truth determinately. But the more it is consistent with itself, the more the appearance of something other to univocity makes its demand. The thinking of this other causes us to think in terms of the equivocity of being. In turn, the coherent thinking of this equivocity drives us beyond equivocity to dialectic. Equivocity absolutized subverts itself, and calls for a more positive mediating mindfulness, in order to be true, not only to the transcending of thinking, but also to the truth of being as other to thinking. Further again, dialectic itself, while dealing with the limitations of univocity and equivocity, is tempted to absolutize itself and its characteristic forms of mediation, especially self-mediation. And yet this seeming completion of dialectic is actually its undoing. Dialectic absolutized reveals its failure to take seriously enough the other that is other to thought thinking itself. It absolutizes the self-coherence of thought at home with itself. And yet the end result is a new homelessness of thinking.

It is this new homelessness that impels thinking to the metaxologi-cal level. Dialectic cannot be fully accounted for dialectically. We require a thinking that is less willing to domesticate the ruptures of the imma-nence of thinking by the transcendent other. This is a thinking more open to what transcends thinking, a thinking more patient to transcendence, just in the highest exceeding of its self-transcending towards the other as other. But this last possibility is not a master category. The language of master categories is simply not appropriate, for this mode of thinking demands a divestment of mind's will to master the otherness of the hap-pening of being. There is a transformation of the energy of self-transcending thinking to which the language of appropriating and overcoming the other is not at all appropriate. What is "overcome" is the will to over-come the other. There arises a new willingness to let the happening of being offer the truth of itself to mindfulness.

Fifth, a necessary requirement of philosophical understanding is its capacity to illuminate the matter itself, what the Germans call die Sache selbst. There are contemporary philosophers who scoff at the notion, but that is their problem, generated by a threadbare understanding of die Sache selbst. We philosophers ask for bread, and what stones are we handed? Commentaries on commentaries on commentaries . . . What is the matter itself? If one could answer this question in a preface, there would be no need for the book. The book as a whole answers this question: the matter itself is the meaning of being between. As it will turn out, this meaning in the end cannot be completely confined to the between we inhabit, but must extend to the originary ground of that between, and this is not the finite between once again. In our passage through the between, philosophy demands a kind of phenomenological fidelity to the matter itself. Along the way, the fourfold understanding of being will illuminate many key con-stituents of our habitation of the between—creation, things, intelligibilities, selves, communities.

Sixth, an important consideration is the ability of a philosophy to illuminate the essential metaphysical positions. I give counsel to myself: Do not smash the wheel and proclaim the glorious liberation of human creativity; you, or someone else, years hence, will find it necessary to reinvent the same despised wheel—decked out perhaps with a new name to assuage the pretense to glorious creativity. I think we have to be able to interpret the rationale, the strengths, and the limits of the basic philosophical possibilities, as diversely expressed in the history of philosophy. This requires a thinking about them that refuses to stay on the surface of the packaged positions that easily get regurgitated in standard histories of philosophy. We must go deeper, approach the originary sources of perplexity and astonishment, out of which the surfaces of the positions have grown. This means we must already be mindful of the matter itself that has occupied philosophers for millennia. Much more than being a historian of ideas is asked of us. One must be a philosopher to understand *as philosophy* the history of philosophy.

One's attitude to past philosophers cannot be defined by simple rejection. One learns from them, even when one disagrees with them. And even in disagreeing with them, one ought to have a hermeneutic generous enough to allow one to make strong intelligible sense of their essential contributions. Every previous philosopher worth his salt harbors latent reserves that challenge continued rethinking. I believe that the fourfold sense of being is extremely fruitful for casting light on, as well as helping us recast in a new light, many of the basic philosophical positions. I reject what has followed from the alleged completion of metaphysics by a Hegel, or a Nietzsche, or a Heidegger. I do not simply reject, but hold that the fourfold offers us some basis to rethink the tradition of metaphysics. We must move beyond the paralysis and stultification generated by this rhetoric of the end of metaphysics. Once again the promise will have to be redeemed in the work itself. I add that I have kept scholarly apparatus to a minimum, which is not to say that extensive study does not inform what I say. But this work is not a piece of scholarship.

 Seventh, I think that a philosopher is a seeker, and that any genuine philosophy is an adventure of thought. As an adventure, it cannot be judged before the search has begun. There will be many who scoff on the dockside as the ship heaves off. They will congratulate themselves on their prudence in valuing the security of safe harbor, and the solid land. They will even feel superior to those who launch out into the unknown, those who risk their thinking. They feel sure in advance it will come to shipwreck. But perhaps these wise homebodies are the already defeated. How dare you do metaphysics? I am asked. I do dare. But you must also dare, if you want an answer to your question.

And if we philosophers took to heart these prudent discouragements, we might never stir from the spot. Alas, we too seek for home, but we must seek for home to be at home. We are fools, no doubt, to dream of something more. But since the world is so wise, and since the standing army of its sages is always swelled with new recruits, the stray folly of metaphysical adventuring will perhaps be excused in us. We have been told not even to try, so we will not blame the fashionable commentators for the outcome—be it what it may.

Let the wise read as the philosopher writes. I do not ask for uncritical readers, but I do ask for disciplined readers—readers who have studied hard and long, who can take their time to think; readers who have not shunned solitude; readers suspicious of themselves before being suspicious of others; readers patient when demands are made on them; readers themselves adventurers; readers who ask for more than the rhetorics fashionable in academic philosophy, and who hate the substitution of "relevant" ideology for the seriousness of truth; readers with souls full of an intellectual, indeed spiritual generosity, beyond the hermeneutics of suspicion; readers who desire to hear fundamental questions addressed with a genuine intellectual, not to say, spiritual seriousness; readers philosophically rich enough in themselves as to be able to laugh at the pretensions of what sometimes passes for "philosophy"; readers who long for a simple human voice to speak again about the essential issues that perennially perplex us. I do not ask for the impossible. I do ask for what now is rare.

WHAT IS METAPHYSICAL THINKING?

From *Being and the Between*

THE QUESTION OF BEING

Beginning, we ask the question: What is being? What does it mean to be? This is the question of metaphysics. It is old beyond age, newer than the most novel thought. It calls to us from the dawn of human mindfulness; it calls for its renewal again, even when we seem to have passed the high meridian of science. It is the dark question of philosophy, and the light without which other questions would be dark. Ageless and ever-fresh, it has been asked again and again, and yet in all the answers, the asking once again stands before us, one more time. The asking will stand before us still, even when our utmost response has been tried.

Asking it again, I know that for millennia it has been variously posed and answered. I ask it again, not to downgrade past efforts as misguided and superseded, but because the question bespeaks an elemental perplexity that perennially calls for renewal. Even where it has been answered, often the meaning of the proffered answer grows faint and needs refreshing. Again and again mindful human beings are troubled, perhaps shaken by this perplexity. To ask the question properly demands that we be on its level, and this requires a tireless mindfulness. For even were a true answer given, this still would not be heard, if the hearer did not have the ears to hear.

This defines our present concern—namely, the nature of metaphysical thinking relative to the question of being. We might say that metaphysical thinking articulates the milieu of mindfulness within which this question can be heard. But there is a respect in which simply to be as human is to be constituted in and by this milieu of mindfulness, and this apart from any concerted and concentrated effort of philosophical mindfulness. For we are what we are by virtue of our abiding in the milieu of being in a more or less mindful way. Hence, the question of being is not first one for philosophers, understood as an elite of thinkers. It transcends the difference of the few and the many, for it strikes our humanity simply in virtue of its being, as mindful of itself and what is other to itself. Of course, this matter

15

may degenerate into platitude, then being will be said to be the emptiest of abstractions—a vacuous generality, indifferently applicable to everything and anything, and hence not applicable with illuminating power to anything in particular. Against this degrading of being we must fight strenuously. There may be a sense of the universal and the community of being that transcends any abstract universal.

There is, of course, a certain initial indeterminacy in all of this. We are indeterminately given over to mindfulness about being, given over immediately and from the start, even though what is given thus presents its face to us as astonishing and perplexing. We might say that this question rouses itself in us, struggles to shape itself into saying. It emerges like a diver rising to the surface from a deep sea, as if an emissary were being sent to the airy surface and the light. For this surfacing of the question is not first generated by some self-sufficient act of autonomous thought. It comes to us from a depth of others, the otherness of being itself, that we cannot claim to control, or completely to encapsulate in our subsequent concepts.

The question is gratuitous in an important, positive sense that will become clearer as we proceed. For it asks the ultimate why of being, but it has no why that we initially can give to it. It is given to us in the power to ask why of all and everything. It is the ground of all whys that we give, but the why of it comes to us from a source that we cannot master. The question of being happens. The happening is in and through us, as the mindful being on whom a call is made, a call we cannot shut out.

I am not saying that being is an object over against us, the knowledge of which we gain by crossing a dualism between us and it. The situation is more subtle. It might be put this way: there is an *ontological intimacy* to our mindfulness of being, which is immediate, and which is not constructed from two fixed poles (say, subject and object) that are then joined together. I am speaking of an indeterminate opening to being that is prior to any determinate question regarding this or that being, or this or that specific aspect of things. This indeterminate opening is not first determinately known as such; it is lived; it is simply our very being, as given to be mindful of being as given. All determinate questions are further specifications of this first indeterminate opening, as we shall see.

We might be inclined to say we are "englobed" by being. But if so, we are not "englobed" in the way a drop of water is engulfed by the ocean. The situation rather is such as to *release* this singular being, the human being, into mindfulness, not just of its own being, but of being *simpliciter*. "Englobed" is perhaps too ambiguous a word, since it recalls, for instance, the homogeneous circle of Parmenidean being. This is not what I intend. Rather it is the release of *difference and transcendence* as other to any such homogeneous whole. The mindful human being is within a community of being that "englobes" it, in the sense of being more encompassing than its singular being; but this is not such as to swallow the singular being within an absorbing totality. Quite to the contrary, the astonishing diversity and differentiation of beings, and precisely within a community of being as common, emerges for mindfulness. Metaphysical mindfulness is aware of difference in itself, as other in thought to being—being with which mind is also intimate.

There is here articulated what I will call the vector of transcendence. "Vector" is not the best word for what I mean, but the truly right word is hard, perhaps impossible, to find. I must note the following ambiguity. "Vector" carries some connotation of "activity"; but I want to call attention to an opening of transcending that is prior to active transcending. There is a *patience* to this opening; yet it is not inertly passive either. It is beyond capture in the standard opposition of "active/passive." Thus by "vector of transcendence" I do not mean a self-conscious intentionality. I mean the advent of original being, as a dynamic process of coming to be, as also a process of becoming mindful. Transcendence comes to us as an *advent*; this is the patience of an original opening. But, one must add, what comes to us in this advent makes us, in turn, *adventuring* beings, beings ventured towards (*ad*) something of which we are not sure, though we are with it, or it is elusively with us from the outset—with us, though in no sense mastered, This adventuring is closer to the more normal meaning of vector. Yet the vector is enigmatic in its origin. There is a going towards being, but this adventuring emerges out of a community with being that already grants the self its opening to being. That is, in us the vector of self-transcendence is both our relativity to being, and our difference from it. It is our being in community with being, and our others to being in this community.

The vector of transcendence, I want to suggest, is already a relation to transcendence, and in a sense not reducible to human self-transcendence. Transcendence as other to us works along with human self-transcendence.

THE DOUBLING OF METAPHYSICAL PERPLEXITY

Metaphysical thinking is precipitated in the between. We find ourselves in the midst of beings. At first, we do not know our beginning; for we have already begun, before we begin to know that we are, and that there are beings, and that we are in the middle of things. Nor do we know at first what it means to be in this middle, or what makes it be a middle at all. Being between troubles us. It troubles us, not in any mode of neutral objectivism, but with regard to the ground of intelligibility, indeed the very worth of being. A cloak of disquiet is spread wide. There is perplexity about the origin, perplexity about the given milieu of beings, perplexity about the essential thrust of self-transcendence. In the adventure of transcending, we wake to the mystery of being, impelled towards an end we know not, from a beginning we comprehend not, in a milieu whose lords we are not.

Our mindfulness here is *doubly* mediated. On the one hand, our perplexity shows us to be *distanced* from the truth we seek. We undergo a kind of indigence at the heart of our being; in that respect, perplexity reveals our *being-other* to the truth of being. Yet this being-other is not absolute vacancy; rather it is a paradoxical indigency of transcending power. Our lack, it might be said, generates the drive beyond itself. However, what drives the lack beyond lack cannot be itself mere lack. The lack points backwards to an inward other in perplexity itself that is the promise of a *relativity* to being that is beyond mere indigence.

Thus, on the other hand, we would not be perplexed at all, were we not in some *communication* with being in its truth. This prior communication, I want to suggest, is anterior to the beginning of mindfulness in lacking perplexity itself. It is the original power of being in us, waking up to itself as mindful, and driven beyond itself to mindfulness of being other than itself. This anterior original power is an excess to lack; indeed this excess articulates lack itself as the mode of a finite mind's self-transcendence. This latter transcending faces outside itself towards what is other to itself; then, it may take itself for a beginning, though, in fact, it has *already* begun; and so, in fact, it comprehends itself as the indigence of lack only because it has already been precipitated out of the excess of the original power of being, as anterior to the finite beginning that already finding itself, as having begun.

This double mediation of our perplexity makes it *metaxological*. By this I mean that perplexity is itself a condition of mindfulness that is between: between nonknowing and knowing, between ignorance so complete it knows not its own ignorance, and a knowing so complete that is it not human at all but that of a god. Metaphysical perplexity is a *tense togetherness* of being at a loss *and* finding oneself at home with being. We must not fail to keep in mind both these sides. This doubleness is both our plenitude and poverty, our grandeur and frailty, our highest call to nobility and perennial reminder of infirmity.

At either of these extremes the demands of intermediacy are inescapable. That is, metaphysical perplexity is not a monolinear epistemic drive from a question to an answer, which then lets us put aside the question. Rather it is the probing for an answer, which renews the question again, and in certain respects may indeed *deepen* perplexity, rather than dispel it. And so, in the poverty of our *nonknowing*, we are impelled to something more and beyond, indeed impelled by something more than lack, already at work behind our back, as it were, in the thrust of our transcending. Likewise, in our *knowing*, our plenty, we do not drop finally into sleep, satiated with some feast of gnosis. Metaphysical perplexity is a desire that in being satiated is renewed as a hunger. There is a restless search for the truth that in coming to be known incites the seeker into further unremitting search. It allows no sleep, though no doubt we repeatedly drowse.

This doubleness corresponds to what I will call the *eros* and the *agape* of metaphysics. There is an eros to perplexity; there is also the promise of agapeic mind. The eros of perplexity is driven to transcendence, troubled initially by a sense of lack. The thrust of mind's transcending seeks to overcome that lack, make determinate what is vague and indefinite, complete what is partial and unintegral. In other words, the eros of perplexity is impelled towards as complete a comprehension of the whole as is possible. It is a movement of transcendence wherein mind mediates progressively with being's otherness to make its enigmatic face available to determinate intelligibility. It is driven to the ideal of comprehensive intelligibility and knowing: knowing of the whole. Sometimes, too, it may define metaphysics as an absolutely autonomous thinking. The metaphysician then seeks approximation to the god of the philosophers: thought thinking itself.

Agapeic perplexity is other. It is not driven to transcendence from an initial lack, but from the effective work of a plenitude that is prior to erotic lack. The agape of perplexity is prior to the eros of perplexity, because the lack of eros could not drive beyond itself at all in the first place, were it not energized by an anterior power of being that cannot be described in purely indigent terms. Put differently, agapeic perplexity is not driven by the will to comprehend completely in a mode that subordinates being's otherness to the metaphysician's categories. It seeks to be genuinely self-transcending in going towards the otherness of being as other, and not simply with the view to appropriating it to the self, or the same, or to mind itself. One could say that *mind others itself* because it is about the *otherness of being* and not just about itself. I am noting here an intermediation with being-other that goes beyond the self-mediation of mind, elevated into primacy by the god of self-thinking thought.

In a word, agapeic perplexity points towards the metaphysical thought of the other as other. Its going towards the other as other is not with the view to subsuming being as a thematic intelligibility simply, but to acknowledge its excess as other, the excess of transcendence itself that gives the world of the between. Agapeic perplexity manifests the heteronomy of metaphysics. As I understand it, metaphysical thinking is not autonomous mindfulness. For in agapeic perplexity there is a giving of mind over to the others of being that transcends mind, transcends it as a plenitude that could never be exhausted. And if there is any fulfilling of mindfulness here it is not just in a completely determinate knowing, or a complete autonomous science, but in the endless renewal of astonishment and perplexity.

METAPHYSICAL THINKING AND BEING BETWEEN

If metaphysical thinking, as I claim, takes shape in the milieu of being, the question of transcendence has nothing to do with a leap out of being into the void, but with the deepest mindfulness of what is emergent in the middle itself. Again the double meaning of *meta* is relevant. "*Meta*" is being in the midst; "*meta*" is also reference to what is beyond, what is transcendent. Metaxological metaphysics must think the doubleness of this tension between being in the midst *and* being referred by self-transcendence to the transcendence of what is other, what is over and above.

I stress that vigilance to the signs of transcendence does not imply the reduction of transcendence to the between. There is a thinking about the beyond in the between itself. What gives the between surpasses the between, though we face towards it, in and through the between. Thus, what I called posthumous mind suggests a rebirth of thinking with respect to the meaning of being in its height and depth, in its spread over the middle, in our implication with being as a community of plurality. The rebirth of agapeic mind demands the articulate thinking of this community.

This is no easy matter. It means a rejection of the idealistic strategy whereby autonomous thought is tempted to impose its categories on appearing and hence only to see what it puts there itself. But the coherence idealism is also its unraveling: for when thought only thinks itself, the emptiness is evident in its reduction of thought's other to the construction of a category. I think we need a complex realistic fidelity that does not dictate to being, but that puts itself honestly before it. This realistic fidelity makes us attentive to the between as the matrix of thought. We must not let the later conceptualizations cover over what comes to concrete nascence there.

In the middle we are on the way, to where we do not exactly know, from where we are unsure. Mindfulness comes in the middle, out of an enigmatic origin, in expectation of an uncertain end. Existential contingency cannot find its substitute in any purely objective system. Nor do we have an Archimedean point to survey the middle as a whole, or to overlook our wavering passage in it. We are amongst, and the density of being touches us; we are participants and intimate with being. As such we live from within what we try to think. But to think from within is hard; some reflective distance is needed; but absolute distance is impossible for us in the within of the middle. To remain true to our intimacy with being, and yet to gain reflective distance that does not distort, is a great struggle. We need an equilibrium beyond objectifying science and idiosyncratic individuality. We need a certain doubling of existential and systematic thinking.

Metaphysical thinking, thus conceived, cannot entirely escape a metaphorical dimension. This is especially evident with respect to the metaxological, and the reborn thinking of the second perplexity. Metaphor itself refers to the double of the *meta*. Metaphor is a carrier in the between; it ferries (*pherein*: to carry) us across a gap; or it is the carrier of transcendence; it is in the midst as *meta*, and yet an image of the *meta* as beyond, as transcendent. It is both determinate and indeterminate at once. It is neither one nor the other, but both in a manner that transcends univocal unity, sheer equivocity, and indeed a dialectic that reduces difference to mediated identity. There is a rich sense of indeterminacy at play in metaphor that functions as articulating a pluralized mediation, and a certain opening of transcending. Metaphysical metaphor is the carrier of agapeic astonishment and perplexed mindfulness in the middle. I conclude with the following remarks, Metaphysics *does* often put a strain on language, seeming to make it other to so-called "ordinary" usage. It sometimes taxes language with an almost intolerable burden. If mindfulness has not been reborn to the second perplexity, bearing this burden will make no sense. For this rebirth makes restless the transcending of mind, with a questioning that will not stop short of the extreme, even though it must weary itself in search. In fact, it may turn out that there is nothing "ordinary" in the ordinary. The "ordinary" as a manipulable aggregate of determinate entities or happenings may be granted as a pragmatic abstraction, indispensable to our muddling through the twilight of the domesticated middle. But to mindfulness reborn in the second dimension of perplexity, there is the promise of a truth more ultimate. Across the middle a light has flashed, and now the "ordinary" looks dark; thinking reborn into second perplexity turns to the "ordinary" with a new astonishment, with a new groping unfamiliarity. Briefly, being was other, and is perhaps still other, despite the clouding over of transcendence.

And so born-again perplexity contests any taken for granted attitude to being. It puts us on trial; it provokes and challenges. The perplexities of being never yield a univocal answer, indeed resist being formulated as univocal problems. There is a constitutive ambiguity that remains. There is a constitutive openness that persists. To these perplexities we must return again and again. We never master or completely dissolve them. Yet if agapeic astonishment is not allowed to die, the perplexities are buoyed by the confidence that something *more* than insomnia, or threat, or despair may be offered.

We might say that there is both a wager and a promise in metaphysical thinking. In a way this whole work is a kind of wager. One ventures a thought, not quite sure of it, whence it comes, whither it will take one. One has to venture with a certain boldness or audacity. Even then, transcendence harasses us out of every hiding hole, every threadbare or superficial thought, every smug conceptual satisfaction. Even then, a promise is held out in the hazard of thought. That the world of the between is at all, is the wonder.

We might say there is an ontological generosity to metaphysical thinking when it embodies the genuine self-transcending of agapeic mind. We wish to think beyond the mind that instrumentalizes. The middle is not given to us as a mere means; it is the place of a way, a passage. Agapeic mind passes towards what is offered in the middle, not simply for some conceptual return to itself, but because the being of the other offers itself for a celebrating, affirming thought. We think the meaning of being, because being in itself is most worthy to be thought.

Yes, we do think to alleviate our own perplexity, our sense of being at a loss, our sense of not being entirely at home in the middle. But not only that, and if only that, the thrust of self-transcendence is contracted. There is the promise in the hazard, promise that now and then is redeemed. I mean that there is a *being at home with being* beyond erotic perplexity, and that lifts perplexity out of its oppression by the burden of the mystery. The mystery does not burden, but lightens thinking. It is as if perplexity gives us a kind of metaphysical migraine, and nothing seems to lift it; it clouds the mind, maybe even crushes it. Yet we can come to mindfulness at home with being, and the metaphysical migraine is lifted; one's whole being is lightened. There is an agapeic mindfulness that is not just a grasp of something in particular, but an enlarged or deepened participation in being itself. We break through into participation in the community of being. Mindfulness is released to dwell more intensively in it. Being reborn to being, one says yes to our mindful community with being, and to its gift.

METAPHYSICS AND DIALECTIC

From "Being, Determination, and Dialectic"

Dialectic is tied to the entire range of ways of thinking about being that we find in the tradition of metaphysics. I will not review that range of ways, as I have done so elsewhere. Metaphysics now, of course, often meets with outright rejection as purportedly dealing with what lies beyond our ken, or as a conceptual projection onto an illusory transcendence of our own powers and impotences, or as the cunning conceit of an intellectual will to power. The intimacy of connection between dialectic and the thinking of being also defines part of the problematic of so-called postmetaphysical philosophy. The claim is that we are now to think beyond all that, beyond dialectic, beyond metaphysics, beyond being. None of these claims is itself immune from question. Hence, I want to consider this contested place of metaphysics, and the complex, indeed ambiguous, role dialectical thinking has played in defining that place.

Often we attribute the sources of this contested place to Hume, and in a more qualified way to Kant. By contrast, Hegel is frequently presented as embodying a postcritical resurgence of metaphysics, a recrudescence of what seemed to have been safely stowed in its grave. True, one finds interpretations in which Hegel as metaphysician is subordinated to Hegel the true heir of the Kantian project. Nevertheless, Hegel's continuity with the prior tradition is so massively evident, and not least in his respect for the Greeks, especially Aristotle, that this interpretation has much to do with the commentator's own embarrassments with metaphysics. Yet Hegel has been a contributer, sometimes witting, sometimes not, to metaphysics' contested place.

The view that Hegel represents a kind of summation of major strands in the Western tradition is not without some truth. This being so, if we wish to follow in his footsteps, we must strive for as comprehensive and nuanced an understanding of the possibilities of the philosophical tradition as he had. Obviously, this is extraordinarily difficult; it is Hegel's *greatness* that has made things more difficult for metaphysics rather than easier. To be a great metaphysician is not only to release essential possibilities of thinking, but it is also to cast a shadow over descendent thinkers under which they must struggle for light. Excess of light blinds eyes unused to the surplus of greatness.

If Hegel is the summation of the essential possibilities in the metaphysical tradition, there seems something unsurpassable about him. And yet just the alleged consummation leaves us strangely disquieted and hungry. If Hegel is a completion, the very completion shows forth starkly that something was missing in the quest, perhaps from the outset. The completion suggests the full richness of metaphysics, and yet the richness seems also to show (in Marx's phrase) the poverty of philosophy. Thus if we are to "surpass" this alleged end of metaphysics, we must do so from beyond the alleged poverty of philosophy. It goes without saying that this language of "the end of metaphysics" is not only the fashionable rhetoric of post-Heideggerian thought. It names a task that a plethora of thinkers set themselves in Hegel's wake, for instance, Marx in his will to realize, complete, and surpass philosophy in revolutionary praxis, Kierkegaard in his desire to be "postphilosophical" in religious faith, and Nietzsche in his eros to be a "new philosopher" celebrating the aesthetic theodicy of Dionysus. As much as, indeed more than the more positivistic or scientistic heirs of Kant or Hume, the continental heirs of completed idealism have been the "surpassers of metaphysics," be they rhapsodic descendants of Nietzsche or deconstructive heirs of Heidegger.

I do not invoke this throng of "postmetaphysical" despisers of "metaphysics" to enlist in their company. I think that much of this contestation of metaphysics is bound up with crucial ambiguities in dialectical thinking. I will explain what I mean in what follows. However, I want to reject from the outset the view that Hegel embodies the culmination of the tradition of metaphysics. I say this, not because I want to surpass metaphysics, in whatever direction, be it to praxis or to rhapsody or to poesy or to scientism or to grammatology, but because Hegelian dialectic represents a very powerful interpretation of thinking, yet one that hides nuances, nuances that, if resurrected for rethinking, shed a different light on metaphysical thinking, and the possibilities of its contemporary renewal.

The claim that Hegel represents the culmination of metaphysics has had disastrous consequences, not because Hegel is a disaster, but because the reiteration of this claim has stood in the way of rethinking metaphysics. It is like a mesmerizing fetish whose bewitching spell we cannot break. Why are we in its spell? Precisely because of Hegel's greatness, and the great difficulty of thinking philosophically at a level comparable to Hegel's. We cannot surpass Hegel because Hegel surpasses us, and the seeming comprehensive system freezes us, or exhausts us, instead of freeing us. It does not have to be so. Nor need one's strategy be just the predatory exploitation of this one aspect of Hegel's system to call that other aspect into account, as if we could beat one bone of Hegel's head with another bone taken from the dismembered body. We cannot confine ourselves to Hegel and his legacy. We must return to the sources of metaphysical thinking.

I cite four reasons why we need to do this: first, to have self-knowledge of what we are doing, and thus to understand the lack of understanding in much talk about the completion of metaphysics; second, to understand better Hegelian dialectic in the flawed incompleteness of its claim to completion; third, to understand better the equivocal legacy of dialectic in respect of some of Hegel's successors; fourth, since the sources are never behind us, to see how and why metaphysics will always continue to be reborn, beyond every claim to determinate completion. The different sections to follow will address these considerations. Since I am primarily approaching the matter in terms of a reflection on the sources of metaphysical thinking, I offer but a mediated glimpse of *what* one thinks when thinking thus.

I think the beginning of mindfulness is in an original astonishment before the givenness of being. Being is given to us; we are given to be, and to be as mindful; we do not first produce being, or make it be as for us; originally it is given as an excess of otherness which arouses our astonishment that it is at all. There is something childlike and virgin about this, but not childish. A child looks into the night sky and sees the silver orb of the moon. He or she may merely point, or exclaim: Look, the moon! There is something indeterminate about this. The point is not a definite indexical reference but an elemental acknowledgment of the being there of that beautiful being.

None of this is determinately known as such. It is lived, with a mindfulness that may be more or less rudimentary, more or less articulate. As has often been pointed out, children tend to ask the "big questions." They are not normally chastised for this; sometimes they are indulged. There are philosophers who will chastise the child in themselves for the seeming indulgence. There are philosophers who believe that if this virgin openness is lost completely then metaphysics has truly reached its dead end. The metaphysician keeps alive this elemental astonishment, and it is never dead even in the most articulated and developed of his categorial thoughts.

Why do we sometimes chastise the child, or more mellowly, indulge him or her? Because we have this inveterate tendency to think that to be is to be intelligible, and that to be intelligible is to be determinate. But— and this is the rub—the original astonishment is not determinate in that way at all. We believe that we must make definite every indefiniteness, make determinate all indeterminacies. Only thus, we hold, do we come to proper knowing of being. Moreover, this movement from the indefinite to the definite is often seen as a progressive conquering of the indeterminate, and hence a progressive process of leaving behind the original astonishment.

Astonishment may be a beginning, but it is one which is left behind as knowing fulfills its own destiny of completely determinate cognition.

I think that this is what is implied, for example, in Aristotle's discussion of *thaumazein*. Wonder may be the beginning of philosophy, but the end of the question is the dispelling of wonder in as determinate as possible a knowing of matters. This is why he uses geometry as an example of knowing. There is a solution that leaves behind the indefiniteness of the initial wonder, and that offers a definitely articulated answer. It is not that wonder is deepened in the end; it is dispelled.

By contrast, my sense is that Platonic wonder is not to be simply dispelled in the end but deepened. I know it was said that over the gates of the Academy the admonition stood: Let none who has not studied geometry enter here! However, this does not say that geometry is all we will study, once having entered, or that it epitomizes the highest kind of knowing. Indeed, if we take geometry as a figure for completely determinate cognition, it is not incidental that it reappears as an honorific goal throughout the tradition of philosophy. We see it in Descartes, Spinoza, Kant, Husserl, to mention some. What Pascal calls the *esprit géométrique* stands for a way of knowing deeply beloved by philosophy. As Pascal knew otherwise, however, there may be needed other modes of mindfulness, captured under the name of the *esprit de finesse*. There may be indeterminacies or overdeterminacies about the ontological situation that demand metaphysical finesse which does not conquer astonishment or perplexity but deepens and disquiets thinking even more radically.

What are some instances of such overdeterminacies? The question of being is one such: why being at all, why not nothing? The question of nothing is another. The question of the very givenness of being at all calls forth an indeterminate perplexity before an overdeterminacy that resists complete conceptual determination. The question of the meaning of freedom is also beyond complete determination. Questions about the suffering of the tragic, about the enigma of death, about the monstrousness of evil are overdeterminacies in the ontological situation, as are the traditional concerns with the being of truth, of the good, and of the beautiful. The questions of the ground of intelligibility is one such overdeterminacy: Can we give sufficient reason for the principle of sufficient reason? Is there a surd to intelligibility—that the intelligible is intelligible at all—a surd that is not just absurd?

Such questions put thinking on trial. They provoke determinate thinking, but they issue in perplexities that do not yield a univocal answer, resisting being conclusively formulated as univocal problems. A constitutive ambiguity persists, a constitutive openness remains, beyond our efforts at determination. Since such questions concern the being or the good or the intelligibility of the determinate, they come to articulation from beyond the determinate. We may not be able univocally to answer such perplexities, but we cannot negate them. They continue to be reborn. Though we cannot master or dissolve them completely, we must return to them again and again, and with thinking informed by mindfulness of what comes to be at the edge of determination.

I have no desire to undermine or deconstruct the emphasis on definite cognition of the determinacies of beings or processes. However, I do not think philosophical mindfulness is simply a progressive conquering of an initial indefiniteness by a more and more complete determinate cognition. There is something about the beginning that is not only in excess of objectification and determination at the beginning, but that remains in excess at the end, even after our most strenuous efforts at determination. I think we need to distinguish between the following: first, the original astonishment; second, perplexity; and third, the curiosity that leads on to definite cognition. Let me explain further.

Astonishment names the original wonder. I prefer the term "astonishment" because contemporary usage of the word "wonder" easily slides into the sentimental. We are struck into astonishment. We do not think our way into astonishment; we are overcome by astonishment. There is a certain shock or bite of otherness in astonishment. There is also a certain receptivity, indeed patience. The givenness of being is offered for our beholding. We are patient to its giving insofar as we do not produce it, or bring it towards ourselves only for it just to be cognitively possessed by us. There is always an excess in astonishment. Something is both given to mindfulness, and yet is in excess of what mindfulness can grasp clearly and distinctly in that given. Astonishment is aroused when there is, so to say, a "too-muchness" about the givenness of something that both overcomes us and fascinates us. Moreover, this astonishing, although not first within our control, and though resistant to exhaustive illumination in clear and distinct concepts, is not a mere vague indefiniteness. It is indeterminate, but indeterminate in a positive and affirmative sense. This is why I prefer to speak of an overdetermination: such a sense of the indeterminate is not antithetical to determination. Rather it exceeds every determination we will later attempt, exceeds complete encapsulation in a definite and exhaustive definition. This affirmative overdetermination of the beginning will be very important in understanding the equivocities of dialectic below, and the fact that there is no end of metaphysical thinking.

Perplexity, by contrast, is a movement of mindfulness that arises subsequently to the first astonishment. The very excess of what is first given rouses thought and questioning on our behalf. Something excessive is given, and we would fain interpret its meaning. Perplexity arises when mind becomes troubled about the meaning of the original astonishment and what is given to thought in it. There is also something indeterminate about perplexity, but there is a more concerted movement to overcome the indeterminate. The very troubling of thought here seeks its own overcoming in a peace of mind that is no longer troubled or perplexed. Thus we find the beginnings of the movement towards determinate cognition, but in such a fashion that the aura of the beginning still wraps itself around mindfulness. Perplexity is not patience to the otherness of being in quite the same way as is the original astonishment. In its troubled mindfulness there works a vector of self-transcendence that would go towards this otherness of being, and if possible overcome its own perplexity. Perplexity is felt as a lack of definite cognition, driving out beyond itself to overcome that lack.

From this drive there arises the movement of mind towards determinate cognition. That is, perplexity becomes *curiosity* when the indefiniteness of perplexity is focused more specifically on particular beings and processes. Perplexity may have an indefiniteness about it, in that one might be perplexed and not know quite what one is perplexed about. Curiosity, however, is more clearly definite; one is curious about this, that, or the other. Curiosity is not vague, though it may be itchy, that is, greedily extend itself to everything coming within its purview. It is with curiosity that definite questions arise about particular beings and processes, definite questions that seek determinate answers. Yet like perplexity, the movement of curiosity is also out of an initial sense of lack: I lack the definite knowing of this, that, or the other; nevertheless, I take definite steps to acquire proper determinate knowing; and the goal is just such determinate cognition as brings to an end the thrust of curiosity, and overcomes the initial lack of knowledge that drives the seeking.

Overall, then, there is something excessive and overdetermined about the astonishing beginning; then there is a troubled indefiniteness and sense of lack in the perplexity of mind that is subsequently precipitated; finally, there is a drive to definiteness and determination in curiosity that seeks to overcome any survival of troubled indefiniteness and lack, such as we find in perplexity.

Why is it important to distinguish these three? Because in the main we have tended to think of the process of mindfulness, whether philosophical or scientific, in terms of the third possibility, and in such a fashion that certain fertile resources in the first two are easily distorted, I think the first two are not reducible to the third. However, because we have often privileged the third, we have a predilection for modes of cognition, like mathematical knowing or objective science, as most fully living up to the inner exigence of the desire to know. These seem to epitomize the ideal of knowing that is as completely determinate as possible, wherein all indeterminacy and indefiniteness seem to be progressively conquered. The *esprit géométrique* is tempted to make redundant the *esprit de finesse*, and to do so with a clean epistemological conscience. For after all, is not this redundancy just the inevitable end of proper progress to epistemic enlightenment? Who could possibly want to sing the praises of the indeterminate?

I ask allowance to offer another way to describe the differences between astonishment and perplexity, with implications for curiosity and determinate cognition. I use the classical language of eros and agape. Astonishment is agapeic; perplexity is erotic. When determinate cognition, begotten of curiosity, forgets or denies its origin in these parents, it becomes an ungrateful child, at times begetting some unsweet issue of its own.

What I mean in calling astonishment agapeic is that it arises from a surplus or excess out of which an affirmative movement of mind as self-transcending emerges. The beginning is already full, overfull, and out of this overfull beginning a movement of self-transcendence towards the other arises. It is to the excessive richness of the origin that I want to call attention. Moreover, the arising movement of self-transcending is not simply for purposes of a return to the self. I do not go out from myself towards the other to appropriate the other and through the other to return to myself. I go towards the other because the other is for itself and always irreducible to what it is for me. It is its being for itself that is affirmed, celebrated in this movement of going beyond self. It is the stunning beauty of *the moon* that the child's exclamation celebrates, not the child's own feelings. This agapeic relation to the other as other must be kept in mind by metaphysical thinking, especially since other possibilities can come to distort its promise, as indeed does a certain rendition of dialectic.

By contrast, I call perplexity erotic because it arises out of a troubled sense of lack and desire: as ignorant, one lacks definite knowledge of the other that is given to mindfulness in astonishment; and yet one desires to overcome that lack of ignorance. The beginning of perplexity is this indigence of knowing, out of which indigence there is a movement of self-transcendence towards the other. I also call this movement erotic because the other sought is sought for the sake of alleviating perplexity's own troubled mindfulness. It is for the sake of returning the self to its own epistemic peace or satisfaction with itself. I go towards the other out of my own lack; I need the other to requite my own lack; I appropriate or possess the other to enable my own self-appropriation or self-possession. There is a return to self through the other; hence the movement is a complex self-mediation that passes towards and through the other on the way back to itself; and now, at the end, we no longer live in the initial lack of perplexity but think we have fulfilled the eros of knowing in its own self-knowledge. The lack of the beginning seems to be overcome in the end that returns to the beginning, which is consummated self-knowing.

Note that if our major philosophical emphasis falls here, the other is no longer for itself, but is a medium in which I become for myself. Then the drive of self-transcendence puts primary stress on the self rather than on the transcendence, whereas in agapeic astonishment there is also self-transcendence, but the transcending is *more* than the self and, in a way, the self is more than itself, in genuinely exceeding itself towards the other.

Curiosity partakes more of erotic perplexity than agapeic astonishment. For it is driven by a lack of knowledge, and this it wants to overcome through cognitive possession of the other it first lacks. Curiosity seeks its own alleviation in the mitigation of its ignorance of what is other to itself. In contradistinction to perplexity proper, it exhibits greater insistence on the determinacies of knowing. The eros of perplexity has an openness to its self-transcendence; and it can be willing to let its deeper exigencies be troubled by questions that may perhaps exceed its present, even future, determination. There may be perplexities about life, about death, that are forever beyond complete determination. Yet the eros of perplexity is not brought to a standstill by this always unavoidable failure of determinate cognition. Its very failure may augur something other that is positive, and may incite a new restlessness of self-transcending thinking. The ultimate failure of complete determination may energize mind in another dimension to determinate curiosity. The eros is infinitely restless.

There is no end of metaphysics, precisely because the sources of metaphysical thinking are in a beginning that always exceeds complete objectification. Moreover, the modes of mindfulness that go with the overdetermined beginning also exceed complete determination. When Heidegger calls for a new beginning beyond the so-called end of metaphysics, he may be right about the need for something other to calculative thinking, and so beyond the determinacies of curiosity, but this other thinking is not just back there before Plato and Socrates did their "bad" work, nor yet before us in the future, in the coming mission of being. The sources are always here now. Agapeic astonishment and perplexity cannot be thought of as before and after a temporal span, since they are promises ingredient in all spans, and hence permeate the middle, as much as the extremes of the middle. The excess is as much in the middle as at the extremes, and it is this overdetermined middle we must think.

In other words, I am not concerned with a move from the overdetermined to the indefinite to the determinate to the self-determined. I am concerned with the overdetermined that is there always with all of these particular possibilities. At any point there can be a resurgence of agapeic astonishment; at any point there can be a resurrection of erotic perplexity. There is a second indeterminate perplexity that exceeds all the hard won gains of determinate science, and that is not itself an instance of a new curiosity that will be answered for in terms of a further determinate solution. It is in another dimension, even while it permeates all the dimensions of the determinate. This second indeterminate perplexity that is not exhausted by determinate cognition drives the restless self-transcendence of philosophical thinking.

Is this all that drives philosophical thinking? I do not think so, though in some cases it may seem to be all that is available to a particular thinker. What I mean is that, finally, erotic perplexity is lacking just in its lack. The very restlessness it expresses is itself grounded in a prior, more affirmative, energy of being that cannot be expressed in merely lacking terms. The self-transcendence of erotic perplexity could not be the self-surpassing it is but for transcendence that is more than self and lack. Lack becomes restless just because in lack there is an affirmative original energy driving lack out beyond itself. This more original source is, from the start, beyond lack. It is agapeic in the sense of being given out of an affirmative surplus. Lack does not exceed itself; rather the self exceeds itself as lack because already it is the promise of more than lack. Without adequate understanding of this, erotic self-surpassing can become a negating self-transcendence that finally comes to nothing. Indeed, it may be consumed by what it takes as nothing, not only the nothingness of things other to itself, but by its own nothingness. All of this is, however, to not grant the agape of being that is first granted.

In a word, we need the resurrection of astonishment. Of course, this is a poor way to put the point. You cannot just say: we need astonishment, and then go out and find it, as if we could whistle and have it come. Calling it forth at will, this is just what we cannot do. We cannot will astonishment. It is a given. It is a gift. There is required preparation, waiting, purified willingness, opening, tireless thinking. There is a willingness beyond will to power. Self-transformation is called for, but this cannot be a process of self-mediation only. Something from beyond self must be allowed to give itself, if it will give itself at all. This is all the more difficult in our time when the general spiritual ethos is pervasively pragmatic and oriented to instrumental problem solving. We give our concern to things about which we can do something, where we seem able to will it and bring them under some control. Since astonishment is in another dimension, we have to place ourselves, or be placed, in that different dimension, beyond all will to power.

THE METAXOLOGICAL

From *Being and the Between*

THE PLURIVOCITY OF BEING AND THE METAXOLOGICAL

Being is given. Its givenness reappears over and over, redoubled in excess of any dialectical reduction to a monism of self-mediation. The excess redoubles itself in the origin, in the middle, and in the end. It is to the pluralization of the mediations of givenness that the metaxological sense speaks. It is not reductive of the pluralization, either univocally or dialectically; nor is it dissipative of it into only an equivocal many. If being is spoken in many senses, these must include a proper understanding of unity, of difference, and of mediated community. These requirements are addressed by univocity, equivocity, and dialectic, in each case with strengths and limitations. The metaxological addresses the same requirements but always keeps in mind the excess of being's plenitude that is never exhaustively mediated by us.

If univocity stresses sameness, equivocity difference, dialectic the appropriation of difference within a mediated sameness, the metaxological reiterates, first a sense of otherness not to be included in dialectical self-mediation, second a sense of togetherness not reached by the equivocal, third a sense of rich ontological integrity not answered for by the univocal, and fourth a rich sense of ontological ambiguity not answered for either by the univocal, the equivocal, the dialectical.

I suggest that as dialectic tries to redeem the promise of univocity beyond equivocity, so the metaxological tries to redeem the promise of equivocity beyond univocity and dialectic. It keeps the space of the between open to mediations from the other irreducible to any mediation from the self. The *dia* of dialectic is to be genuinely preserved in its doubleness, and dialectic's promise thus fulfilled. The mediation from the other converges on the middle out of its own excess of being and integrity for itself. And though the other may meet the self in the middle, the intermediation between them cannot be totally characterized in terms of the mediation of any one of them.

There is a convergence of self and other, and a communication from one to the other. This community and convergence is exhausted by none,

33

just as none is exhausted in its express mediation with the others. There is a reserve of excess in the beings in intermediation, a reserve not itself exhausted by their complex, nonreductive community of togetherness. If rather than self-mediation there is intermediation, this is double and redoubled; so even in its being communicated, the excess of transcendence remains reserved as excess. This is so, in the giving of the beginning of the between, in the supporting of its continued coming to be, and in the offering of its fulfilled ontological promise in the good.

If being is given, it is given both for itself and for mindfulness. Mindfulness is itself given to itself to be mindful of being, both in itself and in its otherness as given. Being is given as the happening of the between; but this between *is immediately given as mediated* between a plurality of centers of existence, each marked by its own energy of self-transcendence. In the human being this self-transcendence becomes mindful of itself and transcendence as other. Therefore, the meaning of the "to be" demands that we do justice to the following: first to the givenness of being-there in the between; second to the concretization there of integrities of being; third to the complexity of mediation between beings among themselves; fourth to the complexity of mediation between the human being as mindful and the rest of being in its difference.

THE METAXOLOGICAL AND THE PLAY OF INDETERMINACY AND DETERMINATION

Since the start of this work, we have been reflecting more and more adequately on the traditional belief that to be, and to be intelligibly, is to be determinate. I do not simply reject this view, but its limitations have been made evident, resulting in our thinking of other senses of being that are not intelligible in terms of some set of determinations, whether predicable features, or forms of things, or thought-categories. As we found, the indeterminate reappears, and not as the merely indefinite that must then be made determinate. It reappears as an overdetermination of being, of an original dynamism of being that cannot be finalized or fixed. It reappears also as an overdetermination of mindfulness in which the thought of being as given in agapeic astonishment cannot be exhausted in any infinite set of thought-determinations, This overdetermination is the manifest transcendence of being as original plenitude, as itself the festive agape of being.

Let us begin by asking: How does the fourfold sense relate to this plenitude? My answer to follow will serve both to recapitulate and move us forward.

First, with the *univocal* sense we find a drive to reduce this overdetermination to the indefinite, on which fixed determinations of being and thought are imposed. In fact, this putative indefiniteness proves dynamic in itself as a process of becoming. But the category of the indefinite is by no means adequate to name what is at work in being prior to fixed determinacy. Likewise, any fixation of the indefinite by imposed category always proves less than final. Both the process of becoming and the process of thinking continually pass beyond that fixation, even while exploiting that fixation and gaining from it some intelligible lucidity.

Second, with the *equivocal* sense there emerges a sensitivity for the indeterminate beyond univocal determinacy. For the process of becoming itself generates this emergence; it is not a merely arbitrary stipulation by an abstract intellect expressing its dissatisfaction with the thought-determinations of univocity. The self-transcending of becoming and mind themselves recur to the indeterminate, because the indeterminate continues again and again to renew itself in both. Moreover, this repetition is not the reiteration of the univocal same, since the repetition of the indeterminate is the emergence of variability and diversity. Because the indeterminate is overdetermined it can throw up differences again and again, such that, while the differences are differences redoubled, they are reiterated as *difference for themselves*, and hence as other to each other, and not as multiplied univocal variations on an underlying univocal sameness. And so there is here recognized an *interplay* of the determinate and indeterminate. Yet, all too often, the tendency to think in terms of the indefinite still persists; then this interplay is itself characterized as indefinite. Instead of a univocal determination of the indefinite, the equivocal sense then offers us an *indefinite play between the determinate and the indeterminate*.

In fact, the play is not simply indefinite; it is an interplay, and hence a mediated play; it is intelligibly mediated, hence complexly determined too. The play itself is not the articulation of the indefinite but of the overdetermined power of being. The *dialectical* sense, and *third*, offers us a way to think the play between the indeterminate and the determinate in more than indefinite terms. This play is mediated, and the rhythm of the interplay shows itself as a passage back and forth between the terms in interplay. The determinate and the indeterminate are said to define each other. Each would not be what it is without the other, and hence each is necessary for the other. Hence the determinate is the indeterminate, but in the form of its being concretely determined. The indeterminate is also the determinate, but in the prior form of yet-to-be determined being; it is the lack of definition that later will be made definite in the concrete mediated process of determination. Both the determinate and the indeterminate as other are finally alike, both defined as different stages of a process that mediates with itself in the interplay between them.

Thus the dialectical defamation of the interplay between determinacy and indeterminacy tends to give the primary emphasis to self-mediation. This is why in the interplay it sees the basis for a transformation of determination into a process of *self-determination* that works through a logic of determinate negation: the negation of the indefinite will not produce another indefinite, but an affirmative determination. Thus the indefinite is increasingly transformed into the determinate by means of an increasingly autonomous self-determination. Through a negativity that is self-relating, the play of indeterminacy and determinacy is interpreted as the self-negation of the indefinite, and its transformation into something definite through self-negation. The transformation of self-negation into determinate self-negation makes the process one of self-determination. In sum, the dialectical interplay of the determinate and indeterminate mediates a move from the overdetermined to the indefinite to the determinate to the self-determining.

What can be questionable about this? Answer: the overdetermined as *other* can be occluded, in the beginning and in the end. For if the logic of self-mediation is claimed to cover *completely* the entire interplay, the indefinite *must displace* the overdetermined as other. But this is a diminution or contraction of the overdetermined excess. It is now, and *fourth,* that the *metaxological* sense enters, for it serves to remind us of the excess that is prior to the contraction, an excess that also remains *after* a logic of self-mediation claims to determine itself absolutely. This also means we are *returned to the interplay*, where we begin to see *beyond* the work of self-mediation to the overdetermined as other. This latter, we begin to suspect, makes possible the process of self-determination, even though it is not a process of self-determination only, nor entirely intelligible in terms of such a process. In other words, the metaxological sense reminds us of the resurgence of excess beyond complete determination. The transcendence of being as other resurrects itself again and again. And there remains excess in the origin, in the between, and in the end.

There is excess in the beginning. What I mean is that the overdetermined power of being is prior to and beyond any beginning considered as indefinite. For to be a beginning the indefinite somehow has to be, and to be it must be already given to be; it does not give itself to be; it is a derivative, not an absolute beginning; it is derivative of the overdetermined plenitude to which it is unequal. The metaxological seeks to restore mindfulness of the *that it is given to be at all.* Moreover, this restoration is shaped in a recall of the agapeic astonishment that is prior to all perplexity and determinate thinking about being. The origin suggested in agapeic astonishment is beyond all determination, and yet it is what gives the possibility of all determinacy, and hence too of the delimited intelligibility of beings. As intimated on previous occasions, the origin is given indeterminately in agapeic astonishment. This is why "what" is given in astonishment proves to be so extraordinarily elusive, exorbitantly enigmatic. Hence also its resistant ambiguity is easily turned into equivocal terms; or its ever-renewed dynamism is shunned in favor of fixed univocity; or its enigma is occluded in favor of the self-satisfaction of autonomous thinking, and determined exclusively in terms of dialectical intelligibility.

None of these latter responses is enough. None dwells deeply enough with the happening of the between relative to the excess of the origin. It is the call of metaxological mindfulness to dwell thus. This is not easy. It may be necessary to wait in an indeterminate darkness, endure lack of self-certainty, grope for what one cannot exactly say, speak as intelligibly as possible of what eludes every final why, or how, or whence, or whither. One suffers the resurgence of the second indeterminate perplexity that has been touched by transcendence in the middle, briefly illuminated and blinded by this touch, made to suffer metaphysical migraine in incessant thought of what might have been given in that communication.

There is excess at the end. Granted the prior more of transcendence at the origin, agapeic astonishment is not quelled by being reminded of being's givenness. Quite the opposite: it tends to deepen the more deeply we think the otherness of what is given to be. The excess of the origin is never rendered completely determinate in the middle. And even though the more determinate our mindfulness becomes, the more the middle is rendered determinate, the excess still escapes beyond all this. We face, so to say, the *too muchness* of being that still at the end is beyond all determination. The restlessness driving our mindfulness to more and more determinate thinking finds, even in its greatest success, that there is still more, still an other side to the most exhaustive determination of being, an other side transcendent to determinacy. We find ourselves turned around, as in Plato's *periagogé* of the soul. The height of determinate knowing turns into a humble consent to the mystery of being, as passing beyond all determinate knowing.

There is excess in the middle. This is evident in the play of the determinate and the indeterminate in *beings*. No being can be rendered so absolutely fixed that any reserve of indeterminacy or promise of being other is completely brought to finalized thereness. Ontological freshness lives on, burns still in finite determinate beings. This freshness is their being renewed in being, again and again. Even when they are passing out of being, the freshness of renewal, passing beyond the dying being of this thing, is never smothered. It still burns on. The metaxological sense serves as a reminder of this inward otherness of things in their ontological freshness.

And suppose we consider the play of determination and indeterminacy relative to the *plurality* of beings. We discover a relativity between beings, one being contributing to the determination of another, another being bringing about the opening of yet another being, in the continuing of a dynamic process of becoming. So not only do beings in their *singular play* resist exhaustion in terms of determination and self-determination; beings in their *communal interplay* escape beyond singular dialectical determination. The community of beings in interplay is not a dialectical self-mediating whole; it reveals a metaxological intermediation between beings who are open wholes unto themselves, without being completely determined in themselves. Their relativity to others and of others to them shows multiple mediations that cannot be finalized, for the ontological freshness still flares there too.

Overall, then, the metaxological sense is mindful *of openings* in the happening of the between. It is also mindful of the *opening of* the between itself, beyond all boundaries of finite determination. Transcendence transcends the happening of the between, even while the between, metaxologically understood, marks an opening beyond itself towards the most ultimate other, whose integrity for itself can never be determinately mastered, The immanent middle opens beyond itself to unconditional transcendence. The relativity of beings in the between do not form a closed circle of mutual self-definition. The very interruptions in immanent relativity remind us that the vector of self-transcending is an infinitely restless seeking of unconditional transcendence. The happening of the between is not completely self-determining, but its unmastered indeterminacy points beyond the middle to the overdetermined excess of the origin as other. This excess is also the excess of the good, which is the excess of the end.

THE METAXOLOGICAL AND THE COMMUNITY OF BEINGS

What now of the *community* of beings? As there is a resistance to self-mediation in both the singularity of beings and the mindful being, just so *between* beings there is also otherness beyond self-mediation. The very word "community" points beyond the unity of the univocal, for it is the "unity" of a plurality of integrities, and we must emphasize the word *cum*, "with," as much as the word "unity." There is a pluralized "unity" of "being with," a togetherness of beings in community. And while difference is needed to make plurality possible, this togetherness cannot be any merely unmediated equivocity.

Beings hold together as integrities; the plurality of integrities holds together, even in the incalculable diversity and stunning prodigality of the many. This "holding together" is not a superimposition on plural terms already finished in their self-definition, such that all that remains to do is to cast a net of relations over them in their diversity. Rather the community is constituted by a coming to be; there is something essentially dynamic about community. The active differentiation we find with equivocity is here retained in the articulations of integrities of being, dynamically interinvolved with each other through a network of relating. "Relating" itself implies an active interinvolving, beyond all established stases and, as we shall see, beyond all determinate objectifications.

The community of being is a coming into the between. "Coming" here signals the work of transcending in each singular entity. Beings come to be in the middle, but coming to be is being in community, for there is no absolutely solitary coming to be. Coming to be is a relation of community, a social relation. If B comes to be, it comes to be from A, and there is a community of relation between the issue and the source. If the source A gives B to be, then the source itself is the promise of community between itself and what has issued from it. Coming to be, even when what comes to be is given its otherness and freedom, is still a social relation; for the free being that is the issue is still defined in its being by its "being with" the source that gives it to be freely. Of course, since the beings that come to be are for themselves also, concretions of self-transcending power in themselves, the complexities of that "being with" are multiple, often multiplied beyond any clear and distinct disentangling. This is the intimation of the equivocal sense, when it feels the promiscuous co-implication of each in all and all in each.

There is a misunderstanding to be avoided. The coming into community does not mean beings first come to be themselves and then enter community. This is not so. There is from the beginning a "being with," relative to which the coming to singular being reaches any determination. Nor is there simply a coming to community before a coming to singularity. Rather there is no coming to singularity that is not also a coming to relativity with the other. Hence there is no coming to be that is not also a coming to be in community. There is a priority to community in this regard, that no singular is self-generated. Its generation as self is the issue from an other; its very being itself is a generational relation to an other or others.

This understanding of the coming to be in community is related to the idea of creation. Creation is an issuing into otherness and an articulation of a relativity to an other, even in the singular determination of an integral being as for itself. We might say that since the community of being is at all, it is creation that provides the embracing context of coming to be, wherein the plurality of singulars comes to self-definition. We sense this prior inherence of community in creation when we are struck into agapeic astonishment. We may not be able thus to articulate it; all we may do is stammer the "It is" or perhaps the "It is good." But these are not negligible, are indeed momentous. In the "It is" and the "It is good," what is implicated is a more universal sense of the community of being, as coming to be in the givenness of creation. I know many will think of this as vague and indefinite. No doubt much of this is and remains so for us. But when we try to think it through, however, the meaning is not at all indefinite, but rather concerns our initial intimacy with the coming to be of the community of being in creation. There is a prior community of being, which is the immediacy of an overdetermined plenitude of being. This is what is given indeterminately to mindfulness in agapeic astonishment, though when we find the right words for what is given, we see something momentously affirmative in this excess of determination.

Within the given community, determinate beings and the mindful human being live their own participation in the energy of transcendence. They come into the coming into the middle which is the community of being. So what we find in the middle, then, is the coming together, with a variety of different determinations, or different interplays between indeterminacy and determination, of a plurality of centers of self-transcendence. The community of being is the conjunction of this plurality of integrities of self-transcendence. Moreover, this conjunction is less the obviation of difference as the concretion of relativity in difference and across difference. It is not the obliteration of difference in a homogeneous sameness, but rather a going beyond homogeneous sameness and the sustaining of a relativity in the very determination of heterogeneity itself.

I said that the coming to be of the singular is itself communal from the outset. We must now advert to the double mediation at work: each being is a center of self-mediation and hence is for itself; each being is defined in a network of intermediating relations with what is other to itself. Its self-transcending energy, as coming into the middle, is defined by this doubleness, with all the tensions therein, as well as the opportunities for creative origination beyond itself. In itself the being is marked by community; hence its being cannot be exhausted by self-mediation; nor can its relatedness to what is other and beyond.

This is what is at issue in the metaxological sense: a pluralization of the event of mediation such that it is impossible to reduce the plurality to one form—namely, that of an encompassing self-mediation. Something escapes this reduction in the immanence of the between. Mediation is so pluralized that there is no singular mediation that will include all others within its own encompassing hold. The enigma of pluralized mediation itself escapes beyond complete mediation, for the beings in community are free from mediating in the mediating itself.

The doubleness *within* is complicated by the redoubling of relativity to other beings, each complexified in itself, relative to its own inherent double mediation; mediation is redoubled within and hence is beyond self-mediation. Mediation is redoubled *outside*, redoubled beyond the embrace of one singular self-mediation. The process of intermediation is just this escaping from the closure of any form of complete self-mediating, no matter how absolutized. The community of being has to be thought in terms other than absolutized self-mediation. Community of being is infinitely complicated, complicated in that there is a co-implication of each being with other beings, a co-implication not exhausted in a logic of dialectical determination. The infinite complication takes us to the limit of this logic.

The reader may find helpful the following summary line of thought, for it leads us to the question we want to pose: Suppose the beings in interplay are each dialectically self-mediating, and suppose that this self-mediation makes them wholes; suppose further than there is a depth of infinitude at work in this self-mediation, such as we termed the intimacy of being, and suppose that this were such as to make each of these beings an open whole, a whole that opens into its own intimacy of being and that opens beyond itself into the between; and suppose that beings as thus complexly defined were multiplied without number; then what would we say about the mediation *between* such beings, such as to constitute the community of being?

This is the answer I suggest: the mediation between a plurality of such open self-mediating beings cannot just be any form of self-mediation. Remember that such beings are pluralized within themselves. Were we to answer that community is simply a more encompassing self-mediating whole, we would have truncated the immanent self-mediation of each being in its opening into its own intimacy of being; we would have glossed over the singularity of self-transcendence that each such being is; we would have also closed off its inexhaustibility, and made it a partial, finite manifestation of a more inclusive mode of dialectical self-mediation. In a word, this absolutization of self-mediation is hence a betrayal of self-mediation. Dialectic thus absolutized betrays dialectic. The doubling within, and the pluralization without, escape beyond this absolutizaticn.

It should be clear that the double here at issue cannot be determined in the standard terms of a dualism. Where there is otherness, of course, we always find the potential for opposition, as well as for equivocites resistant to mediation. But since the present meaning of doubling is defined with reference to the community of relativity, standard dualistic language is inappropriate, for it is a corollary of rigid univocal thinking. Nor is the double a vanishing phase of a more encompassing process, an opposition that in its lack undermines itself, to be superseded by a more inclusive unitary process of dialectical self-mediation. This is to reduce the doubling to an ontological level less complex than dialectic. In fact, the doubling is more rich that dialectic as self-mediation; it is the *dia* beyond self-mediation. And since it is itself beyond self-mediation, it is not in need of being subsumed into a community beyond lack. The community offers a pluralization of freedom beyond all self-mediation, and hence beyond freedom defined as self-determination.

Remember that the dialectic that privileges self-mediation takes its sights from the ability of thought to think what is other, and to bring the other into relativity to itself. The conclusion then drawn is that the thought that thinks the other overreaches the other; hence in thinking the other as a thought, it ends up as the thought that thinks itself, but now inclusive of otherness. And its image of community rides piggyback on this self-transcending power and its purported inclusion of the other. Its conclusion is: the absolute community would be the absolutely inclusive process of dialectical self-mediation.

Metaxological metaphysics contests this way of thinking community. It recurs again to the double mediation operative even when thought thinks itself. It recurs also to the self-transcending of mindfulness as not reducible to an erotic knowing that in knowing the other really completes its own lack as ignorance and returns to itself in self-certain satisfied knowing. By contrast, metaxological metaphysics goes towards the other, out of the double mediation of thought, but lets the thinking of the other be guided by an agapeic mindfulness that goes towards the other as other, and not on a mediating detour that recoils back on itself, once having appropriated the other. Agapeic mind is an exemplification of communicative being; it is a being mindfully there for the other as other, and not for the self itself. It goes towards the other, it delivers itself over to the other; and this making itself available for the other is its communication of itself to the other. It communicates itself not out of lack merely, but out of an excess or surplus, out of a generosity of being that gives to the other for the other.

Agapeic mindfulness, as communicative thinking of the other, is an intermediation which, in going towards the other, gives itself to the other as other, and does not think about what it gets from what it gives, if indeed it gets anything at all. Its generosity of transcendence is a giving for nothing, nothing beyond the goodness of the giving itself. Agapeic mind gives its understanding over to the position of the other from its otherness, seeks to see the other from within the intimacy of its own integrity of being. It is eccentric relative to self-mediation. There is compassion in this knowing, an undergoing with the other, not a standing above in the mode of mastery or domination.

Clearly, too, the standard models of *atomism* and *holism* will not do. The atomistic model sees a set of primitive univocals and then knits them together in terms of a set of extrinsic connections. The atoms have nothing to do with each other inherently; they are indifferently external to each other. It should now be clear that such atoms are really the sclerosis of singularity, its hardening into a knot of being, devoid of immanent mediation and the energy of transcendence. Inevitably atomism conceives of community in terms of an impoverished version of merely external relations. Externality is also understood on a very impoverished univocity. The sense of singularity we have developed opens up the intimacy of the being of beings and also their energy of transcendence, such that there are no merely external relations in this aggregational sense.

That said, there is also a holism to be avoided, one which stresses the *mutual definition* of beings in a manner that dissolves this hardened knot of atomic singularity into a network of relations, outside of which it is nothing. This holism sees the relativity of the singular to the others, but *dissolves the singularity* into this relativity. Moreover, it claims a prior implicit whole at work which defines the singular, and a subsequent whole that subsumes the putative singular. Given our account, such holism is not adequate to what is at play in the singular; nor is its definition of the internal relatedness of things adequate to the immanent doubleness of things and the co-implications of transcendences in the relations between things.

Plurality is not precipitated by the splitting of a prior whole into parts, parts then reintegrated into a more articulated whole. Rather the giving of plurality in its otherness and togetherness is a giving of plurality as for itself; singular integrities are not merely parts of a larger whole, but wholes unto themselves, that are also open beyond themselves. As opening beyond themselves, they do not constitute their inherent relativity to others by being subsumed into a larger whole of which they are subordinated parts. The community of being they constitute is transcendent to such a dialectical whole. There is no totalism of the whole within which the plurality of integrities is sublated, contributory parts.

So we must say that there is the excess of transcendence at all levels, from the beginning through the middle to the end, and the end closes nothing off but rather renews the promise of freedom. The community of being is not an inclusive totality, but a being together in transcendence of which there is no totalization. For this being together constitutes the happening of the middle as the promise of radical freedom from absorption in all totalities. The community and its metaxological togetherness, and the modes of intermediation that shape the energy of transcendence, are beyond all totality. The spaces between beings upheld by community are not subordinate determinations of an all-inclusive totality, but indeterminacies that welcome the advent and adventure of the freedom of its participants. This community involves a pluralization of the excess of freedom.

Indeed this very excess makes the community possible. There is no final determination of what a community of freedom is, for freedom itself is a determining beyond determination. Nor is it just self-determination, for there is a different sense of freedom into which we are delivered by an agapeic relation to what is other. The freedom beyond self-determination is a gift, first *of* the other, then *for* the other. The community of transcendence beyond all totalization is the pluralization and togetherness of this agapeic giving. Community reveals the mystery of ontological generosity.

Let me offer the following image, as suggesting something of the requisite respect for singularity and otherness. I have in mind the catacombs. This might seem a startling image relative to community, since the catacombs are mass graves. Human beings are mashed into the earth, homogeneous humus again. And yet, in death, beyond death, there is a sign of community that seeks to acknowledge absolute singularity.

Consider. One descends into the catacombs outside Rome. The weight of the earth above one crushes with the inexorable weight of death which no human being can bear. In this company of death one is awakened to thoughts of posthumous mind. One assumes the mind of the dead, thinking of what being looks like from the placeless abode of the dead. One is overcome by the view from nowhere, and looks again on being, more slowly, stunned into silence, made pensive by perishing. Wrenched out of mindless immersion in being, one tries to see and think what it is one is immersed in, given over to, tries to think its unmastered mystery.

One goes down into the bountiful earth itself, home of the living, home of the dead. These chambers of burial are often conceived as hiding places for persecuted Christians, but it appears this is overstated. There is another, perhaps more important sense of hiddenness in the earth and in death. One goes down into a mystery that exceeds all thought, contracting into the darkness. In the ensuing enclosure one is mindful that there are thousands upon thousands dead here. There is the numberless pluralization of the dead. These too were once, but now are no more, never again to walk into the air and the light, to feel the solid earth beneath, the soaring sky above, the bobbing blossoms on the trees, the swaying grass to which the breeze whispers, "It is good."

As one goes downward and downward, one enters the graves of the paupers rather than the sepulchers of the rich above ground. One sees the places of individual burial, the singularity even in death itself. There are the places, now empty of all bones, of small children. One cannot but sense the loving of singularity even in death again, beyond death, with the hope of being again, even despite the crushing "never," being again as this singular beloved one. There are the altars where the early Christians celebrated Mass, the eucharistic agape of Jesus.

These are not simply mass graves. Hundreds of thousands are buried, but these are not the mass graves we know from the modern totalitarian evil. In the latter mass graves, there are no singulars, there is no respect, no God. Posthumous mind, so to say, demands a metaphysics of being beyond

Auschwitz: a thinking of singularity and community beyond absorbing total-ity. The catacombs look like a mass grave, but the meaning is not mass humanity. Each hole of death, each gap of gaping absence, every empty tomb, is a reminder, a sign of the community of irreducible singulars before God. Everyone can step into that space of singularity, is already in it, and every singular will go under into the space of death. But these holes of the dead, these holes in the earth, are also holes of love, holes of the "I" and the "We" that cared for the dead "I"—beyond death, worthy to be loved for itself, beyond what life and death do to it, beyond even the happening of the between. And all this, because the singular "I" is loved as a singular absolute in a community before God, the absolute original.

THE IDIOCY OF BEING

From *Perplexity and Ultimacy*

Philosophers sometimes exhibit a species of metaphysical anxiety when singularity is taken as ultimate. Yet the question arises: Is there a kind of absolute singularity, particularly in relation to selfhood, a singularity at the edge of inclusion in any conceptual system? Is there a certain thisness to self which from the standpoint of universal science is idiotic? Is there not something idiotic about this singularity that strains logos? I do not say that it must send metaphysics sulking away in misology. Rather it strains logos to the limit of any neutral universalism, hence demands modes of saying other to more traditional discursive ways. I want to explore this idiocy of being, in terms of both its availability to discursive articulation and its recalcitrance to complete univocal determination.

By the idiocy of singularity I intend no privatistic atomism, though I do mean a privacy of the intimate. I intend it also in this sense: there is a certain excess of being characteristic of what it means to be a self, which can never be completely objectified in an entirely determinate way. This is an affirmative overdetermination. Thus, the "presence" of a self can be understood to point to this all but incommunicable intimacy of being; and yet this all but incommunicable intimacy, in fact, is at the very origin of genuine communicability. In many current debates "presence" is defined in the critique of the so-called metaphysics of presence, but this meaning is almost the exact opposite to what I intend: "presence" as the reduction of being to a completely available univocity and determinacy; "presence" as completely transparent and available for intellectual consumption by Cartesian conceptions. This is a wrong contraction of the idiocy of being as intimacy.

"Presences" is something shimmering and elusive. We know what it is before we say anything, though when we try to say exactly what it is, we know not what it is. Nor is this unexpected, because presence is an excess of being. It is the promise of self-transcendence that is especially characteristic of personal being, though it is prefigured in all being. This

47

shimmer of presence, as the elusiveness of intimacy, is an indeterminacy in a positive sense, and might perhaps be called absence too: absence in the sense that there is no one definitive thing, univocal determinate entity that completely answers the call of what is here at play. Presence is absence, if our sense of being is completely ruled by the logic of a rigid univocity. The indeterminacy of selfhood is ultimately grounded in a freedom of being which can never be reduced to one determination or even an ensemble of determinations, since in itself it is a very source of determination. The origin of determination is itself indeterminate in this dynamic, open sense. This is absence, but only because the atomistic logic of a flattened privacy, in insisting that self be a completely determinate entity, sees nothing there, cannot see anything there.

Again I do not want to deny the universal, but we must rethink it in terms that do not sacrifice idiotic singularity. The deconstruction of the transcendental ego does not get us to the intimacy of presence, since presence is reduced to univocal determinacy, and the deconstructionist, like the empiricist, sees no such presence, sees nothing there. But the intimacy of being, while not completely articulable in determinate univocal fashion, is communicable; it is communication itself. We are thus pointed to the deeper meaning of presence. Presence is self-communication; presence is already a vector of intimacy which is self-transcending, a vector that goes towards the other, even for the other. Presence is outside of itself, other than itself, because it is the self-communication of an original center of being to an other that too, in its own right, is presence, is self-communication. Presence lives the doubleness of being, between self-mediation and intermediation with the other.

We need, then, an other idea of the universal that cannot be just the Platonic *eidos*, nor the immanent Aristotelian form, nor the consciousness in general of idealism, certainly not the *flatus vocis* of nominalism. This other universal is not one term of a logical or ontological antithesis. It is the happening of the between. This universal is the community of the between where presence meets presence. This universal is the community of the middle, that space where being ceases to be an anonymous thereness, where self and other, each in their self-communication and their communication with the other, cross and crisscross. If the idiocy of personhood in its singularity is self-communicating presence, we are always beyond univocal presence, and the two, self and other, always go together. This universal is a community of being wherein idiotic particulars meet, in a meeting that is not a logical conjunction or an empirical contiguity, but a mindful being-together that is ineluctably ethical. There is no "being-with" without the intimacy of being.

Nietzsche claimed that the opposition of Plato and Homer was life's basic antagonism. I doubt that Plato would grant the antagonism as Nietzsche stated it. For there is a *philosophical art* that, even in its logical pursuit of the universal, seeks not to betray the singular in its proper singularity, nor the community of saying even between antagonistic human seekers. This art is suggested by the Platonic dialogue itself. It is as if Plato himself is the *internal* tension between art and science. Plato reveals the tense communication of "Plato" and "Homer," in Nietzsche's sense.

The standard opposition of art and science is presented in terms of the contrast of the particular and the universal. It seems to me that the idiocy of being demands a kind of metaphysical thinking transcending this standard contrast. Science does have a drift towards the general, even when its evidences are garnered from the particularities of the given. It tends towards general explanatory schemes or cognitions that intend a universal range of reference, none of which are to be confined to the particular as particular. Art genuinely evidences a tolerance of otherness and embodies a rich way of naming the "this" as "this." Nietzsche is so far right. It is not that philosophers must give up general analysis and become writers of poems. They may do this, but this is still to accept the standard contrast. Rather the sense of being manifest with the idiocy of the "this" must be let pose its challenge to philosophy, must be let seep into the sources of thinking its otherness.

No prescription can be offered of the thinking that might result, were we to allow the idiotic to seep into metaphysical mindfulness. There can be no method or analytical technique here. The intimacy of being points to an idiotic source beyond determinate thinking. To ask for a method would be already to determine this source, in advance of the challenge it might pose to metaphysics, and hence to domesticate this challenge before it is even allowed to pose itself. We do not give up determinate thought, but this source in idiocy must be let sprout, and in the determination of metaphysical thinking itself. Certainly the categorial pigeonholing of art and philosophy must be suspended. This is not to advocate their confused promiscuity, but a certain philosophical fidelity. The fidelity may sometimes demand resort to metaphysical metaphors, or concepts that are mindful of their own imagistic nature.

If the idiocy of being makes an intimate claim on the philosopher, one cannot escape into the thought of mind in general. The singularity of the philosopher has to be acknowledged. One must deny oneself the consolation of denying oneself. Even such a consolation is equivocal, since one is still oneself as consciousness in general, even while claiming to have put oneself aside as *this* thinker. Paradox is hard to avoid, for there is a kind of loss of self in the return to singularity; but this is not a return to the ego, but to the I as abroad in the field of the intimacy of being. In other words, there is an energizing of the sources of agapeic mind which loves the particular as particular, and as for itself, and not simply for the subjective ego. The "loss" of self in the idiocy of self is just this willingness of the singular I to be mindfulness for the other, to be this singular source of radical self-transcendence towards the other in its otherness. This is what I call agapeic mind, not nameless mind in general. Properly speaking, metaphysical thinking and aesthetic openness both are concretions of agapeic mind, which is mindfulness for the other in its otherness, and yet also in its community with the intimacy of the I.

It is relevant to recall again Plato's repeated reliance, on the story and image. This is not a mere concession to the many, who are incapable of the pure selfless thought of unindividualized *eide.* It is a necessity because we philosophize in the middle. The middle requires of metaphysics some articulation of the concrete texture of *being there,* through the particularities of the image and the likenings of myth. The self as singular is philosophically put to the test in the middle. Nor is it by accident that so many Platonic dialogues are given the titles of proper names. One might expect dialogues to be named in terms of the general themes said to be their subject matter. And yet the proper name of the singular interlocutor is offered as the identifying mark of the philosophical conversation. The proper name points to the self as a "this," just as a "this": he is on stage in the drama of the dialogue, itself a community of intimacy, since it is the very deepest selves of the interlocutors that are put to the test of conversation, of philosophical communication. The abstract universal is only one "character" in this much more complex and rich drama of philosophical dialogue.

This community of aesthetic and metaphysical mindfulness, and both as different expressions of agapeic mind, points us also beyond science to the affiliation of philosophy and religion. Religion offers us the ultimate images of ultimacy. Of these we must be metaphysically mindful. We are called to restore to mindfulness a certain religious respect for the "this" as "this." Ultimately I believe it is impossible to do justice to the "this" as "this" outside of a metaphysics of creation as agapeic. The ultimate origin is an agapeic source that gives the finite other its being, not for the origin itself, but for the finite being as other in its own right. The finite entity is let be in its thisness as other and its own. The intimacy of being, we might say, is the memory of God's creative breath that sustains every being as a singular "this."

While I do not want to suggest an "aestheticization" of being, in the more normal sense of "aesthetic," in some ways *music* is the art that most restores us to the idiocy of being. Music touches us at a depth below and beyond self-consciousness. Through it sound the voices of the silent intimacy of being. No doubt, musicologists will point out the intricacies of formal structure involved in music. They will resurrect their Pythagorean ancestry and see the link between *ta musika* and *ta mathematika.* No question, there is intelligible structure in music proximate to mathematical determinacy. But the living performance is not the structure. It is the aesthetic sounding of the intimacy of being, given form in the score. This is something always other, in that every performance more or less redeems the music, or betrays it, but no performance exhausts it, though the score is the same. The playing of the music is the thing, and there is something beyond mathematical system about this play. It is a happening of the idiocy of being itself. We play it or find ourselves in its being played. It comes upon us when we listen attentively to it; it carries us, though we have to let ourselves be open to it. We have to have ears to hear, and this is no biological function but is a condition of the intimacy of being. Having ears is to have a heart that listens. We are taken out of ourselves by listening, transported into openness.

The music that comes closest to the condition of prayer is closest to the intimacy of being, for such music is the word of intimacy with the sacred other. In such music, it is as if the sound dissolves into an infinitely upward movement towards transcendence. It catches us in the vector of transcendence; and we are moved from depths we cannot comprehend, moved towards an other we cannot determinate. Neither the inner depths that stir, nor the other that draws can be univocally determined, yet while in the milieu of the music, they are together.

Prayer may be the deepest enactment of the intimacy of being; for the praying self is the most idiotic. It is senseless and yet divines sense beyond sense. It is given over, yet it is the audacity of trust. It is elemental vulnerability and appeal, elemental perplexity and consent, elemental confession and renewal, elemental adoration and fragile glory. It demands nothing, yet waits in expectation of all good. This is the infinity of the simple. Augustine said that God was *intimior intimo meo*. This is the intimacy of being beyond the ego, and beyond the intimacy of self. It is the idiocy of God. Of God we are made mindful in an idiot wisdom. If death is the final idiocy in the between, then the only way to die is with a proper prayer. We may spend a life looking for the proper prayer. Can idiotic metaphysics close its mind to this audacity and this appeal?

AGAPEIC MIND

From *Perplexity and Ultimacy*

Is there a community between mind and being? If so, how does it agree with being between, being at a loss, and the idiocy of being? What is its character? How do we speak of it? Does the field of the intimacy of being suggest something of it? Is it bound up with that mysterious word "home?"

This is an old and elemental metaphysical question. It is also a perennially renewed perplexity. Parmenides' affiliation (frag. 3) of noein and estin, thinking and being, suggests the question—though he says they are auto, same, where we ask about community. Nor has the question been definitively solved, and put in place. At the height of contemporary science, Einstein remained perplexed by a version of it. If never definitively answered, yet it ever recurs, and to it we also must recur, with perhaps a deepening of the proper perplexity.

Such perplexity is qualified by our sense of *difference* to the rest of being. Testaments to this include the unquestioning dualism of common sense, as well as the scientistic hubris going with a conceptual dualism of mind and nature. These issue in two opposite results: on one hand, the objectivism of denatured mind, relative to nature; on the other hand, the subjectivism of denatured mind, relative to mind itself. These extremes have formed the legacy of post-Cartesian philosophy. They reflectively accentuate the dualistic difference of common sense into a systematic alienation of mind from being in its otherness, and of mind from itself in its own deeper intimacy of being.

It is now increasingly recognized that this legacy is used up, bankrupt. It is the inheritance of an ontological deracination. The question then is: What resources do we have after this judgment of bankruptcy? Is there any source of renewal, exceeding this inheritance, or perhaps preceding it? We are brought again to question the community between mind and being.

The renewal begins minimally in the recognition that no conceptual reflection of being is absolutely autonomous or self-determining; rather it originates in a prereflective mediation, an already given togetherness of mind and being. This togetherness is not exhausted by the conceptualizations of being that science or philosophy produces, though these can be mediated transformations of it. Thus, the acknowledgment that science originates in the *Lebenswelt*, for example, by Husserl and others, is one expression of what is at issue. Does this expression go far enough? Does not the *Lebenswelt* itself raise the question of a more originary community of mind and being which shapes the possibility of the *Lebenswelt* itself? Does not the modern reflective mediation all throughout carry with it the residues of its own dualistic starting point? Must we rethink the prereflective community of being, prior to both scientist and commonsense dualism, rethink not only the commonsense community of being, but a more originary sense of ontological community?

Objective, subjective, and transcendental mind will not suffice, for they are subsequent to this prior community. We must rethink the dynamism of minding as an orientation to being; we must rethink the otherness of being, as both for itself and for this minding. To this end, I propose an exploration of what I call "agapeic mind." The matter, of course, has ramifications other than the deracinated mediations of post-Cartesian thought. Agapeic mind can find expression in aesthetic, in religious, in ethical form, in metaphysical form. No neutral condition or monological state of affairs is intended by the activity of being mindful. I explore a mode of mindfulness in which thinking is for the sake of the other, thinking for the sake of what is other to thought itself.

Traditionally *agape* is a form of love, often contrasted with eros, and also with *philia*. These contrasts are not irrelevant, with a relevance I will specify as the occasion demands. Agapeic mind names a mode of thought thinking what is other to thought, in which there is a release of thinking from itself towards the other as other. At stake is the power of mind to transcend itself. The point to be explored is whether and how, in this transcending, mindfulness is already in community with being-other towards which it transcends.

There are different modes of this self-transcendence, including that of what I will call "erotic mind." By contrast to agapeic mind, by erotic mind I will mean a relativity of mind to what is other to self, but a relativity that subsumes what is other into the self-relativity of the mind seeking its own self-satisfaction and self-certainty. Erotic mind goes to the other beyond itself, but its self-transcendence is impelled by its own lack, which it would fill by appropriating the other. Its relativity to the other serves this fulfillment of its own initial lack. The truth of the other affords the truth of self-fulfillment.

The truth of agapeic mind is not this self-satisfaction. It includes a disquiet about every such self-satisfaction, a perplexity before the other it cannot include in its own conceptual schema, a loss of self-certainty, and at best a trust that its motion towards the other calls for a faithfulness beyond guarantees. Traditionally philosophers have often favored erotic mind, since this coheres with the very strong desire to make thinking absolutely self-consistent, and so to glorify thought thinking itself as the ultimate, and the philosophical god.

In terms of the fourfold sense of being, objective mind is dominantly tied to the ideal of univocity; subjective mind easily lends itself to the equivocity of being; erotic mind corresponds to the dialectical sense; the metaxological view finds its expression in agapeic mind.

Let me now attempt to speak of agapeic mind. Are we confined to the "ego-centric predicament?" Is there a transcending of mindfulness beyond this, beyond subjective, objective, and erotic mind? What I want to explore is a generosity of mind beyond lack, an openness beyond need, a vigilance with respect to the beyond, beyond self-interest. My claim is not that humans ever *completely* embody such agapeic mindfulness, yet in our failure, we are aware of the ideal at stake, even if its demand is only episodically approximated. It says something essential about what we are, and the promise of what we are to be. Again we cannot avoid our intermediate condition, between our finitude and an absolute demand. Agapeic mind expresses something that is both a regulative ideal and an ontological reality, somehow constitutive of our most intimate being. There is no direct univocal way to say this. Given the nature of the case, my path will have to twist and turn in a sometimes serpentine way.

How think the possibility of mindfulness that, in some elusive sense, is from the beginning already defined by a certain fullness, and not simply by lack? Full of what? It cannot be full of different kinds of determinate knowledge, knowing everything about this and that. This is impossible. Yet mind can be implicitly informed by an enigmatic sense of the "whole," and this prior to all determinate knowing, and more than every item of determinate knowledge. Thus, agapeic mind is related to the *second indeterminate perplexity*. The latter is not a specific curiosity about a determinate problem, but is activated beyond even the answers to such specific problems. If it is activated beyond such answers, it suggests that there is more at play in minding, even *before* the specific questions such answers meet.

Suppose we take our sights from Aristotle's previously cited saying that somehow the soul is everything. The soul is not a determinate form since it is the power to receive determinate form in itself. Aristotle might equally have said that the soul is everything, because somehow it is nothing. How then something, indeed everything, and nothing? This: the mind is nothing because it is no thing; it is in excess of every thing; it manifests self-transcending dynamism. If it were simply a univocal determinate thing, there is no way we could explain this self-transcending power. And we need to acknowledge this power, even if perhaps we cannot completely explain it. We must acknowledge it because if knowing is a relativity of self and other, we have to explain how the self is outside of itself in this relativity. The self as mindfulness enters the middle between itself and the other, mediates this difference, and constitutes a self-aware relativity. This, of course, is only one side of the matter, since the other gives itself into the middle also, and mindfulness relative to the other is doubled over to meet this giving of the other. In any case, a thing that is beyond itself is not a completely determinate univocal thing. It is a thing that is a no thing. It is a determination of indeterminacy. This indeterminacy can be given a number of modulations. Consistent with the paradoxical language that is called on to conjoin seeming opposites, this indeterminacy is the nothing that is also the more, as the original of the self-transcending power of minding.

Consider how, when I mind something, I am no longer simply myself; in minding a thing, my mind is about that thing. Example: I am driving a car and someone shouts: "Mind the child!" Mindlessly—so it seems—I swerve and avoid the child. But the seeming mindlessness is really minding that forgets itself by being catapulted out of itself, by its being riveted on the other. I forget myself in minding the child. But this forgetfulness is just the activation of myself as sheer mindfulness of the other. I give myself, am given over, to its life as other. I become that life, at least partially. Mind is free of itself, released from itself but as itself, engrossed in the other which it becomes, even as it makes itself nothing for the other's sake. This enigmatic power of becoming the other is possible on the basis of the mind being a kind of free nothing, a creative indeterminacy that can assume, without subsuming, the being of the other.

This nothing of creative indeterminacy will receive different interpretations, depending on whether we see mind as erotic or agapeic. This nothing is granted in both. In erotic mind, the nothing is the lack of indefiniteness which has to be overcome in a process that makes the indefinite progressively definite. The nothing is defined through a process of self-definition which appropriates the determinate other, and uses the definiteness of the known other to confer increasing definition on the self-developing mind.

And this, of course, is ingredient in the maturation of mind. Mind can overcome indefiniteness through a dual process: One, reaching out to determinate objects which, on being known by mind, give the mind itself the definition of the thing known—mind becomes determinate in knowing determinate things. Two, through a process of self-development that goes along with increase of determinate knowing; for in knowing definite things the mind comes to self-awareness of itself, as precisely a power of definition, and hence knows itself as self-defining. Hegel's account of mind is erotic in this sense. He combines these two senses of definition, coupling them with an understanding of the negativity of mind. The nothing determines itself through a process of self-development, which itself goes along with increasing knowledge of determinate things. We culminate with an understanding of the nothing as self-determining negativity, and of mind as in possession of itself in its appropriation of the other.

When we turn to agapeic mind, we find a different sense of the nothing and indeterminacy. The indeterminacy is not just the lacking indefinite; it rather refers to a sense of plenitude that undergirds even the lack of the indefinite. Indeed, the lack of self-determining negativity is itself only possible because it is grounded in an affirmative power of being. We desire, seek, quest, not just because we lack, but because we are, and we are as the power to be self-articulating. We are the positive power to overcome our own lack because we are already a particular concretion of the plenitude of being. A sense of plenitude is written into even the indigence of our lacking and needy form of being. The indeterminacy is not merely an indefiniteness to be given complete determination; the nothing is not a negativity that is completely self-determining. The otherness of the power of being intrudes at the beginning, in the middle, and it outlives our end.

This otherness calls for a different affirmative relation right from the outset. The call is coeval with our being, indeed it is prior to the self-articulation of being for which we claim autonomy. The power to be self-articulating is given and called forth, called forth by the otherness of being, *before the self can call itself* forth. In a word, there is a prior giving of self-determination which is not self-determining. This giving is from a surplus of plenitude, not from an indefinite lack. The movement of mind is not impelled by a doubting that insists on being allayed by self-certainty. The nothing of agapeic mind is awakened in an expectancy that is not self-insistent. This expectancy is not an epistemological defect. It is the desert of an elemental love of being.

Previously, I hinted at this love in relation to the way the senses feast on the agape of being as aesthetic presencing. But the point can be applied to philosophy itself—commonly viewed as the opposite extreme to aesthetic feasting. Philosophy might be an agapeic knowing. This relates to the metaxological view and its double mediation. The first movement of mind (but this does not mean absolutely first) is from the self to the other but for the other, perhaps even to the point of sacrifice of self. "Sacrifice" here is meant metaphorically. This is the death of the self in the knowing of the other. Eros has been described in terms of "the little death," and one sees the point. But one might say that if agape is more truly death, it is also more truly life, in that one is nothing, the other is all. The second movement concerns openness to the return from the other to the self. This is not a return to the self of itself; it is the self-revelation of the other to the self. In agapeic alert the other may come out of itself. This is *its unfolding*, not mine, its self-unfolding as given for the self, given in return from the other as other. The coming of the other is welcomed.

And so the directionality of agapeic minding is not linear in any straightforward sense. It demands a patient thinking, a staying with the being that is before it. This is not, as it were, an apathetic patience; it is an active patience. It is a watching, where watching implies a ready attentiveness for what may break cover before one, and come out of itself and towards one. It is a vigilance. To be vigilant means to be willing to wait, to be patient in the sense of letting things take their own time, unfold in their own time, and not be forced into premature, hence false, revelation. To be vigilant also means to be in a state of high alert. The patient thinking of agapeic mind is this state of high alert that paradoxically has nothing insistent about it. It demands a strange mix of active mind and patient readiness, energy of being and of being nothing.

The movement of agapeic mind can sometimes be a kind of hovering, or expectation, or solicitation. Expectation: one is not sure what will emerge. As stillness overcomes the mind—the movement is a movement of stillness, of quietness—one is waiting. Hovering over the middle: waiting for the spirit of the place or event. One may miss it; there are no guarantees. It may be too subtle; it may be so obvious, and we look in the wrong place or way. The time of the self may be out with the time of the other. They cross, but do not cross.

I am in a place called Inchydoney, near Clonakilty, West Cork. I look out at the sea and watch. The waves come in, retreat, come in, retreat; there is the background murmur of a low whoosh. On the other side of the bay, the hill is a motley of greens; there is fog on the horizon. I have just offered a set of simple empirical observations. These might be confirmed by anyone at all who would occupy the position I now occupy, who would step into my perspective or something relatively close to it. The empirical observations are relatively anonymous in that respect. Anyone might make them.

But now consider: I might offer these observations as I pass through this place. I drive to Inchydoney in my car, get out, make a number of observations, like a few quick snapshots, and drive on, drive away. The mind has served as a good registering instrument but is barely touched by the scene. Instead I have come here, and have stayed. I have been here a time now. This is the staying that is important, and the giving of time to mind to loose itself, the giving of time to the things before one. With such a giving of mind and things a chance to be themselves, with this mindful giving of time to things, the self-same observations can cease to be simply neutral descriptions. The self comes to sink into a place with time; the place tends to pass over into the mind. The mind is in the place; the place is in mind. This is a deeper mediation of the self and world than the minimally implicated observation of one who passes through the middle. The one who passes through, if he does not have enough time, merely surfaces, skims over, instrumentalized the middle. The interplay between self and world is superficial, albeit correct, accurate, even exact.

Not so simple with the one who mindfully stays with the place. Agapeic mind must stay with that kind of patience, for only then can there come to realization a deeper relatedness between the minding and the showing in the world. The greens of the hills are gestures, signatures of difference; the sound of the waves voice the endurance and impermanence of things; the fog on the horizon is the line of indeterminacy beyond which hides mystery. The mystery is not in here, or out there; it is here and there and nowhere. The mind must be steeped in the things, sink into the things; alternatively, the things must become tinged with minding, become presences, lively or brooding, but presences, not neutral objects. Presences seep beyond their own determinate boundaries and communicate their implication with their surrounds. Agapeic mind goes out to such presences; things present themselves, out of themselves to agapeic mind.

And so as a noninstrumental vigilance, agapeic mind is not an interfering mode of thought. Or, since the human mind almost unavoidably is interfering, it is an effort to still that self-insistent will to interfere with the other. The presencing of the other is often reduced to its determinate thereness. We identify it as an object by pinning down this its determinate particularity. In the process we diminish the suggestion of something more in the thing. We want to see the things as simply that determinate presence and nothing more. In fact, no thing is simply that thing and nothing more. In itself it concretizes an energy of being that is individualized in things but that exceeds every such concretion. Every such concretion reminds us of this "more" that it concretizes and that it is not fully, that it does not exhaust.

Relative to other things, we find the seepage of this more in the presencing of the thing to things beyond itself. No thing, we find, exists univocally in itself; its very identity is shaped in its relativity to other things; it is outside of itself in this relativity; its presencing to the world is its passage beyond rigid univocal identity into the community of others; the presencing of things is their mute communication of an identity that is revealed in relativity, and that in a way celebrates self and relativity together. The flower sings to the hill on which it grows; the wind dances with the grasses that it enlivens, quickens; the birds glory in the sky that gives them freedom; the heavens rejoice in these open spaces of unconstrained liberty. The community of being sings, sings silently. Presencing is the silent word; or there is no silence really. Agapeic mind tries to be attuned to the voices of otherness. Attuned to the "more" in the determinate things, it welcomes its freedom, calls it forth. The yes to things of the agapeic mind somehow confirms their identity, redeems their presencing.

PART II

ETHICS AND ETHOS

AUTONOMY AND FREEDOM

From "Autonomia Turannos"

THE GOD "AUTONOMY"

In modernity generally substantive conceptions of the good have been pervasively criticized, and not least in our own time. All values seem open to critique or question. Indeed, the claim is that they must be open to such critique if they are to pass muster—especially if we claim to live in an accountable, transparent, and democratic manner. Nevertheless, there seems to be one value that is accepted as basic in a widespread way. This is the value of freedom. The god who presides over the epoch of modernity seems to be named "Freedom."

Often, in fact, it is in the name of freedom that other substantives values are subject to critique. Over the centuries the suspicion has gathered pace that such values curtail or derail or railroad freedom: curtail its promise; derail its realization; railroad its forms into what is acceptable or not to one group or culture or sex or lobby. There is the slightly embarrassing problem that while we all seem to bow before "Freedom," this god retains something of an unknown character. It seems the more striven for the more it can become a *deus absconditus*.

There are many forms of freedom and interpretations of its meaning, none indubitably self-evident. Freedom might be a substitute for the old Good or God, but it shares with them a similar problem: a plethora of pretenders to the throne. One of the pretenders that seems to have crowded out many rivals is the once princeling "Autonomy." This princeling has become sovereign monarch. The name "Autonomy" is now so pervasively invoked, especially in Western societies, that it is often used as a synonym for freedom. Freedom as the one incontestable value has become autonomy as the dominant name for that absolute value.

This dominance is not at all evident in early modernity, and Kant's use of the word transposes it from the context of political self-governance to the self-legislation of the moral individual. This migration and transposition have passed into the general culture, such that, as I say, autonomy indiscriminately passes for freedom. The name is linked with the notion of self-determination also, another term that is often without further thought identified with freedom. In the glory of this god there is much that falls into the shadows. We pay our respects at this shrine, but there is more implied in our worship than appears in the words of our rituals or spells.

There is a context to this. I would say something like this. There are significant shifts in how the ethos is understood in modernity that condition the rise and dominance of autonomy as freedom. Suppose we grant that there is something incontestable about freedom as a fundamental value. But how define this? Through itself alone? But this initially makes no sense. Through another? But this seems to be contrary to the meaning of freedom, which at a minimum entails "freedom from." Let us start with this as a minimum. Freedom from what? I would say that the epoch of modernity wills to be free from the *otherness of being as equivocal.*

I mean: being as other presents itself to us, and does so as often beyond the range of our knowing and practical power. This puts us in an equivocal position vis-à-vis its otherness. Suppose we come to find this equivocal appearing intolerable? We set out to mitigate this equivocal face. How? By subjecting its uncertainty and ambiguity to clear and distinct cognition. By increasing the range of our power over its otherness through mechanical means, themselves developed from the growing univocity of our cognitive mastery of that other, reflected in mathematical and cybernetic expertise. Knowing is power, it has been said. This is clearly not true in all instances. Increase in some forms of knowing does not increase power. For instance, certain forms of religious knowing, certain tragic knowledges, offer a freedom that does not increase our power, a freedom that releases at the limit of human power. But we seek a knowing that will yield power, and define a new ethos as one given by and for our autonomy.

I name some manifestations of this orientation. There is the struggle for autonomy from the hegemony of a theological orientation in the rise of secular modernity. We find the claims of autonomy with respect to art, culminating in doctrines like art for art's sake, or in the putative higher freedom claimed by artistic genius. Philosophy may assert its autonomy in its demarcation from theology; but even here the god of modern metaphysics shows its absolute autonomy as self-cause: god as *causa sui.* More, we find the affirmation of reason not only as master of its own house but as the ground of self-mastery. Thus the ideal of self-determining knowing: knowing validated through its own immanent resources, not by appeal to something other or putatively extraneous. Think of the tension between the self-validating directionality of Descartes' *cogito* and his appeal to God. In response, we find a groundswell of suspicion of the latter as merely a deus ex machina: a redundant other to be progressively expunged as the project of self-determining becomes more radical and complete, up to the ideal of absolute knowing in Hegel where knowing, as he puts it, no longer feels the need to go beyond itself.

In politics, obsession with the idea of the sovereign centers on the exercise of power within its own domain of mastery, not to be interfered with by other intrusive powers. The implicit dynamic of sovereignty is tempted by the lure of absolute power; for where there is an other, there is ambiguity between the trustworthy and the untrustworthy, and it seems that only by being master over the other is the threat of the hostile and the untrustworthy overcome. Let suspicion of the other infiltrate the will to sovereign power, and we begin to draw the line of connection from political sovereignty to totalitarian will to power.

In morality or ethics, the ideal of autonomy becomes fixed in the Western mind-set with Kant for whom the form of all false moralities is heteronomy. One seeks self-legislation over oneself as one's own sovereign possession. The power of Kantianism is still very strong, while other philosophical ethics seem to have been eclipsed. Moral autonomy seems to speak to something fundamental—some pervasive need or demand in the culture as a whole. It is not only secular morality that refuses reference to anything beyond the human. We all seem to seek independence from any demeaning dependency on another—be it master, or God or father or priest. Plato and his priestly progeny are to be erased; ditto, morality as derived from God the father. All fathers must be put out to grass, or if they will not go quietly, replaced or dethroned. And humanity in the new youth of its self-defining originality will mount the throne or sit at the head of creation, and a new age of reconciled humanity will come. I am sometimes reminded of a kind of *expressive Stoicism*: the ideal of self-sufficiency *redivivus*, but no longer in an apathetic soul, but in an expressive self, aflame with a romantic or postromantic rhapsody of itself.

The issue: we seem to have come to a form of self-governing ethics, but have we really left behind the old obedience and submission? Do we find *new obediences* to indeterminate powers we know to be and not to be our own? I will call these powers, gods or the counterfeits of God—the equivocation is essential. I now want to explore the equivocal presence of different submissions, nesting in the very radicalization of autonomy.

I will be dealing with what I will call a dialectical equivocity. This is not just a dialectic that overcomes an equivocity, but a dialectic enmeshed in equivocities it seems to mediate, but does not. Indeed, it cannot do so, on the terms of freedom as self-determination. This dialectical equivocity is related to what below I call the antinomy between autonomy and transcendence—an antinomy not to be resolved in terms of any dialectical self-determination, since there is an involvement of an other that is not a dialectical other. Why look at some major classical sources with respect to this dialectical equivocation? Anglo-American reflection on any ethics of autonomy tends to be a mixture of Kantianism and utilitarianism, but one can also detect a crucial line of unfolding from Kant through Nietzsche that has had immense significance (not least through Marxism, and now in the form of postmodern Nietzscheanism). These forms of self-determination (sometimes ambiguously or covertly) push its logic in ways that Enlightenment callowness, commonsense complacency and Anglo-American pragmatism do not do. Coupled with such dialectical equivocity, we find counterfeits of creation (nature neutered), false doubles of freedom, and counterfeits of God. Since God is infinite, and human desire infinitely restless, the names of these last counterfeits are legion.

AUTONOMY AND THE EQUIVOCITY OF THE ETHOS

What can we say of the ethos of freedom? The ethos is the basic milieu in which determinate values come to form, but in itself it is in excess of determination. Ethos is indeterminate in an overdetermined sense: not merely neutral, but an equivocal medium of possibility or an in-between of promise. Here ethics and metaphysics cannot be entirely divorced; changes in one are reflected in or influence changes in the other. The modern project, at least initially, is one of the neutralization of the ethos, though in the interests of a revaluation of it in terms of human self-determining power. The ethos, as understood in premodern metaphysics, viewed the happening of being as not inhospitable to value or the good. Thus the Platonic view of the Good as providing the most fundamental horizon without which all life and intelligibility was to be situated: without some knowing of the Good all is really pointless: the whole has no point. Likewise in the Aristotelian context the good is what all seek; all being is teleological in some basic regard. In Aquinas and others: *ens et bonum convertuntur.*

These seem to be the platitudes of the tradition. But as platitudes they are the well-worn formulations of an appreciation of the inherent hospitality of being to the good—and the basic inseparability of ethics and metaphysics. It may be true that this hospitality cannot offer us univocal certainty. How univocalize Plato's Good, since we require imagistic speech—simile and metaphor—even to talk of it? Likewise with respect to Aristotelian teleology: there is no univocal certainty about the determinate ends shaping nature's becoming; and yet the conviction persists—nature does nothing in vain. Aquinas: the discourse of the transcendentals has an astonishing character in this sense that it cannot be determined in the language of determinate entities, and the univocalizing that would fix on this or this or this. Similarly, the analogy of being is not devoid of its own intelligibility, but it makes demands which cannot be captured by univocalizing thought at home with definite things or the geometrical clarity of formal patterns.

The will to mathematicize nature owes its inspiration to the mind of geometry rather than the mind of finesse (Pascal). If the good is identified with the final end, and we reject final ends, the process of nature becomes a valueless process of ongoingness. It is a happening without inherent end, lacking point and purpose. Perhaps God might know, but since God is as enigmatic as ends, he too will be made redundant. Despite what thinkers like Kepler and Galileo might claim, finally there is no geometry of God's will. God is finesse. But if you will to absolutize the geometrical mind you cannot quite see this.

In fact, the will to absolute univocity ends with a sense of the valueless whole. This is, of course, convenient for us to assert ourselves, if there is nothing of inherent value in being other than ourselves. Can we live in a valueless whole? No. Even the new way of looking at things shorn of value is itself the result of a set of values that considers a univocalizing objectivizing the best way towards the truth of things. Valueless objectivity is itself the outcome of a project of value in which the "subject" continues to play a game of peek-a-boo: now you see it, now you don't. The rejection of inherent ends has also the effect of putting an inordinate stress on efficient cause as *the* cause par excellence. Things become intelligible in terms of their efficient causes and the relations between antecedents and consequents. Things become units of effective power. The human being is also a unit of effective power. To reduce all being to effective power is to make more efficient man's own project of effective power over the equivocity of heterogeneous being. Homogenize and determine: if it is all the same, then one principle alone is needed for this determination. We are the principle—we are *to auto* that will be the *nomos* of the earth. To determine the *nomos* of the earth is to be self-determining, autonomous. Here we already see the initially hidden connections between power, will to power, and autonomy.

Suppose we say that nature neutered is a counterfeit of creation and its glory. What then is "glory"? It is our *being above* nature neutered. Suppose such an ethos of "neutralization" is itself an ontological contraction of the given milieu of being as saturated with value. Why then be surprised if such an ethos is implicated in "autonomy," as perhaps itself a contraction of freedom?

Our equivocity concerning other-being and the other as good shows itself in a diffidence about any ethics of "obedience," in which I am subject to command. Our preference is for an ethics of will or choice, in which I exercise my own power of command—even when I find myself commanded. (I come back to this tension between obedience and willing my own choice.)

All forms of being externally determined must be suspect of being obstacles to the free expression of my own being. Examples are numerous, but a notable one is the way the language of originality and creativity infiltrates all aspects of life, and not only the artistic. We are to be originals—not imitations or copies of an other. We are to be ourselves through ourselves; we are not to be ourselves through another. We are to be like the genius who gives the rule to art, but is not himself a rule, and not completely subject to rule. It is the original, not the imitation who bestows value. Who is the original? We are the original: our truer being for ourselves is not in obeying the given law, but in giving the law.

Is this then the *positive outcome*: the self as the value, the end in self, legislating value in an otherwise valueless ethos, answering to itself and legislating through and for itself? If here we seem to come to Kant as the high point of autonomy, he is not alone. An ethos of self-determination pervades modernity, to be found in other thinkers critical of Kant, even though they radicalize what is latent in Kant also.

I sketch a line of connection leading from autonomy to will to power. The latter does not simply come after the "deconstruction" of rational autonomy; it is already there at the very roots in the ambiguity of autonomy's relation to what is other to self. Indeed "below" both autonomy and will to power is the ethos as valueless and a devalued soil of otherness. Different constructions may be built upon this soil—Kantian, Hegelian, Marxist, Nietzschean, and now the further fruit of groundless will to power in some forms of postmodern thought. We move from the desire of the ideal to the project of the ideal to the dissolution of the ideal. Certain forms of "post-modern" thought seem to suggest more the *disillusion* of autonomy rather than its *dissolution*. We push away our autonomy, yet equally hold onto it. This is the self-laceration of autonomy, not its abandonment.

THE POTENCIES OF THE ETHICAL

From *Ethics and the Between*

I would I did not have to attempt these thoughts so early. If the jolt helps, well and good; if not, a slower caress may be better. But I still need to anticipate. To understand the promise of the ethos, do we need what Nietzsche sought—a transvaluation of all values? In the main, he offered us a flawed critique of "Christianity" and "Platonism," from the standpoint of a Dionysian will to power. I think what we need is less such a transvaluation as a renewal of discerning reflection on the basic sources of value, in terms of the plurivocal possibilities of the power of the "to be." The ontological promise of the power of the "to be" receives such plurivocal articulation in terms of what I will call the *potencies of the ethical.* These potencies—the idiotic, the aesthetic, the dianoetic, the transcendental, the eudaimonistic, the transcending, and the transcendent—will be more fully defined in due course, but they refer not to abstract possibilities but to the dynamical ethical endowment of the human. We are plurally endowed with the ethical promise of diverse potencies of the original power to be. These potencies assume different definitions, depending on the dominance of this or that sense of being, or of being good. To understand them is more fundamental than a critique of "Christianity," or "Platonism," or "Kantianism," or for that matter "Nietzscheanism." That understanding allows us to see these configurations of the ethos in new light and not simply play one off against the other. Since these potencies recur throughout this book, it will be helpful to note, again in a preliminary way, something of their metaxological meaning.

First, all potencies spring out of our immersion in the ethos as offering us an opaque intimation of the *surplus* of the good. There is nothing transparent about this; it is metaphysically enigmatic. Patience to this surplus otherness is especially significant for metaxological ethics. It awakens us to something inexhaustible about the good of being at all. But this is too much for us. It sustains us, but we fall into a familiarity that droops to its marvel. It is at work in giving us, astonishingly, the gift of being, the elemental good; at work when we develop ourselves and our determinate lives this way or that; at work when perplexity overtakes us and troubles

Against
(Nietzsche)

us into anguish at the equivocal enigma of the good; at work when we determine to become ourselves, facing oppositions that rend us and stretch us on the rack; at work beyond our fullest stretch of self-determination, aiding fidelity to the "more" beyond every claim to final wholeness; at work in letting the giving others again come to us in a more mindful frame, and greeting us, as we greet them, as intimates become strange, and as strangers anew standing before us as givers of good beyond merit. This surplus good is always beyond measure, in all of the genuinely good things we do, though they seem anonymous and slight and merely routine.

Second, there is a sense of the *idiocy of the good in the between*. I refer to an elemental *intimacy* with the value of being: a predeterminate sense of the "rightness" of the "to be." This does not mean that we have made this "rightness" determinately clear to ourselves. Mostly it is in an unstated background that may come into sharper focus under the pressure of different stresses of being. This idiocy is beyond our determinate reason, but it is intimate and other at once. We are native to the world as good, but we are native with a mystery that demurs before our domestications. The idiocy of the good is especially important relative to the source of intimate worth in the human being. Humans wake up to this intimacy, and so begin to move beyond the living of this, to an express understanding and gratitude for it.

Third, there is the *aesthetic* potency. I mean that the otherness of the ethos involves a *showing* of the worth of being that is aesthetic—given to our senses and our bodies. The incarnate good of the world is in rapport with our response to goodness and our being as good. Most often we live this in our response to beauty; but we also create works of beauty; we bring to be, so to say, a courtesy of incarnation. The ethos of the body, as well as the "eco-system" as other to our will to master, is to be respected by metaxological ethics.

Fourth, there is the *dianoetic* potency. I mean that we seek some intelligible, law-like regularity to the ambiguities of the aesthetics of the good. This aesthetic showing is more full than we can manage, yet as we become discerning, we discover constancies and regularities. Metaxological ethics is attendant to the intelligible constancies emergent in the between. If this is a respect for sameness, it is not reductive. There are intelligible bonds that hold diversities together and that command or ask for respect. Metaxological attendance must avoid the superimposition of orders on the inexhaustibility of being or its surplus worth. This does not mean that the constancies are always adequately formulated by us. We must guard against the false fixation and securing of ourselves through the spurious certainties we often mistake for dianoetic constancies.

Fifth, some constancies occupy a special position of being *transcendental* in this sense: without them, determinate ethical living would not be possible. The metaxological relation between self and other is transcendental in that regard: it is the condition of the possibility of more determinate forms of selving and "being together," of self-becoming and of being in community. Then there is the good as agapeic origin: the ultimate condition of the possibility of the between. This is not a "condition" at all, but if we call it a "condition of possibility," it is more in a "Platonic" than in a Kantian sense: the being of the good and the relativity of the metaxological as "original sources of possibilizing," presupposed by determinate approaches to the ethos and specific human formations of the ethical.

Sixth, there is the *eudaimonistic* potency of the ethical. In a way, the fullness of human flourishing resumes, with reference to the daimon, the idiotic and aesthetic potencies. There is a primordial "being pleased" with the fulfillment of powers: the determination of the indeterminate such that what was being sought and implicitly loved in the idiocy comes into its own and into its neighborhood with the good of other-being: comes into fullness, and in coming into fullness, rejoices even the more that being is the inexpressible good that it is. This is easier said than reached, but all the travail seeks it, though too much travail darkens the secret directedness on the daimon. We have to come to terms with this darkening in the chiaroscuro of the ethos.

Seventh, the *transcending* potency keeps in mind that the overdetermined comes to expression in human being as exceeding itself. We are determinate and more than determinate, and much of what we are, as determinate, is itself the crystallization of an indeterminate power of self-surpassing. This transcending potency cannot be fully understood in univocal, equivocal, or dialectical terms. The inward source of this transcending is a strange otherness in innerness itself, and it cannot mediate with itself entirely; for the presence of enigmatic otherness is always there before we come to ourselves in more determinate form. There is the surpassing mystery of self-surpassing itself; as we live it in the between—always something more than we can fix in our moving to something more. There is excess to that which we are seeking: the "end" is beyond us, even as we come into its neighborhood.

Eighth, metaxological ethics seeks the best way to keep our living in the ethos open to the call of *transcendence itself*—not just our self-transcendence but transcendence itself as the ultimate power that possibilizes all transcending, indeed all being, and possibilizes it because transcendence itself is good. The best word in ordinary language for transcendence itself is the extraordinary word, "God." The extraordinary asks us to respect the ordinary usage. Metaxological ethics names the ethos as the space wherein the ultimate good intimates itself in the idiotic, aesthetic, dianoetic, transcendental, eudaimonistic, and transcending concretions of life in the finite between. This good is communicated into the between, opening its finite otherness, and through this, opening to the self-becomings of different beings, each becoming towards what is good for it. We are pointed to a community of the good beyond self-determination, a community already there from the start, enabling the powers of self to be determining of itself, giving it to be itself; giving also the ethos of possibility wherein that power can be more fully realized.

Relative to the ethical potencies, we need a fuller appreciation of the relation to otherness than dialectic offers, a more affirmative sense of the mystery than equivocity has, and a more open sense of determination than univocity fixes. And if all we say is a speaking from our human perspective, this need not be a mere projection of the human good, if from the outset the human is an undergoing: human being is a suffering of being, and a suffering of the good, before it is a doing of the good more proper to itself. Metaxological ethics is not a substitute for God's mind, but a human essay, always in the between, to read the opaque signs of being good. As a suffering, as well as a doing, as an opening to the other, as well as a self-forming, it must be alert, on edge, to what comes to it from beyond itself; otherwise it closes itself to traces of transcendence in the twilight of the middle or its dawn. The surplus of the good *asks for plurivocity*: not only because we are poor; not only because we are also rich in our poverty; but because the good of the between is beyond our measure; because we must do our best to stay true to what is given from it, and what is best in it. We need many ways. Nor is this antagonistic to the One, if this One is the agapeic giving of the plural between, and the broadcast of the good of being.

METAXOLOGICAL ETHICS

From *Ethics and the Between*

THE ARCHEOLOGY OF THE GOOD

Where are we? Still in the play of indetermination and determination of the ethos. What there is the difference between the dialectical and metaxological ways? Both mediate the play of univocity and equivocity, the first with respect to self-determining being, the second with a fuller intermediation with otherness. The latter calls for a different *archeology* of the good, not just its teleology. For dialectic, the beginning is an indefinite, to be made more and more determinate, to the end of self-determination. In the end is the true good. This is faithful to the Aristotelian line or the Hegelian erotic teleology: the end is self-realizing, or realized being for self. By contrast, the metaxological is recalled to the *otherness of the origin.* The beginning intimates the overdetermination of the good—not indefinite, but too much: out of this surplus, determinate forms of good come to shape. This is the origin as agapeic good. This overdetermined good companions all moves from indefinite to determinate to self-determination. An exclusively dialectical view is not fully mindful of this companionship.

The origin as agapeic suggests an elemental worth to the "to be" (see *BB*, chapters 6 and 13). To be is to be given to be by the origin; but given being is other to the origin, and for itself, and good as for itself. This "being good" is not antithetical to being in communication with other-being. To give being is to communicate the good of being. Finite beings also communicate the good: in some cases, simply by what they are, fulfilling their natures according to allotted destinies; in other cases, greater openness goes with a more extensive range of self-transcending, as well as more intensive selving and depth of original power. In the latter cases, by responding to the call of being good, the creature answers for what it is. This call and answering are themselves communications calling for communities. Being good is a doing of the good in community. And if in our open transcending we find the promise of allowance, there can be no one simple way to fulfill that promise. The goodness of being is surplus, and we are guests of a feast that surpasses us.

Singulars within creation also are good—concretions of the "to be" as good. Singulars are harmonies of integral being. Their coming to be is inseparable from such integrity; were they not "one" in a fundamental sense, they would not be at all. But this is no block creation. There is a pluralism to creation, reflected in the pluralism of original powers marking different beings. The good of beings is shown in the ontological integrity, out of which a being's powers emerge into expression, and shown in the harmony of wholeness it seeks to attain in fulfilling these its powers. Given to be, beings are open to the promise of realizing themselves, as for themselves. The good of beings is thus inseparable from the original power of transcending (the very doing of its being) that the gift of the finite "to be" concretizes.

The openness of creation means that it is not the self-determination of the divine, not the necessary block of nature that is the body of Spinoza's God, or the necessitated finiteness that is the self-externalization of Hegel's God. The agapeic origin gives a world for itself, and as in promise to be itself through itself. The promise seeks out fulfillment, and in that regard the good is in the end; but this is possible because the good as original releases the finite into its own being for itself. This is not to be forgotten, even as we transcend towards an end. Ends sought in the between may be genuinely good, but they are not the absolute good. Nothing finite is a final measure of what this is.

If promising beings seek the redemption of their promise, do we have the dominance of being for-self? This is not so, since the range of powers of being remains metaxological rather than exclusively self-mediating. This range involves other-relating as well as self-relating powers. We find a tense doubleness here. In fact, this is the basis for the intense equivocity of good/evil, as well as the labyrinth of the heart. This is the juncture of plural possibilities at the heart of the potencies of the ethical: the coming together of self-transcending and transcendence as other, or their splitting or wounding. This doubleness defines the communicative promise in the original power of all beings.

The range of goods cannot be separated from the range of metaxological power to dwell in the fullness of the between, open to the other as transcendent in the very unfolding of self-transcending. Communication with the other goes hand in hand with intensive self-relation, which is exhibited variously at different levels of ontological richness. The range of transcendence towards the other is expressive of depth of ontological intensity. Thus communicative power as metaxological, the ability to be self beyond self with the other, cannot be separated from the richness of the concretion of singular power, reflected in the intensive innerness of selving. This is why the human being (as far as we know) is the most communicative in creation and the most intensively singular: most selfless, most selfish; most open and out in the open, and most idiotic, reserved and secret.

The doubleness directs us to these two sides. First, there is the good of "wholeness" that expresses the integrity of being as seeking to fulfill its power most completely. Second, the relation to the other brings us back to the surplus of the good. The good as more than our good becomes more of moment. Our transcending to wholeness gives way in itself to an infinite restlessness that seeks what as good in itself is no finite good. There is no rest in a self-determining autonomy but a breach beyond finite wholeness, which offers the breakthrough of a freedom beyond autonomy. This freedom releases the energy of the good in giving towards the other. Beyond autonomy it brings us to goodness as agapeic giving, as well as sends us in search of a different telos beyond self-determining: to be ourselves agapeic and in community with the origin as agapeic.

This doubleness is reflected in the difference between erotic sovereignty and agapeic service. These are the flowers of our self-transcending as coming to itself and its justified autonomy, and as exceeding itself and its autonomy in the release of a more ultimate freedom that communicates in a being for the other that is a giving of good. What is intimated in the arche here becomes community in humanity, itself now called to be a concretion of agapeic community and witness to the ultimate agapeic source. This end is participation in community with the arche and hence itself is a finite form of the community of agapeic service. This is the good we must seek to be, failing again and again, and beginning again and again, as we must. I now explore the metaxological meaning of the potencies of the ethical, but first a word about the surplus of the good.

THE SURPLUS GENEROSITY OF THE GOOD

Sometimes the "too muchness" of thereness is oppressive; other times it falls into the invisibility of everydayness; and still other times it is alive with a shimmer of inexpressible worth. To be in the between is to suffer the thereness. This is first an undergoing; we do not choose it but find ourselves in it, now buoyed up, now flat, now weighted down. In every instance, thereness is saturated with some communication of value. Even insipid life is not flat of value, and this is clearly so with being weighted down, or elevated. There is an otherness to *being at all* that now seems void of meaning, now assumes the urgency of a message, communicating a good that teases, or torments, or turns tender on our terrible exposure. Univocity and dialectic seek too much to determine the surplus; metaxological mindfulness, like equivocal attunement, comes into the knowing of surplus beyond our mediation. The equivocal attunement does not always see that, beyond our mediation, this surplus sends its own shoots of communication and thus mediates with us: to feel the oppressive weight of being there, or to be lifted by a release, both are beyond mediation as self-mediation. They are opaque communications, intermediations from beyond us. We alone do not intermediate the good.

Suppose we have the presentiment even in the oppressiveness: it is good. What communicates this? Are we ourselves communicating with ourselves? Something other? Would there be any between did not that other come? The very being of the between is constituted by communication. Creation is a communication, and in the middle we have a presentiment of its mysterious goodness, as we live the feeling of "it is good to be," and are called to live up to the "it is good" of being. The communication is extremely enigmatic to us, and first we have no ken what it is we touch or what touches us. We are like tiny insects, laboring to climb a spiky stalk, and we put out feelers into the wide and empty air; and when we know a warmth on our surfaces, it is beautiful, but we do not know it is the sun that shines, and that the vast expanse of open air is the inexhaustibility of the between. Our feelers twitch, and our small minds are given the spasm of a glimpse that all this is the great mystery of the good. We baptize as "world" our twitch and feel. Some twitches, say, some dialectical and univocal ones, even feel their "world-historical significance," or feel assured of their "scientific-technological progress." Yet something about the touch of air and warmth has passed into us, and life is more difficult yet more true. The metaxological way is chastened by knowing the meagerness of its knowing, knows it does not know. More affirmatively than the equivocal way, it lives on this border of mystery. This too we may come to know more wakefully as the chiaroscuro of the good.

Our argument comes later, but if it is not grounded on the givenness of the ethos, then it is the insect flying through empty air and thinking that the freedom of the air is its only ground. The argument comes from what we cannot know at the beginning, for knowing of a more determinate sort comes later. The later argument tries to construct determinate accounts of the surplus given in the beginning. We come to be out of an origin that initially we cannot know determinately, for there is an indeterminacy prior to such cognitive determination. Being given to be is not best described as a thrownness into absurdity, or a condemnation to a hostile environment. It is being offered the gift of life as itself the elemental good we live. No doubt this gift is not Paradise, and there are too many occasions when the gift of life itself is communicated in circumstances hostile to its receipt; or that conspire against its joy; or that evoke hatred in those who are being gifted; or that sometimes come with a baffling deformation that tempts us to see evil there, not good.

Image: A deformed child is born. We recoil. Why? The child lacks the full promise of the good we anticipated. We need not recoil; we can have faith that there is good in this, though this faith is hard, maybe divine. But that we recoil is a secret compliment to the good that seems to be not given; we have expected the properly formed, perhaps taken it for granted; we may have forgotten that all of life, formed or deformed, or what we take as such, is given, is gift. This is not something we can demand, or over which we have command, or can count on, absolutely. We are dependent on the giving source. And when we see the (to us) deformed, we may be tempted to see the source as other than good; as no source, or perhaps as impotent, or perhaps as malicious.

But why *recoil* at all? What is it in us that recoils? Can it be pinned down, made completely determinate? Does it not suggest an anticipation of good inscribed in our being, an expectation that is our being? The ontological inscription of that indeterminate anticipation suggests that the recoil is an *indirect mediation of our relativity* to the source as good. The recoil testifies to an elemental expectation that the givenness of being is good, more elemental than the determinate deformations and disappointments that will later come on the scene and trouble us and make us suffer, and maybe rebel or revolt. The indeterminate intimation of the good of the giving source is mirrored in the indeterminate expectation of the good of being that we are and live. Our dwelling in the ethos, our being in the between, testifies to an original indeterminate togetherness of these two overdetermined sources.

You say: all this seems quite "metaphysical." Very well: this is because "being good" has to be understood all the way down, as well as all the way up. Can we otherwise avoid being pulled into the orbit of ethical nihilism? For this nihilism is not first the failure of humans to be ethical, to live up to genuine ideals. More elementally, is it not a loss of a full feeling for the fullness of the ethos? Loss signaled by the loss of presentiment of the giving source as good, and the trust that there is a good in the giving, not of our doing or making but in which we enigmatically participate? The loss of the ethos takes the form of the so-called death of God. And this is correct in that this is the loss of the elemental good of being in the between. It is not primarily a matter of finding the arguments for God unconvincing, or finding oneself living fine without God, or indeed even of turning against God. It is a loss of the mindful attunement between the indeterminate openness of elemental expectation in us and the goodness of the source.

This loss can take place behind our backs, occasioned by the formation of ways of life that cumulatively turn the ethos more into a mirror of the human being than the source of otherness which gifts all being with the goodness of its being at all. We live the ethos with an emphasis on our own powers of self-mediation, but in the process we crowd out, slowly, inexorably, with a gentle stifling, the subtle communication of the source as good. We are responsible for the loss and not responsible; responsible though we do not know it, and we think we are being the most responsible, since we answer primarily to our own powers of self-mediation, and not to anything other. But this answering just to ourselves is the rub. The ethos communicates the source as other, and this the metaxological way must recall, but this recall means breaking the circuit of self-mediation that has crowded out, or subordinated, or refused the more elemental character of this primal relatedness to the other. The fundamental enabling power of being is forgotten, in our being enabled to be ourselves, as we claim to define the good for ourselves and through ourselves. Metaxological mindfulness returns us to a new rapport with the between as good, as ethos in communication with the origin.

Is not late modernity anomalous in this regard? We have set ourselves up over against the surplus of otherness; stripping it of the charge of the good, we also have stripped it of the signs that point towards the ground of the good. As we saw, being there becomes worthless. In tandem, we set ourselves up as ground of value who impose on this valueless thereness values of our construction. This construction is really based upon a destruction and itself is an aggression that congratulates itself on its own superiority to other-being as other. All of this is the result of certain developments of being in the between, especially the absolutization of our being as self-determining. Previous epochs, we may say, were less powerful, in being determined by what was other; and yet this "impotence" was not without its glory, in that beyond the wretchedness, humans were sometimes visited with glory, in the breakthrough of the gift of the origin, the vision that the between is truly beyond our power, and that this is a good thing, that it is just the good of the between that its good is not our production. Its gift is the good, albeit ambiguous to us, sometimes threatening, sometimes destructive of us. Just this appreciation of gift can nurture a gratitude to the ground of good. We are not in our own hands. We receive the gift. We can be thankful; we can rage, or whine, or find sly ways to get our own way, to the end of finding that it is not ours, and will be taken from us, as we go as naked into death, as when we first came into birth. Naked, we spend our lives covering ourselves, but in the end, as at the beginning, there is nakedness: exposure and vulnerability beyond all human power, beyond the power of nature itself as a totality; vulnerability and exposure beyond the whole.

The nakedness can be lived with hard-won consent, or perhaps with a gift of "yes" that comes out of nothing, or with anxiety and trembling, or with wrath. And yet for all of this, an *ethics of gratitude* can be called forth. This ethics is not supinely impotent because the ground is beyond our power; it generates a response in us, a corresponding *ethics of generosity*. We are grateful for the generosity of the ground, and we respond to this with thanks, and with thanks lived as a form of existence. For it is not only the generosity of the giver that is important but the generosity of the receiver. We are the receivers, and strangely, it is the generosity of the other that possibilizes our comportment of generosity towards the other. Generosity entails no servile reception or abjection before the other. In fact, the other's generosity does more than occasion our gratitude; it charges us with the living of generosity. Only a generous person can properly receive a gift. The *receiver* must have generosity to receive the generosity of the giver, otherwise the gift is perverted in thankless grabbing. Think of a person who cannot receive a compliment. Think of those who are unable to be gracious—their inability turns the gift into something else, turning it aside. The gift needs the graciousness of the receiver to be itself fulfilled as gift. Thus the gift is the promise of a fulfilled community. The promise can be lost in more than one place. The gift is an occasion that occasions giving, as much by the receiver as by the giver. There is a reception that is a giving, for it is an opening of the self to the other, and this opening is the greatest gift—not the thing given, but the mode of being of the giver and receiver, as with the widow who gave her last mite.

So also generosity is not only relative to the giver. Those who cannot receive a gift lack the spirit of generosity. We must be generous to allow the generous other to offer its gift. It is the spirit of generosity that is more than us and makes us more than ourselves, and that comes over us in the gift of the ground. If we are obsessed with doing all for ourselves, of proving that we are in charge or in control, even if we seem utterly noble in insisting on giving to others, we may, in fact, have perverted the occasion of generosity. Our "generosity" may be the pride that insists on itself and hence may not be generous at all. The depth of generosity is sustained by humility in relation to the ultimate.

This means the willingness to put oneself in the relative position, not the unconditional. Strangely, the relative position is the absolute position, insofar as it is the position of relativity in which being there for the other becomes an ethical reality. Being relative in the spirit of generosity is the unconditional relation, not the unconditional self-relation that would only relate to the other out of its prior securing of itself. Relative to the surplus, this prior securing is a perversion of what the prior is, for what is prior is the gift of being as good. Securing ourselves as mastering powers cuts us off from the fullness of the gift, even though it is the gift itself that allows this cutting off of the gift. If the project of modernity is this securing of itself, it must risk the loss of the metaxological between and hence of the ethos as ambiguous cipher of the grounding good. Before that, and still for many in their heart of hearts, the good is God and nothing but God. The singularity of this good is alone what makes more than aloneness possible.

This good communicates the being of the good as being in relation to the other, and of enabling self-being in the web of relations that constitutes the between. That there are communities of being in the between is already a sign of the communication of the good. We have taken up domesticated residence in these communities and have forgotten how astonishing it all is. There is an ethical need for the rebirth of agapeic astonishment, for this is the opening in which the ethics of gratitude and generosity is born for us.

You sigh with faint exasperation: But are we not all now postmodern—not modern, not premodern? I sigh too. The equivocal again dons its seductive mask. There is a "postmodernity" that, in all humility, seems to be coming around to a new insight into the patience of the human before God, and the active patience that is the ethics of generosity, and the life of service going with it. There also is a "postmodernity," and this seems the more frequent, which is an accentuation of the modern, an aggravation of the powers of self-determining, but now grown skeptical and bitter about themselves: wanting still to be absolute, insisting on themselves always, secretly now, overtly now; and yet knowing that these cannot be absolute, for a presentiment of the other has made its way into the heart of humanity, puffing itself up as a project; but the project is wounded by a shadow or a compassion or a terror or an abyss or . . . some indeterminate nothing.

Then the self-determining human lacerates itself, as it still clings to itself; preaches about the other, while still shouting about its right to be in control; vacillates between knowing in its heart of hearts that the tale is told and the impotence to let go of its own power. The laceration brings us to no self; no God; and we are in the between with a bewilderment we hysterically call creative freedom, all the while without wise counsel about our bewilderment and our hysteria. "Having your cake and eating it" is an old phrase for this; but the cake that is had is just as deficient in nourishment as the cake that is eaten. The simple answer is to rethink the good of the human as more ultimate than the human; to have the humility to say that numberless generations of humans were there before us, closer to the divine traces of the ethos than we are, and for all the sound and fury and mire of man, quietly aware that the ultimate "yes" is the "yes" of the divine and our "yes" to it.

TRANSCENDENCE AND THE METAXOLOGICAL: THE AGAPE OF THE GOOD

Is it possible for humans to sustain an ethics of agapeic service? Extremely hard. We are always drawn back into the being of selving as for-itself. The doubleness of our transcending, as seeking its own fulfillment and going beyond itself to the other, resists definition by one or either side. Yet no absolute closure on ourselves is possible; we always stand in relation to others; though there can be a retraction of self back on itself, as if, in its necessary relation to the other, it would that it were only in relation to itself and nothing but itself. But in this "would," it is always fighting against the exigence of transcending to be for the other.

Equally, on the other side, we cannot absolutely leave ourselves behind, in our being for the other; there is no transcending for us so absolutely self-less as to be nothing but a service for the other; for our self-transcending, even when maximum, is still the self as other, in its being beyond itself, and so it always brings itself with its self-surpassing, hence there is always a "for-itself," even in the purest form of its being for the other. This means concretely that just as self-love cannot be defined absolutely to exclude the other, neither can love of the other exclude self-love. Moreover, there is a proper self-love; this is the love of the good of the "to be" as singularized in the I; this I is to be loved as good, as much as the good of the other. Concretely, this proper self-love is mixed with more retracted selfishness so that agapeic service also is mingled with other considerations: the need to get something back, to get something out of the relation, to get a return, whether thanks, recognition, a smile, or a mere nod. The agape of being is entirely forgiving and will laugh at these mischiefs of selfishness. The human is to be loved still.

Acting on the call of agapeic service is not sustainable by our will alone. It is not enacted by autonomous will deliberately setting out to be beyond itself in service for the other. Transcending desire discovers that, in being fully itself, it is more than itself and called forth by transcendence as more than itself, transcendence as superior to it. The call is a sustaining that is prior to the hearing of the call. The hearing is sustained by the call that, in being sounded, opens up the middle of communication, even before the middle serves as the medium of its transmission and reception.

That is why I speak of a willingness before and beyond will, or any will to power. For this willingness is the laying of selving open to this calling. And it is in the strength that comes to one in laying oneself open that the support is offered for living something of the life of agapeic service. Strength comes from laying oneself open, or being opened. The power of being good grows with knowing that one is not the good; the power of doing good comes from knowing that good is being done to one; the power of willing the good comes from beyond the powerlessness of will to power.

Needless to say, the call of the transcendent good is enigmatic in our self-transcending. Hence our laying of ourselves as open seems like a constant striving, or like a pathway through a wilderness that often vanishes, making us think we had been fooling ourselves, only then to reappear suddenly further along and hearten us that our faith in the good, faith without certitude, is not without unexpected fruit. The life of agapeic service is impossible if we are alone and without the sustaining power of the good as other. As I suggested before, the familiar word (and I think best word) for transcendence itself is "God." The fullest community with the good is reflected in the openness of the metaxological way towards God as the ultimate other. The metaxological is a way of trying to give articulation to the ethos as the finite between wherein God is intimated and reserved in the idiotic, aesthetic, dianoetic, transcendental, eudaimonistic, and transcending potencies of the ethical.

There is a reversal here: being open finds itself being opened. The ultimate power is turned towards us: transcendence itself possibilizes all transcending, indeed all being, and possibilizes it because transcendence itself is good. It is not only good but the good. The good communicates itself into the between, communicating the space that sustains the community of finite being and the variety of self-becomings of different beings, as each strives towards what is good for it, or what is good. There is a community of the good beyond self-determination, given from the origin, giving the ethos and the power of "to be" as good, giving the self the power to be determining of itself, giving it itself to be itself, giving all beings their distinctive promise of agapeic community with other beings.

The ethos as good is not any projection of the human good. The gift means an undergoing of the good from the origin. The supreme suffering of self-transcending reveals ultimate receptivity, not mastering power. We do not understand the mystery of God. Metaxological mindfulness mulls over the signs of God in the between, alert to what comes to it from beyond itself. Traces of transcendence are communicated in many ways to the twilight or dawn of the middle. The many ways and the one good are not antagonistic, for the one good as agapeic gives the plural between, communicates to it its being as good, whence comes the good of the "to be." The many ways are possible ways to serve the communication of the good in the community of agapeic service. This is true even of our finite vulnerability, which strangely heightens the good rather than simply being the occasion of despair. It is because we love the good that we despair, when we are not with what our being secretly tells us we should be with. Despair is love of God frustrated, frustrated by overwhelming perplexity about the equivocal face of evil, or perhaps by our frustrating or corrupting the exigence of transcending in ourselves.

The relation to the good as other is more complex than dialectic comprehends; the mystery is more affirmative than equivocity knows; determination is more open than univocity allows. The intimation of transcendence as other is not within our univocal or dialectical grasp, though the equivocal brings us to its threshold. Those who have the finesse of the equivocal often are closer to the divine, though their finesse seems like a laughing mockery of the certitudes of univocity or the premature inclusions of dialectic. Nor is the intimation separable from the glory of creation, its show of aesthetic value in the ontological splendor of the incarnate "to be." Love of creation is secret love of God, for the time of creation is our time to sing.

There is no univocal proof of what is suggested in the intimation. There is probing with respect to the ultimate perplexities, especially, "What is the good of it all?" This perplexity we have shunned in our obsession with this or that finite good. Yet if there is no response to it, our busy obsession is much ado about nothing, and we had better face this honestly, for the emptiness will stalk abroad as hatred of life and leave us finally in the lurch. The probe is dependent on discipline that purifies itself in the direction of spiritual discernment. This archaic truth is neither old nor new; it is elemental and perennial, always promised, always betrayed, but in strange ways, also redeemed. The agape of being is first given to us, but we are called to an agapeic being that is the doing of living, in an ethics of gratitude to the origin, and of generosity to self and other. The agape of being intimates a fullness, but it is not being full of oneself. One does nothing to merit it, and no payment is exacted, for it offers itself simply as the life of the good, a life we are to live. It has no reason, beyond itself, which is to be beyond itself, in being itself.

PART III

RELIGION AND THE
PHILOSOPHY OF GOD

AGAPEIC ORIGIN

From *Perplexity and Ultimacy*

I am sometimes visited by the mockery of Dostoevski's Underground Man when he sneered: if man is not stupid, then certainly he is monstrously ungrateful! Agapeic being? Come, come! Lear learned about ingratitude from his daughters and paid for his folly with madness. Agapeic being? Come now!

I did say before that being agapeic is almost an impossibility for us. We are spiteful, grasping, thankless. And if there is something monstrous about the Underground Man, there is also, it seems, a monstrous audacity in the thought of agapeic being. That audacity drives us to think of agapeic being in relation to God. How then might the matter look?

We would have to break with any dualism of being and the good, and any divorce of ethics and metaphysics. Consider how Levinas, for instance, claims that the concern of traditional ontology with being ends in a philosophy of power and a subordination of the other to the same. He does grant that what he calls "metaphysics" allows for the other as other. Plato's Good beyond being is invoked by him, and the claim is made that metaphysics in his sense must become an ethics of the other. What I call erotic mind and the ontological outlook going with it might be correlated with what Levinas calls "ontology." By contrast, agapeic mind is related to metaphysics. But agapeic metaphysics is a philosophy of being, agapeic being. Contra Levinas we do not need to dualize being and the good. It is crucially important not to do so. If the ultimate is agapeic, it is the good. To be is to be good. Absolute being is the agapeic good.

If we think of God as agapeic being, God could not be defined just as thought thinking itself. The latter suggests the closed circle of absolute self-mediation. Ultimately it stems from an understanding of the good primarily in relation to erotic being. By contrast, agapeic mind makes way for the thought and the being of the other, beyond the circle of thought thinking itself. Every closed circle is broken open. Moreover, the model of exit and return, *exitus* and *reditus, monas, prohodos,* and *epistrophe,* so dominant in the tradition of speculative theology and metaphysics, must be qualified. What I mean is the following.

The erotic absolute might be said to mirror this movement: origin as the indefinite abstraction or lack; self-exit into otherness; return to self through and from the otherness; now in the end explicit self-constitution, finally determined as fully real. By contrast, the metaphor of the agapeic absolute would run: origin as excess plenitude, transcendence itself as other; creation as finite concreteness, but not for the return of the origin to itself; the "exitus," if we call it such at all, is for what is given as other in the middle; and while there may be a different "return" in the metaxological middle, this is not dictated by the logic of a circular erotic self-becoming; it is gratuitously emergent in the created other as itself trying to be agapeic being; "return" is the cocreation of community by the finite other. In other words, the teleology of erotic being is finally closed, or looks forward to a closure in a completely self-determined whole. By comparison, the teleology of agapeic being is there at work as the opening of being as free community. It is also more rupturing, more anarchic relative to finite ends.

Were the origin conceived in terms of agapeic being, the origin would be creative in a more radical way than could be ascribed to any finite being or process. In this absolutely singular instance, agapeic mind would be creative of the finite other. Would this finite other be simply the externalization of the agapeic original? If that were the case, the origin would not be agapeic at all but erotic, and the created finite other would be the mirror in which the self-relativity of the origin was effected. Instead the agapeic creation of the finite other is for the finite other as other. Finite creation is given its true otherness; and this is irreducibly given, given as irreducible.

This, in fact, suggests the primal meaning of gift. This is the original meaning of the givenness of being: a generosity of being that gives for no reason beyond the goodness of giving being. This, I believe, is the ultimate basis on which also we must think the value of finite being. The worth of being is its being agapeically given. We might say that the "yes" to the being of the gift is ontologically inscribed in the being of that gift. The very giving of the being is itself an ultimate "yes" that is for the being that is given. This is why, as we saw before, when God says, "It is good," He does not say simply, "I am good," or that it is good for me, or for humans, or for some extrinsic purpose. It is good. It, the being there of the being, is good in itself. This is the primal "yes." This is something different to the elemental "no" and "mine" shaping the psychogenesis of the human self. These are themselves given by the primal "yes," which they ambiguously reveal, and inevitably can come to disfigure. The power of freedom is the power to let the "no" shut out the primal "yes," closing itself in, by closing transcendence as other out.

Here we come across the generosity of freedom as a gift. The absolute origin as agapeic, as it were, sacrifices its own for-itself. It gives, and supports, and preserves the other as other. It lets it go as other. Freedom is not originally given in the expectation of a return on the gift. One gives for nothing. God gives for nothing. This is why in one respect being is for nothing. Being is without a why. There is a kind of agapeic nihilism implied by this, but the *nihil* is not any negating or destructive *nihil*. God does nothing for Himself; everything is done for the other. There is a sense in which nothing is *for* God. God lets be, since everything given by God is for that thing, given for that thing itself.

Since our minds and being are so insistently erotic, such absolute agapeic being seems hardly conceiveable, much less believable. Should this surprise us? The whole thing is something exceedingly perplexing. The agapeic origin is infinite transcendence, hence always beyond dialectical self-mediation. As overdetermined plenitude it is more than any definite whole. "Mystery" is constitutive of its excessive being. No determinate intelligible structure could capture its "essence." Its "essence" as plenitude is beyond every determinate why.

This gives us an inkling of why God's justice or mercy can so appall thought. We suspect a radical *disproportion* to our definition of what is a true measure. Our understanding of measure is generally defined in terms of a determinate calculable standard—an eye for an eye, say. Our measure is generally the measure of equivalence. But there is no equivalent measure in the case of the agapeic origin. The origin as an indeterminate plenitude is beyond measure, beyond all our measures. The measure of the absolute original is beyond every equivalence. There is a divine disproportion in this measure that can cut across and subvert every finite standard we erect.

The inequality of the agapeic origin is its unequalizable plenitude. This is why we can never really think it, since all our thinking tends to reduce the other to the measure of our own thought, or make its otherness intelligible in terms that, more or less, are equivalent to ourselves. The plenitude of the absolute original overflows determinate wholeness. It is transcendence, a surplus, an excess, an overwholeness. It is not perfect but pluperfect: pluperfect not in a past or present being achieved and having being achieved; not pluperfect in terms of the promise of the about to be achieved; its pluperfection is impossible to measure in terms of the dimensions of past, present, or future; it is pluperfect beyond the measures of time; it is pluperfect in the immeasureability of eternity.

The pluperfect excess is for the finite other, as already having been given being as other. The greatest gift is independent being in which one would not ask for anything back. The absolute origin gives and demands nothing back. Again this is beyond measure, for our giving and return are subject to determinable measure. A giving without the expectancy of return is beyond our measuring. This is pure gift. God demands nothing. This is agapeic expectancy: nothing determinate is expected in return, which is not to deny a solicitude for the other. Solicitude is expectancy that the gift will be not only well received but well *lived*.

Does this mean that we must give nothing back? If nothing is demanded of us, must we turn from the giving source without any expectation on our part? The situation is more complex, if expectancy is solicitude for the other. One can give for nothing, but that giving for nothing is informed by goodwill to the other; so its expectancy is such as to want no malice or violence to befall the recipient of the gift. This gift given for nothing is in the light of its *goodness* to the beneficiary.

So it is not that we must give nothing back, like ontological ingrates. Nothing is asked of us, yet in that nondemand there opens up the mystery of free generosity. That is, the nondemand of the source solicits freely the giving of agapeic mind *from our side*. "It is good"; and we humans taste the "It is good" knowingly. The mindful taste of the "It is good" arouses in us a call to *live beyond ourselves* the "It is good." *We* become the expectancy of nothing. *We* are asked by the expectancy of nothing that we try to give for nothing, beyond the goodness of the giving itself. The gift of agapeic being solicits in us the gift of agapeic being. We, too, must be the release of the divine freedom of generosity. Is this "the glorious liberty of the children of God?"

As finite others we are free; but our freedom is a gift of generosity. There is no univocal reason for it. The reason for it is that it is good. This freedom becomes itself creative in generosity. We give back because this is the ontological *ananke* of freedom. The deepest character of being, human and divine, is agapeic freedom. We give back because nothing is demanded of us. There is no external coercion. We give, demanding nothing for ourselves. We give ourselves to and for the other.

BREAKING THE SILENCE

From *God and the Between*

There is a natural hesitation in speaking about God. One fears presumption. God exceeds if not our reach certainly our grasp. We overextend our powers and wound ourselves. There is also something intimate in so speaking. God is not to be bandied about in the highways and byways of facile discourse. One wonders if, rather, one should speak to God, and not with human witnesses to overhear. There seems to be an intimacy about being religious to which philosophical thought will never quite be true. Yet there comes a time when one must break silence, and break a silence that has been philosophically chosen or enforced in recent centuries. If one dares to speak, whether in interrupting that philosophical silence, or in venturing to say anything at all, one had better have something considered to offer.

Through much of the history of philosophy, to be a philosopher at all seemed to carry with it, as an inner part of the philosopher's vocation, concern with the question of God. In recent centuries, perhaps dating from around the time of Kant, it has not been possible to take that concern for granted, and, in our time, it seems rather that silence about God is the norm. That this silence seems to be so self-evident and self-evidently justified to many philosophers strikes me as perplexing. Relative to the longer history of the human family, and indeed most human beings today, such a silence is the anomaly rather than the rule. True, there is a certain analytic tradition that keeps alive the issues of natural theology, and, since the early 1990s, there has been a so-called phenomenological turn to religion. Nevertheless, the more general rule is an atheism that has been common among intellectuals since the Enlightenment, an atheism now in a phase of seeming to be entirely undisturbed about itself. I find this disturbing. For there are silences and silences. There is a silence of reserve and respect. There is a silence of reverence. There is a silence of disinterest. There is a silence of indifference. There are philosophers who affect this latter silence. Not for them the passionate repudiation of the monotheistic God of some earlier atheists, like Nietzsche. The matter is no longer an issue.

91

One can discover that once one scratches the surface of indifference, flashes of an old hostility flare up. It may take the form, for instance, of an irritation that anyone should invest this issue with seriousness at all. Nevertheless, it still is perplexing that there should be indifference at all, since surely it is the most natural thing that such a question should strike one as of the most ultimate seriousness. I began to wonder if the hostility might be like the irritation of someone who, sleeping or half-sleeping, wants to be left alone and not bothered. I began to wonder if our being asleep to the question betokened a kind of bewitchment. Is it possible that an age could fall under a bewitchment? Could it be that especially since the early nineteenth century many of the major intellectuals of the era live under the bewitchment of godlessness? For the question of God is no longer a matter of reason or argument. Nietzsche, as usual, hits the nail on the head: God, he says, is not now to *our taste*. But who are we, and what is our taste? Why have we no taste for God? I have come to think that a postulatory finitism (IST? especially chapter 1) polices the kinds of questions allowed to arise as significant, and God is not among those questions. But what if one were to hold that this question not only should but does arise? Arguments alone will not wake people who are under the spell of an enchantment. More is needed.

The arising or not of the question of God has much to do with our understanding of the ethos of being wherein we dwell. If this ethos is dominated by, for instance, a devaluation of nature as other-being and an apotheosis of human autonomy, the issue of God as a superior transcendence other to our own immanent self-transcendence will not easily arise. We inhabit the ethos of being, but we also reconfigure the given ethos in terms of what we consider to be most important and ultimate. It is within this reconfigured ethos that questions proximately arise. Nevertheless, the proximate questions allowed to arise are dependent on a whole set of background assumptions and presuppositions that them-selves never or rarely enter the foreground picture. These presuppositions take on a life of their own, and function as enablers and censors in terms of the questions that emerge in the foreground of the reconfigured ethos. They may block the arising of the question of God, or dull our taste for it. They may cast a spell in which atheism seems self-evident.

What then would it be to address a bewitchment? Among other things, it would mean trying to understand the recessed as well as the expressed, the backgrounding presuppositions as well as the foregrounded claims and articulations. We live and think *in* the foregrounded articulations, but we live and think *out* of these backgrounding presuppositions and sources. To see again if the question of God can arise, and how properly it must arise, would mean investigating not only the reconfigured ethos in the foreground but also its background sources and presuppositions. It would mean asking whether there is any sense of a primal ethos of being within which all our reconfigured ethe participate, for there are different reconfigured ethe, and differences might be noted between the premodern, the modern, and now the postmodern, and yet what each configures is the ethos as the given milieu of being. This ethos I also call the between. If the ultimate question is to be addressed, we must ask about God and the between.

GODLESSNESS

From *God and the Between*

There is no question more ultimate than the question of the ultimate. This is the question of God. Nonphilosophers may well be willing to grant this claim. They may even expect philosophers to come to their assistance. But we philosophers have long listened to the voices of suspicion, voices that when they do not make us hostile to the question, paralyze our thinking on the ultimate. We have become embarrassed by the question.

This is something astonishing. The most important question, the most fascinating question, the most enigmatic question, makes us squirm—squirm though we wear the unmoved mask of agnostic indifference. How make sense of this shame? Can we mark some of the way stations on this path of shame? And when we have passed along it, can we then ask: What then?

We in the West are heirs of a number of religious traditions, but as descendants we have turned our inheritance into hostility to itself. We emerge from religious traditions, notably the Jewish and Christian, but certain developments of just those traditions have made trouble for any untroubled living of those traditions. I mean that certain forms of theism are not to be absolved from atheism that seems to be their opposite. Godlessness emerges from our being in relation to God. We think of ourselves as at the end of a "good" progress, even when we debunk progress. We are enlightened even when we pour scorn on Enlightenment. We see our scorn as our light—but suppose we are freaks. How freaks? Freaks because the natural condition is to be religious: it is unnatural to be atheist. This crime against nature arises from nature as we interpret it.

We open our eyes, we smell, we breathe, we touch, we are touched, by rock, by the satin of a flower petal, by skin. We are amazed, even delighted; we attend on a certain music of things. When much seems rough and repulsive our horror is the shadow of our astonishment. What is strangely there is strange because it intimates an other—in and through its very own otherness. There is no shadow of a question, yet: the divine is there, though there as also not there, for there is nothing to which one could point univocally and say: That is God. But what that means one does not know.

Or say, one hears one's breath, in the quiet of sitting still, or in trepidation as if trailed, and one hears oneself in an intimacy idiotic to every conceptual objectification, and one does not know what the soul is, beyond knowing that one does not know. There is hinted a depth to selving beyond self, and the haunting of self by an other that slows one into uncertain expectancy. Is this then our being, this uncertain expectancy? But we do not yet know what this means.

Or again, another stirs delight and disquiet in us. We behold a beautiful boy or girl, woman or man, and the beauty can lift one up unbidden and yet also be unbearable, almost. It flows over one, and away from one, though one reaches to it, but it is always in excess, and gone. It comes forward to meet one, and yet is fugitive in its forwardness. A gift has been offered; it seems everywhere and nowhere; and one might be surprised into asking, is this gift a sacramental sign? But what this all means, one does not know, and perhaps may never know.

But—knowing or not-knowing—there is *nothing contrived* about the question of God. It is elemental and enigmatic—elemental because of the givenness of self, other, nature; enigmatic because one is struck into an as-yet-uncomprehended astonishment by the givennesss. The astonishing gift perplexes us about what offers it, or who. And our question is not something to which history determines us, even when it is historically mediated. It is not something grammar imposes on us, even when our speaking is grammatically conditioned. It is not the sly unconscious that presses it on us, though its roots go down deeper than the conscious or unconscious. It is not something to which our social status condemns us. It is not something insidious metaphysics imposes on us, though we cannot escape metaphysics, twist and turn as we will. The question is elemental and inescapable. But we have to be with the elemental, and face what cannot be evaded, to know what this means. Nor will we "overcome" the question, when we have baptized our chains as historicist chains, grammatological, psychoanalytical, sociopolitical, philosophical chains. There are other fetters, harder to unbind, for instance, the lie in the soul, not to mention vices not always dignified with names in philosophy.

Why has the face of being come for many to seem void of communication of God, when everything within and without seems to press on us the question? The changed attitude to being marking modernity has much to do with the matter. This has been recognized by many, and with many different emphases. My emphasis falls on our reconfiguration of the primal ethos along a particular line of response to the equivocity of givenness. This produces a certain devaluation of being stripped of signs suggestive of divine transcendence. This is coupled with a culture of autonomy which, tempted to absolutize itself, eclipses transcendence as other, though behind the mask of autonomy is a will to power usurping absoluteness in a world said to be void of absolutes. The specter of nihilism, now expressed, now recessed, in which all other-being is instrumentalized haunts our claim to mastery, finally inverting into an outcome in which it all seems to come to nothing.

Suppose one holds to a God the creator of all, a God other than creation. Suppose, further, that the creation is given its own being for itself—given to be, it yet has its own otherness. Suppose God is other yet intimate, and other with an unsurpassable transcendence that nothing finite in creation can match. Suppose we seek to relate genuinely to this transcendence. If the transcendence is absolute, the search seems futile. If the search augurs of success, the transcendence seems not absolute. What then are the options? If we say the transcendence is absolute, we drive God away from us into a beyond, and our futility is just our search itself: the search drives away from itself what it seems to be driving towards, and hence lacks the basis to yield even a half success. Better then to search by not searching at all? If to seek God is to drive God away, cease to search, and let God come towards one. But if no God seems to come? Let us wait. How long must we wait? Since we wait for eternity, must we wait for an eternity? But we grow restless and impatient. We have waited and nothing seems to come. Or perhaps it came, but we did not see it pass? And perhaps it is there, and there is no wait, only the call of transformation? We have waited, and still wait, and no God seems to come. What then? Why then transcendence seems to turn over into immanence: first, immanence grieving over its own failure of self-surpassing; then immanence hostile over its previous desire for God; then immanence hostile to God as depriving its own self-surpassing of its own esteem in itself; finally, immanence as willing the immanent esteem of its own worldly self-transcendence. And then there is no more waiting and expectancy. We have arrived—God has arrived. Transcendence overturned. We—God—Ourselves.

If thought is too condensed in these statements, I will thin things in the sequel. To round off this opening sortie: we search other-being as *outer*—nature's astonishing thereness. We search other-being as *inner*—the enigmatic abyss of our own selving. Each of these teases us into thought of God. (Kant: the starry sky above, the moral law within.) And yet God is other to both. But what if we conceive of divine transcendence in *dualistic terms*, as can easily happen? Then no community seems possible between God and creation. Not only does it seem that God withdraws into self-sufficient independence; world and we can seem to do so too. Or it might seem as if the flood tide of the divine ebbs, and world and we find ourselves beached on the solitude of a Godless shore. Something like this ebb of the great tide seems to occur in modernity.

What causes the ebb is very perplexing. Is it the self-withdrawal of God, as some have thought? Or was that space of transcendence always empty? Or have we, in a series of slight shifts—slight as singular, but momentous as a continuing series—blinded ourselves, deafened ourselves, numbed ourselves, though we call our sightlessness, our silence, our anesthesia enlightened? Something of the latter, I think, though I think so as one hard of hearing and as squinting. Yet, given the mystery of God, and the potential for equivocity in our openness to communication, there is some truth to the first suggestion. Our reconfiguration of the primal ethos produces a second ethos, and this makes more difficult our attunement to the signs of the divine. We can see this relative to the ebb: first relative to other-being as outer; then relative to other-being as inner. I mean, first, the desacralizing effects of the devaluation of being in modernity; I mean, second, the atheistic consequences of the self-assertion of human self-transcendence and its idolization of autonomy.

Kierkegaard — - Infinite Resignation
- Despair
(That is when you are ready
to start thinking about God)

BEYOND GODLESSNESS

From *God and the Between*

THE ANGEL OF DEATH, BEING AS GIFT

What is our concern now? To see if we can start on a way beyond godlessness. Can our return to zero enliven again our taste for the ethos of being and its signs of transcendence? I detect the lineaments of a countermovement to the absolutization of immanent autonomy. This absolutization shows the extreme temptation of self-transcendence (T^2): self-divinization. This happens in the flood tide of the *conatus essendi* that overwhelms, overtakes the *passio essendi*. Godlessness suggests a certain recession of the *passio essendi* and a certain accession, a "takeover" of the *conatus essendi*. Moving beyond godlessness suggests a renewed relief of the *passio*, and a qualification of the conatus that brings it home to its proper reserve. There is a turning in the flood tide of the godless endeavor to be. For though the return to zero can seem like the ebb tide of the *passio essendi*, it can also be a turning around which allows flow in our porosity, a new communication patient to the divine. In the inner otherness in excess of our self-determination, there are signs of transcendence as other (T^3) in our self-transcending (T^2).

For the return to zero may be the nihilism of despair, but it need not only be that. It may be a different nihilism: a nihilating of despair in despair. Does despair call us beyond our contracted configuration of being and to a new communication of the ontological promise of the primal ethos? Likewise, does the return to zero bring the I of self-insistence, even the I of ideal self-determining, closer to its own being as nothing? Can a reborn I, beyond self-insistence, beyond self-determining, come to be in the nothing, in a new release of transcending, as willing to be other, both in itself and for other-being? Is there not, as religions have often indicated, a saving despair? You object: Is this not just religious nihilism? But the point need not be intended Nietzsche-wise: that is, religion—the "bad" nihilism. Quite other to Nietzsche's "strong nihilism," this other "nihilism" can be profoundly affirmative.

99

One wanders a desert that bleaches with burning light, or one is exiled to a Siberia of soul that freezes, or one is fleshed together with perishing, as with one's Siamese twin; one has become as nothing, and one is kissed, before one knows it, by the angel of death. What is the kiss? It is a Golgotha of our human hubris. The kiss opens our sightless eyes. One sees the same things but sees the sameness as other. The wings of the angel beat quietly but in the unbearable terror of her approach being suddenly shows the beauty of thereness as absolute gift. Being is given, and it is given for nothing—nothing beyond the goodness of its being, and of its being given. The terror liquefies the world that one has fixed. The world configured as worthless also seems to dissolve. Something else is offered: a taste of the elemental goodness of the "to be"—abundance without a why, beyond the sweetness of its being at all. Here commences a reversal of nihilism, and a redoubled search for God, for we seem to be given to be again, redoubled in being.

Is this to speak of signs—and speak of signs in signs? Perhaps. A shadow falls as the angel of death spreads its wings over us. The shadow is shadow only because a light is cast from beyond the wings. We do not see the source of this light. We see the glow that bends around the wings. The glow communicates a startling halo to the thereness of things. One goes towards the death that crushes one; one goes down, one goes under; one is as dead; reborn to a different mindfulness, one sees beyond purpose: pointless seeing that sees in the pointlessness. The point? Not proximately a new finite teleology: neither an external teleology imposed by a specific end for us, nor an immanent teleology of autonomous self-determination. To what point then? The return to zero releases the energy of coming to be into a *new interface with creation*. Another sense of goodness matters, purposeless and purposing at once: good beyond determinate good and evil and our self-determination. The redoubled beginning: to be, to be again, and for no reason beyond the good of being, as if one were given to be anew, like a child, or as if, in another way, vouchsafed a light by the angel beyond the terrible struggle of life and death.

OUT OF NOTHING: POROSITY AND THE URGENCY OF ULTIMACY

Put the point another way: *nihilism strangely makes the light itself strange.* Were nihilism the ultimate truth, we would expect no light, and yet light there is. We see the "truth" of nihilism in a light that nihilism, were it true, would render impossible. What is that light? Is it something in which we are, in the more primal ethos of being, which we do not bring to be, but rather *we are simply what we are as participants in it?* Has it also anything to do with the shining that bends around the wings of the angel? Does the resurrection of astonishment in posthumous mind also imply a rebirth of what I call the urgency of ultimacy?

Different possibilities are here suggested. The ultimate can be named in a variety of ways. Some of these will fix on what is not ultimate, and then our name will tag an idol. Even nihilism sings its *Te Deum*: nothing is ultimate. It seems impossible to step outside some relation to what we take as ultimate. A very revealing fact is that we humans are capable of idolatry at all. I take this as indirect confirmation that our being is religious. Even when we deny ultimacy, as in nihilism, our being is to be in relation to ultimacy. Ultimacy is not nothing, otherwise there is no relation, and no ultimate, and we would not be what we are.

Consider the urgency. We do not create the relation to ultimacy; we are in the relation, are what we are in it. What urgency shows is the exigent articulation of the relation in our mindful desiring. An urgent happening is not first the outcome of some deliberate choice. It may communicate from within or from without, or both. Its source may be immanent or transcendent, or both. An obscure passion is precipitated, and we are importuned. Opportunity comes in the importunity. Something disturbs our more settled forms of domesticated life; something more absolute importunes us; a gap of difference opens, through which we are coaxed into a deeper rapport with the primal ethos.

Such urgency is ecstatic—it catapults us *beyond* ourselves. From within out it surges from abysmal sources beyond secure self-consciousness, and so communicates the secret intensities of our being. Its movement is also from without in: there is an opening inward—an inbreaking that is a startling outbreak of obscure intimation. In the urgency a *dawning* comes over us. There is the bite of the unbidden about the urgency that breaks up our smug self-satisfaction. It brings unquiet to our vaunted autonomy, stressing it, even shattering it. A longing springs up in a descending darkness that we do not determine, though gropingly we cast around for direction. Drawing us deeper within, it drives us further out beyond. The urgency of ultimacy can erupt any time, anywhere, from any direction, from no one direction in particular, from no direction we can detect, in dreams and waking, in gravitas and frivolity, in laughter, in reverence, from above, from below, from the secret places of earthy immanence, and from the humbling immensities of cosmic exteriorities.

Consider now the ultimacy. Urgency of ultimacy: the "of" is ambiguous. Is the ultimacy of our urgency, thus revealing only our transcending (T²)? Or is it *of us* only because more fundamentally the urgency is *of ultimacy* (T³)? "Ultimacy" seems to refer us to an end, but here, as seeding urgency, it is a beginning. Ultimacy makes our being urgent, but one might say we would not be urgent about ultimacy *at all*, were not the urging of ultimacy somehow already leavening our being. The urgency brings the urging of the ultimate to desire, to mindfulness. Urging points us beyond ourselves because it communicates a source in us that disquiets, rouses, moves, and quickens. We are moved by, we strive towards, the ultimate out of the urgency of ultimacy.

Of course, often in determining the ultimate we inappropriately reduce it to this or that thing, and so we secrete a pantheon of idols. The urgency of ultimacy shows us to be participants in a process that is equivocal, reflecting our ontological situation in the middle. We cannot but reconfigure the primal ethos, and so we always risk vainly reading *our own face* into any initial intimation of the ultimate. Our condition is conducive to ambivalence, distortion, obfuscation, impertinence, and refusal. To be released to the otherness of the ultimate we have to undergo a transformation of mindfulness.

A great danger is to construe the "urgency of ultimacy" too much as just *our* urge: *our* will to be in relation to the ultimate. This is not entirely wrong—we are such a willing. But there is something more primal at the roots of this urgency of ultimacy: the *passio essendi*. Before the *conatus essendi*, our urge to be, to be in relation, there is the *passio essendi*, our passion of being, our already being in relation. The word "*conatus*" itself points back to this in its meaning of "born with, co-birth." Co-*natus* refers back to a being with, to generating community. One might even think of a prior porosity that is like a fructifying womb, a mother who becomes fertile. The *conatus* points back to the *passio*, as well as carrying it forward. The urgency of ultimacy is itself an expression of the *passio essendi* in which our being given to be is more primordial than our endeavoring to be. Before the seeking in which we are put in question and put ourselves at risk, there is a porosity of being which is always already presupposed by all our acts of self-transcending. Being religious brings us home to the primal porosity of being. This is the living middle between the soul in its most abyssal intimacy and the divine. In this porosity, the communication of what we later call prayer happens. Thinking itself is a later formation of the self-transcending of mind which is rooted in the primal porosity: the self-transcending power of thinking is derivative from this primal porosity. Is this our being, what we are: porosity to the divine? porosity which gifts us with the power to be beyond ourselves; porosity that allows us to be beside ourselves, for already the beyond is beside us, beside us before we are with ourselves in a self-knowing way?

The porosity of being is not a vacant emptiness but is endowed and empowered. It is a "being nothing" which is the potency to open to everything. Describing it in terms of the return to zero implies a *fertile void*, not

Charles
Taylor

just a nihilating one. Its endowments are important for how we conceive further the redoubled beginning beyond godlessness. I give mind to fundamental ontological endowments that make us porous to the hyperbolic in immanence: the elemental, the idiotic, the aesthetic, the erotic, the agapeic. These endowments exert various influences in different ways to God, as well as in different notions of the divine, as we will see in detail later. The redoubled beginning concerns a kind of ontological hermeneutic of the primal ethos via these endowments. They offer us signs of the origin, as communicated in the between as the ethos of being. In a way, our question now becomes: Does a Hermes surprise us in the wake of the angel of death?

AGAPEIC RESURRECTION

There is a self-transcending beyond erotic self-surpassing which yet is not the latter's opposite. It comes forth from the fertile void—in the equivocity of its plenitude/lack—unclosed in erotic self-surpassing, but it arises from an intimation that we are already given to be with (co-natus) a certain fullness, out of which we go beyond ourselves, and not always to detour through the other back to ourselves again. Its ecstasis is not from defect and as compensatory, but from abundance and from gratitude for being as gift. The ground of this transcending is obscurely felt to be a fullness in the beginning, remembered in the process of our unfolding, and not forgotten even in the determinate fullness of attained self-becoming. The fullness, given in other-being, given in self-being, is greeted with a gratitude, newly arriving out of refreshed astonishment. If erotic self-transcending tends to come forth from perplexity beyond determinate cognition, agapeic self-transcendence arises beyond self-determination, with astonishment, once prior to perplexity, now won again, at the end, out of perplexity, or perhaps suddenly simply given to an expectant soul, long burdened by perplexity without relief. It arises beyond determinacy and self-determination and rouses in us an overdeterminate expectancy relative to the ultimate source of the givenness of determinate being, and the endowed promise of our own being as self-determining.

I mark a fourfold deliverance towards the ethos of the between and its signs. First, release towards the givenness of creation as an other, not there just for us, but having its being and value for itself. Delivered to the world, one delights in its elemental being there, in the glory of its aesthetic beauty, the unstrained gift of its availability. Agapeic release towards creation is a love of the finite and mortal. This release—episodic and too rare in us—may extend to beings normally deemed repulsive. One is abandoned to purposeless admiration at the strange good of other-being, suffered as unutterably precious in its stunning thereness. Often this only happens in an extremity.

A person confined beholds the frail spider daily build and rebuild her web, beholds with a love keeping alive the flame of faith in life. Laid low, one senses the same flame flare from the tiny patch of sky, barely visible through the small window high above one. Failing one looks at the long familiar tree, but the looking is a longing, exceeding every finite name. The signs are in the *incognitos* of the everyday middle.

Second, there is a certain release of the *abyss hidden in self-being*. One goes out, out of a porosity of selving that is also a too muchness. One is in excess of oneself, in excess towards the other, because the idiocy of self-being is in excess of itself. And yet one is also a kind of nothing. Selving too is a great mystery, enjoyed even more vitally when released towards the singular inexhaustibility of the other. One has opened a door to this dark abyss, too much and almost nothing, and found there many spectral residents—hideous guests, vile parasites, one's own gargoyle self. One has entered into fearful converse with the monstrous. A delivering may come, another energy of selving freed, by warring with and making proper peace with one's gargoyle shadow. The war does not destroy but bends the deformed energy into a diviner form. Agapeic self-release is a release from what one is, and a release of what one is, and was, always, though what one was and has corrupted the purer energy of ecstasis towards the other. The abyss of inward otherness is a source within selving of radical release, out of self towards the other as another inexhaustible source for itself.

Third, there is a release towards *the community of creation and self-being*. I mean a certain agapeic rapport between us and beings. It takes places in the aesthetic rapport, in ethical solidarity, and in sacrificial love between us and other human beings. There are many forms of community, but at the best it takes shape as agapeic service in which being for the other transcends the insistences of being for self, even in the self's warranted claim to autonomy. There is a heteronomy revealed by agapeic release that has nothing to do with an *ab extra* superimposition by a tyrannical or dominating other. The other becomes the source of a solicitation that is a welcome rather than a demand, that delivers both self and other into a liberty beyond autonomy that lightly, even anonymously, is there for the good of others.

Fourth, the otherness of given creation, the inward otherness of self-being, and especially this heteronomy beyond autonomy deliver us to *wonder about an other transcendence*, other in a truly ultimate sense. The finite other, natural or human, releases us to mindfulness of transcendence as the ultimate other, and especially in the heteronomous community that is agapeic service. This service is an ethical and religious service. Given the absoluteness of availability for the other that is solicited, it is not defined relative to various forms of instrumental relativity that have their place in the economy of self-insistence and serviceable disposability, and even self-determining autonomy. Agapeic service is a transcending beyond these, disproportionate to such finite systems of finite exchanges. The service is not done from constraint or perplexity. It is the most elemental thing to do. It is done as if without thought, and yet it asks the highest thoughtfulness for the other, released from thought for self, from thought as for itself (see, inter alia, EB, chapter 16). One can, of course, be released towards oneself in the same spirit of surplus generosity. This is true love of self.

We philosophers are sometimes poor servants of this agapeic release. It is hard to assimilate to more familiar modes of explanation. The why at all of this service, this should trouble us. It does not seek self-justification, but as a transcending of self, it is self-justifying; and yet it is not done simply for itself. It is the enigmatic reversal of self-transcendence into true transcendence of self, making us ponder if it is really transcendence as other (T^3) that is the ultimate solicitation of our going beyond self. When self-transcendence becomes transcendence of self, one goes out of oneself and counts for nothing. This "counting for nothing" is the affirmative double that in its love counter-parts the nihilistic form of "being nothing." This "counting for nothing" is implicated in the becoming of our highest self-transcending. It is the porosity of being between as a love of the other. In another reversal, there is a peace to self, a satisfaction that is no self-satisfaction, rather a resting in the good because one is being true to the good, and again not because one can be happy with oneself because one had done the right thing; the peace is that the good has been allowed to be, released to become in the travail of life. One is at peace because one has been privileged somehow to participate in its passage.

See overall, then, the redoubled beginning beyond godlessness as the release of the passion of being: the passio essendi intimate to the elemental "yes" and the aesthetic re-charging; the passio secretly fermenting in erotic outreaching, despite the tendency of the conatus essendi to take over; the passio now consumed in the porosity of agapeic communication, for love's openness is not an empty lack but a passionate porosity, and at the limit gives itself as a compassio essendi. The sacrificial compassion: this is the compassio that makes sacred (sacer facere), and whose "being nothing" is the resurrection of the agapeics of being.

How does all this relate to nihilism and the ethos of godlessness? The ethos appears now as entirely other to devalued being. Such ontological valuelessness strikes one as profoundly untrue. It is a catastrophic impoverishment, a lie against the abundance and prodigality of life. Our perplexed wonder about God insinuates itself in this richness, in the pleasure, enjoyment, and gratitude of agapeic release for this feast of being. The release is entirely other to the will to power that rebels against, or exploits, or instrumentalizes valueless being. Will to power might seem to make sense relative to the latter ontological poverty. It is entirely inappropriate at this feast: a greedy boy grabbing at a table with more than enough for everyone, including the greedy. There is a religious poverty of being beyond this nihilistic poverty.

Agapeic release is more affirmative of being than even will to power that affirms its own abundance (see IST? chapter 6); for the goodness of the other, as well as the self, is to be affirmed; a more unequivocal release of self towards the other is entirely consonant with the deepest truth of being. Our "counting for nothing," lived in its full paradoxicality as a poverty of plenitude, can be the abandon of self-release that makes a way for transcendence as other (T^3) and always more than self-transcending (T^2).

Will to power is conceived relative to an original ground understood as valueless. By contrast, agapeic release to the ontological worth of creation solicits a rethinking of the grounding origin, as giving being thus to be at all. This calls for a new quest of the divine ground and its relativity to the finite between. There is a kind of ontological marveling, in which thought is drawn towards its own deepening into praise. Thinking can itself be, so to say, surprised by a kind of praying. Seeking God cannot be by way of merely negating finite being; it must be by way of the surpluses of finite being. The gratitude of agapeic release impels us to ask: What it is about the original ground that gives such a release? Can we call it agapeic origin?

I stress: rebirth is still only a beginning. And I hear the snort: all this pretty talk about "beginnings" is nebulous prating; a serious philosopher respects only what can be determinately and intelligibly articulated. Yes, yes: we do need more determinate articulation. Yet, given the complex dimensions of this redoubled beginning, it is no mere indefiniteness, to be conquered by new conceptual univocities or speculative systems. Rather, it enjoins a further turn towards the primal ethos, in mindfulness of a fuller feel for the being-there of being and beings. Our opening to the surplus in the otherness of given being can be complexly articulated, even if it exceeds all the determinations of intelligibility we muster. For again, if the other to thought thinking itself must be thought, and thought otherwise, we are *not* giving up on thinking, but trying to think otherwise than along the way that dead ends in nihilism. We now turn to more determinate thinking concerning the divine, as defined by the guidances offered by the fourfold sense of being. Along a winding way the question awaits us: Can we understand the ontological potencies of the ethos as the *hyperboles of being* that, read metaxologically, communicate in the between the overdetermined signs of God?

HEGEL'S COUNTERFEIT DOUBLE

From *Hegel's God: A Counterfeit Double?*

THE QUESTION OF THE COUNTERFEIT DOUBLE

There seems something ineradicably plurivocal about being religious. It resists reduction to one univocal meaning, and seems marked by a certain constitutive ambiguity. There is a doubleness to this: on the one hand, we might see this as a defect of thought to be overcome by a more rational approach; on the other hand, we might see it as something affirmative, in reminding us of the ultimate enigma of the divine, and the impossibility for humans to be completely on a par conceptually with God. One of the tasks of being philosophical is certainly the cultivation of mindful discernment of this ambiguity. But how? That is the question. Hegel's own resort to the *Begriff* in relation to the *Vorstellung* represents one way. We will occupy ourselves more fully with this, but my point concerns philosophy's relation to religion as the original sphere of significance to be understood, through which the sense of God is more originally mediated.

Monotheistic religions offer an image of God as the absolute original; philosophy claims to reflect on the truth, or untruth, of this. Philosophy's discernment must be attentive to what is shown, or not shown, in and through the religious image, and also to claims made about God as the absolute original. Religion may play false. Philosophy may also play false, if it fails to do justice to both the religious image and the original it claims to reveal. How to tread these very slippery slopes? Every way we turn a demand to *be true* is being made of us: being true in being religious, being true in being philosophical, being true to religion in being true philosophically. Everywhere the danger is that images of the original will be constructed that play false as well as prove true.

The difficulty is raised to the utmost when we consider the diffidence we must show in making claims about the absolute original, Godself. God is God, and nothing but God is God, and nothing finite is to usurp that absolutely unique Absolute. The first commandment is the most terrifying and the most demanding: Most terrifying, for our nature seems to be to secrete idols, and hence to betray the first commandment, even though we think we keep it. Most demanding, since it asks the ultimate in discernment of us relative to the counterfeit doubles of God, the secretion of which seems to happen to us, as if we lived our lives sleepwalking our way to the altars of idols.

Suppose we need, cannot but need, images to speak of God as original. (This does not exclude the need of concepts, nor that images may be informed by concepts. An idol, as I suggested before, is not any the less an idol because it is made of concepts rather than wood or gold.) The problem of the counterfeit double is that the image will mimic as well as show the original, and mimic by presenting itself as the original. Sometimes it may seem so like the original, we have difficulty telling it is an image. If such an image, so to say, usurps the original, how can we tell this, since it looks the same as the original? Consider a figure interestingly mentioned by Hegel, echoing Boehme: Lucifer. Lucifer is the bearer of light, first son of the morn, but he is also the figure of evil. But is it not just light that we seek? What then could an *evil light* be, how tell a light as evil? How could light counterfeit light? An extraordinarily difficult question, since we must also presuppose light to distinguish true light from counterfeit.

Suppose being religious is situated in an ultimate relation *between* ourselves and God. This is the first middle. But we can construct a *second middle* in the given middle. Suppose the second middle is a crystal palace—with a bow to Dostoevski. Then the images in the second middle may well be false doubles, say, doublings of ourselves and the circuit of self-transcendence clogged with itself. We traverse the middle space but now as only the medium of our own immanent transcending. What then can we claim as the true original in this second middle? A religious person will still claim the original as God; atheism will say there is no divine original; postmodern thought will say there is no original at all. Are we then in the midst of images of nothing—except ourselves perhaps? Do we come to the ultimate double: either God or nothing; religious trust or nihilism? But how discriminate the difference of this ultimate double, since all our efforts seem to circulate in the images of the second middle?

Even in this equivocal middle, the monotheistic religions enjoin absolute trust in the absolute God. Despite all difficulties of discernment, for monotheistic religions some sense of transcendence as other (T3) is *finally not negotiable*. How then would the issue of the counterfeit double look? Think of it this way. A counterfeit double is an image that is almost exactly like the original, but something has been altered that vitiates its claim to be true. I have a counterfeit banknote. It looks good, but there is something missing, or something added that is not quite right. A true note, with genuine reserves to back it up, has, say, a line of silver running from below upwards, and this vertical thread can only be seen when it is held up to the light. But when I hold the counterfeit to the light, I do not see the vertical line, but, say, the water mark of a circle closed on itself. If I do not hold it to the light, I will not see, even suspect, the absence of the vertical line. More complexly yet: What if there is a banknote that mimics the vertical line, though the foregrounded line is backed by the water mark of a circle closed on itself? How then identify a counterfeit? And what is *the light* up to which I hold each?

Close discernment is needed, and more and more so, the *better* the counterfeit. The better a counterfeit, the more it is *true* to the original. Its *achieved falsity* is dependent on its *being true to the original*. This is a very paradoxical situation: *perfected falsity is a function of being true to what is not false.* The perfect counterfeit looks almost exactly like the true currency. But somehow (and much of the difficulty lies in this little word "somehow") the claim it makes, or the authority it claims, is not to be sustained. It may even be that the falsity of the counterfeit is that it is *too perfect* (a thought that sometimes worries us about Hegel's system). Of course, much hangs on whether there is any original to which reference can be made to sustain the claim to be true, or false. If there is no original, there is no counterfeit; there is not even an image, since any image, without an original, images nothing, hence is no image. If this were so, there would be no question of truth, and no question of discernment. There would be no question of *being true*, in the many senses this can have.

But this cannot be true. For every denial of truth happens *within* the exigence to be true. This exigence is not something we first determine or construct, but it determines us to be the kinds of beings we are. Every truth we claim to "construct" happens within this exigence we do not construct. Otherwise, in the present instance, we destroy the difference between an idol and God. But this destruction of difference is itself idolatry, and so reinstates, by enactment, what it claims to destroy. If every image were self-authenticating, then there would be no authentication in which differences of better and worse have a grounding. It will amount to "say-so." It is because I say it is. Everything is "made up," but when everything is "made up," we cannot even speak of something being "made up."

The question then: Do we need an *original as other* to sustain the claim made by an image to be a genuine image? A genuine image not simply of itself? For then it would be only a self-referring image, a self-reflexive image, a self-creating original, or (as Nietzsche claimed for the world) a work of art giving birth to itself. Is it surprising that the exclusion of God as the other original leads to the self-divinization of immanent finitude as its own self-original? But where do we get that sense of the original as other? And how do we discern claims that this or that is the original, since every such claim seems itself open to the suspicion of being a counterfeit double? And what if the original can never be identified with this or that, or even the totality of this, that, and the other? In such an equivocal situation, is there any finesse that will help? Where would that finesse come from?

There is no easy answer. The religious image itself, even if it is genuine, is here also tested by this perplexity of the counterfeit double. I know antireligious thought will point the finger at religion as itself counterfeiting human being. Apart altogether from the justice of this finger point, religious thought cannot just point the finger back at its antagonist, but must put the question to itself, most especially, if its vocation is to cooperate in keeping unblocked the ultimate porosity between the human and the divine. Keeping open that porosity is to be in attendance at the communication of the divine and the human, and thus to enact a vigilance to the insinuation of the idol or the counterfeit double.

What then of Hegel? I have already suggested worries about his apotheosis of self-determining being, and his dialectical-speculative relativization of absolute claims made on behalf of God's transcendence. We will have to proceed further. One cannot just say that Hegel's God is a counterfeit double, as if, by contrast, and without further ado, one knew the original. But also one cannot judge Hegel just in terms of the immanent coherence of his claims. His speculative reconfiguration of divine transcendence (T3) may have been effected with just this in view: the closed circle of immanence at home with itself.

Rather, one must have dwelled in the ambiguous plurivocity of being religious, enacted philosophical reflection about the ultimate astonishments and perplexities there occasioned, strained one's soul to the utmost to remain true to the God that is God and that may be shown, or not shown, ambiguously or not, in this milieu of finite being. While internal instabilities and even incoherences in Hegel are not unimportant, there is something more important—fidelity to the "matter itself" (die Sache selbst); fidelity that is enacted in thought that seeks to be true to the fullness of what the "matter itself" shows. Hegel, I think, mixes something of this openness with a way of thinking that reconfigures what is being communicated, leading ultimately to its being recast in a form that closes this openness to the ultimate transcendence of the divine, and the hyperboles of finite being that are the reminders of God communicated to us in the between.

HOW HERE SPEAK OF COUNTERFEIT DOUBLES OF GOD?

This is an almost impossibly hard question, if what is at stake is human knowing of the immanent nature of the divine. Aquinas said we can know *that* God is, not *what* God is. Hegel claims to know the "what." But to make any claims about counterfeit doubles seems equally to imply that one knows something of the original that is not counterfeit. Is this too to know the *what* of God? But what does one know? And what is the mode of the knowing? Can one know anything, what can one know, from self-thinking thought? And know anything of God, even if one must enter most intimately the most original source of being and thinking in immanence itself? What would one say—say *philosophically?*

I think one would have to say: in an important sense, one knows nothing directly of the original—the truth of the trinity—against which one can judge whether Hegel's trinity is true or counterfeit. There are qualifications to add. "Knowing nothing" may be a poverty of philosophy in which something of the richness of the original as other may be communicated, communicated and articulated in terms of the hyperboles of being, that is, happenings of finite being which are rich in significance in an excessive, overdetermined sense. (What this means will be developed in *God and the Between.*)

Just as I cannot make the judgment *simpliciter*—I know the original God—Hegel cannot make the judgment that he, *sed contra*, does know the original. Why? Even were Hegel to say, as he does, *this original shows itself*, what we know of it comes from the show, and so we are *necessarily other* to the original itself. Hence all our knowing, even the most intimate, images the original, but is not it. The difference of original and image is a condition of the possibility of our knowing it. *Our knowing it is not, and cannot be, a matter of its knowing itself.* Hence it can never be rendered on the model of self-determining knowing. Our difference from the original is itself original in a manner that is *not* the *self-differentiation* of the divine original. We live and move and are mindful in the images, possibilized by the self-show of the original, and in them we seek to glean something of the original, but this (God) *qua* original remains other, and in excess of our determination. In showing itself, it shows its overdetermination, communicated itself in excess of what is *determinately* shown, and so again it is always other to a showing that exhausts it, for the showing itself is also overdeterminate. There is a fullness shown to this poverty of our knowing which it fills, but neither the knowing nor the showing is absolutely determinable as the self-knowing or self-showing of God. There is always the (reserved) otherness of God that is *not* God's self-othering.

It is a cause of wonder that speculative dialectic seems, in the final count, so to qualify the necessity of imagistic knowing (representation), that it elides the functioning of its own discourse about God, and the trinity, on the basis of a deeply rooted *likeness* with self-conscious thought, as known to us in our own thought. Likeness, I say, not identity. One wonders then if the indispensability of the imagistic is dispensed with or suppressed rather than, as is claimed, surpassed. The metaphor, or symbol, or analogy, or hyperbole by which we think the original is decisive, but our thinking must be honest about its own always intermediate condition which remains finite, even if it embodies a self-transcending (T2) to transcendence as other (T3).

I think that it is more at *this* level—concerning faithful mindfulness of the deeply rooted images, or metaphors, hyperboles—that the slide towards counterfeiting can be set in motion. No one can stride together with Hegel into the inner chamber of the absolute original, and compare one's "image," or "concept" to the original. This applies as much to Hegel's critic as to Hegel: neither can just say "I have the true original, you the counterfeit." The question is put to *both*. Both Hegel and his critic are involved in discerning the images, and in that discerning seeking to say something true about the counterfeit and the original. The slippage and potential counterfeiting occurs, in my view, with respect to *the images themselves* that we inhabit: with respect to our attentiveness to *those images* that suggest themselves as most communicating the divine; with respect to faithful mindfulness of *what* lines of communication those images open to the divine original. At this level, a difference can *already* be smudged, or an otherness elided, *before* we come to reflective thought; and what we claim speculatively on that basis about the original itself will be correspondingly smudged or skewed. In fact, the speculative reflection or concept might well compound the smudge or skew.

All this is true, even if Godself has absolutely communicated God. We are in the midst of images; we are ourselves an (extraordinary) image; but we still see through a glass darkly. And we can see differently in the glass, and we can look differently. Hence the issue is not only of seeing the original as other to the glass, but of our mindfulness of the glass itself and what its darkness portends. Moreover, the temptation to elide differences is all the greater when *we ourselves are the dark glass*. If the model of self-determining knowing is absolutized, we are tempted to think that we are the light which dispels this darkness. Then we do not say: "Divine self-knowing *is as* human self-knowing." We say: "Divine self-knowing *is* (absolute) human self-knowing." In fact, say what we will, we are still the dark glass, and the light we shed itself shares in that darkness, and hence cannot be the absolutely self-illuminating light it may claim itself to be. This claim to absolute knowing is itself a darkness, and in that respect, it is a counterfeit absolute knowing. We seem to speak of human knowing, but if we say that this *is* divine knowing, the claim of absolute light is doubly dark to itself: dark as eliding the shift from "as" to "is"; dark as forgetting that we have just shifted the dark glass from ourselves to God.

The poverty of philosophy here returns us to an ontologically elemental level in which the ultimate loves of the human being are at stake. The question of God is indeed extraordinarily elemental. It is the question of what we love as ultimate. It turns out, in fact, that what we love as ultimate already participates in a love of what is ultimate that constitutes our being at all. To be is to be in an ontological love of being, the love of the "to be" as good. The question of God is inseparable from mindfulness of that love, and the discerning of what it betokens.

Overall, Hegel's concept of the immanent life of the divine reflects the metaphysical metaphor of an *erotic absolute*. Its contrast with the metaphor or hyperbole of an agapeic absolute will be instructive, especially since traces of the younger Hegel's concern with *love* resurface relative to the spirit as the binding of love that constitutes the self-mediating communication of the Father and the Son. A failure in properly discerning different forms of love may affect our understanding of forms of transcendence, and forms of relation, as well as the metaphysical metaphors that speculatively mediate our image of the divine.

GOD AND THE METAXOLOGICAL WAY

From *God and the Between*

All ways seek God and may be opened differently to God, in and through mindfulness of being in the between. Each is attentive, after its own manner, to the ontological potencies of the primal ethos. Each allows passage towards finite beings and passing beyond. Each opens metaphysically to what is beyond finite beings. Each encounters hindrance and bother. What marks out the metaxological way? Among other things, the six following distinctions. First, a presentiment of the promise of the primal ethos in and through the second reconfigured ethos. Second, vigilance to the ontological surpluses of immanent being. Third, fidelity to these surpluses expressed in a new being true to our self-surpassing as a metaphysical transcending. Fourth, care not to compromise divine transcendence as it is intimated in the surpluses of immanent being. Fifth, mindfulness of the immanent between as showing forth the milieu of the absolved relativity. Sixth, concern for the dialogue of philosophy and religion, in which religion is not a mere representational prelude to philosophy, and in which the philosopher essays intelligible reflection companionable with the enigmas of religion. But, perhaps a brief digest of the four ways is in order.

Broadly put, the univocal way stresses definite sameness rather than indefinite difference. Seeking determinate solutions to determinate problems, impelled by curiosity, God is made a problem, even if the highest or ultimate. This does not "solve" the "problem," it, rather, makes God more deeply problematic—problematic in the paradoxical sense that the question here exceeds what can be fixed as a determinate problem. By contrast, the equivocal way is attuned to what cannot be thus fixed. It accentuates the shock and provocation of ambiguous difference, sometimes steering into unmediated manyness, sometimes even being wrecked on extreme opposition. Result: We are overcome with restless perplexity about God. God is not just a determinate problem but troubles us with a more intractable enigma. Driven out of the houses of incontestable surety, we are exposed under the pitiless and serene sky.

Our loss of univocal certainty may become, though there is no guarantee, our gain of mindful finesse. The dialectical way can help with refining this finesse. Generally, it emphasizes the mediation of the different by the conjoining of opposites. There is a more subtle "sameness" than the univocal way accesses. Beyond the normal binary oppositions defining finite knowing, there is a mediated togetherness of God with finitude more than the univocal unity that fixes or the equivocal difference that disperses. Modern dialectic privileges an inclusive sense of the "same" in this conjunction of opposites. The "system" of the same is given ultimacy over the "systematics" of togetherness, as well as priority over finesse for what exceeds system. Finessed dialectic can engender truer mindfulness of the togetherness of the human and divine, *perhaps* even a taste for their absolved relativity. But given recessed equivocities in the dialectical sense of the "same," we must refuse just this temptation: to hold that this togetherness lets us reduce the difference of the two. The togetherness is crucial, the reduction perilous.

And now the metaxological way? It lives between peril and crux. As a figuring of the primal ethos, it divines the nature of the togetherness, the absolved relativity, with heed to the difference, and without forgetting the transcendence of the divine and its reserves. We need a finessed, transdialectical *logos* of the *metaxu*. The community of God and the between concerns us, but as *not exhausted* by any dialectical self-mediation of the same, nor any whole claiming absoluteness by its immanent closure on itself. This community is *between* immanence and divine transcendence, as ultimately more than every immanent whole. The fourth way tries to think this divine "more" by calling on a metaphysical mindfulness finessed for the surpluses of being manifest in the immanent whole.

This fourth way opens to a pluralized intermediation, beyond self-completing self-mediation, yet hospitable to the communication of what is transcendent to us, out of its own otherness. Beyond any self-totalizing whole, however dialectically or speculatively qualified, in the community of immanence and transcendence, otherness in the between remain open, as does otherness between God and the between. Ruptures shake the complacencies of finitude at the limit of the dialectical way, and we are as a reawakened receptivity to mystery, intimated in the overdetermined givenness of immanent being. This givenness regards not some bare fact of being but the ontological worth of what has been given to be. Beyond univocal determination, beyond equivocal difference, beyond self-mediating totality, God is to be thought through the between as given to be, and given to be as good.

Here we gain a richer sense of the primal ethos of being. We do not create the between, nor does it create itself. As given, it is not absolute; it is given to be, and as coming to be in the absolved relativity. It is not a neutral given, or valueless thereness but charged with the good of the "to be." This is communicated in a pre-objective community of mindfulness and being, inarticulately given to us in original astonishment. The *metaxu* is first a happening, then we try to articulate it metaxologically. All three other ways participate in this happening, but do not manage to articulate it metaxologically. The fourth way shows the fuller truth of the other three, seeking the right words for what is communicated in the primal ethos, and what is given in the overdeterminacy of the original astonishment. The other three ways are conducive to, even as they truncate, the truth of the fourth, but we cannot absolutize any way, as if it were the absolute. We must abdicate the claim to have categories to determine finally what itself outstrips every categorial determination.

GOD AND HYPERBOLE

From *God and the Between*

Here we have stepped to the edges of the hyperbolic, though in monstrous form. The monstrous is sublime, but there are diviner sublimities at that edge, diviner ways of crossing, or being crossed. Generally, by contrast with the symbolic, the hyperbolic indirection turns us to the *excess of disproportion*, but this time in terms of transcendence "above" rather than immanence "in the midst." The hyperbole gives us a figure of the overdeterminate in the determinate and the self-determined, the overdeterminate that cannot be exhausted by determinacy or self-determination, the "beyond" of immanence in immanence that cannot be immanently (self-)determined and that "throws us above" immanence. The symbolic throws together, but stuns us with disproportion *in* immanence; the hyperbolic "throws us above" (*huperballein*) in the disproportion *between* immanence and transcendence, just out of that being stunned with excess of being here.

Though we may have an equivocal sense of the divine immanence, we always are nagged by its too muchness for us. This divine disproportion intimates *that it is, at the most, that side of the ultimate transcendence turned towards the immanent between*. There is intimated an *other side*, turned into the mystery of its own being for itself. This is the reserve of the divine. The agapeic origin is nothing but its giving to the other, but it is also more than any of its determinate gifts, and hence the heart of the agape is both poured forth into finitude and reserved in itself, reserved perhaps just to let the finite be as finite. The finite let be as finite points back beyond itself again, and in its given inexhaustibility points to the radical excess of the absolute origin, reserved in itself in its light inaccessible.

This is why we need hyperboles to say what we mean, what indeed *we alone* cannot mean. We feel we need to pile excess on excess, and then some more, and then we are not any closer to what we do not even have to approach, because it is there always, though not always there, just because we are not always there for it. For we cannot get any closer to that which is absolutely close. Being absolutely close is also being absolutely reserved:

close but not closed, rather resource of absolving communication; utterly intimate always, always further intimated; never passing, ever passing.

Hyperboles call to mind excesses of praise. Both symbols and hyperboles bring our saying nearer to the rich poetics of religious practice. In their own way they might be, so to say, prayers of thinking and indirectly redirect us to the ultimate superiority. This is no squashing heteronomy but a releasing transcendence drawing us upwards. The hyperbole gives shape to the arc of ascending thinking like a kind of praying that can descend into its own depths, know its own excessive nature, know the fragility of its reaching beyond, because it does not proceed through its own will (to) power alone. It is being thrown beyond, rather than throwing itself beyond. Its being beyond, its altitude can be as much in the dimension of depth as of height; for "*altus*" (like "*meta*") is metaxologically double, meaning "deep" as well as "high." As with praying, there is an ultimate patience in being in the throes of hyperbolic thinking. The *passio essendi* comes to the fore in the throw of the hyperbole, which cannot be just a matter of the exceeding of our own striving to be, a hypertrophy of our *conatus essendi*. Being thrown by the hyperbolic is being in the throes of an undergoing which is an overgoing, an abovegoing in receiving, or being received by, the *huper*. The hyperbolic is not a hypertrophy of will to power, but a poverty in extreme porosity that is filled full with richness from the superior other.

Religious utterance, we say, is not only a "carrying across," but is "carried away." Is it just "carried away" with itself? Or does it get "carried away" by an other? The agapeic hyperbole (we will see) implies the second rather than the first. Though, again, there is no claim that the equivocal has been entirely dispelled, and sometimes our being "carried away" by ourselves is taken for a divine "being carried away." We must dwell in these religious equivocities with precautionary mindfulness against being "carried away" in the form of our own transcendental bluster, or self-effusion, or existential overreaching into nothing. Do not worry. The discipline of finitude will keep us in check. What is this discipline? At the least, it is proper metaxological mindfulness of the ontological sources and resources of the between, its richness and its snares.

In what now follows, I attempt a more intensive discernment of the divine by way of the between, and in a movement which approaches the ultimate hyperbole of God as the agapeic origin, through the indirections of different hyperboles of being. The movement is from the idiotic to the aesthetic, through the erotic to the agapeic. It passes from an immediate givenness of ontological community, through the glorious aesthetics of happening, through the exceeding energies of human selving, towards the releasing of free community, all the way to ethical community and beyond.

The idiotic, aesthetic, erotic, and agapeic give articulate expression to the ontological potencies of the primal ethos and their metaphysical promise. While none of these potencies is to be neglected, and while a properly ample philosophical mindfulness must find the just place for all, undoubtedly for many the question of God takes on its most intensive form in relation to ethical community. To this we will come, though there is more.

Coming to this "more," we will also resume with more intensive mindfulness the deeper promise of the other senses of being. I mean that univocity is metaxologically resumed with the hyperbole of the idiotic "that it is," equivocity with the hyperbole of the aesthetics of happening, dialectic with the hyperbole of erotic selving, while the metaxological itself comes to fullest showing with the hyperbole of the agapeics of community. Likewise, just as the metaxological way resumes the other three ways, so when speaking of the hyperbole I mean also to resume in this figuration the indirections of the metaphor, analogy, and symbol. These four indirections and what they figure might be resumed through these four words: "is," "like (as)," "with," and "above." So also through the four hyperboles the passage of (metaphysical) mindfulness is moved in and through the between from the "is" that is immanent to the "above" that is transcendent.

GOD AND THE BETWEEN:
FIRST HYPERBOLE — THE IDIOCY OF BEING

A first metaxological approach takes its direction from the excess of given being. Call this the *first hyperbole*. Being is given before any of our conceptions and remains always in excess of our determinate categories. Can one address God out of wonder at the sheer *givenness of the given*? How to understand this givenness? Is it the sheer fact that is, and that is all? Anything further we cannot ask. It will be granted: it is presupposed by all efforts to make sense, indeed by all forms of life, but since all questions take place within it, there is no question about it; we must accept it, and again that is that.

Yes, there is a consent here, but of what kind? A tendency here is to conflate the familiar middle, reduced to a surd thereness, with the astonishing or perplexing middle. Then meaningful questions only regard connections between determinate beings or happenings, or an origin as first or ultimate determinate cause. The univocal sense of being then reigns, with God perhaps denominated as the first or highest being. Against this, however, there is an astonished perplexity about the "that it is" which is not itself such a determinate question. One is not asking about how *this* relates to *that*, or how determinate beings relate together in some totality the sum of determinate beings (Kant inclines to think thus of the unconditioned). Rather there is the excess overdeterminacy of the "that it is" of all finite beings that are there. The issue of God then is: why the "that it is at all"? not why this or that, nor how and why some total sum of determinate beings.

If this question addresses an overdeterminacy, then the answer, if we can call it such, is *not a determinate solution to a determinate problem*. It too is overdetermined: excess calls to excess, relative to the superfluity of the "that it is." There is something surd about the "that it is," for it is not self-explanatory. It happens, and does not explain itself. The question is whether this surd is absurd. If it were a mere surd, we would say, it is finally absurd. It is there, and either it makes no sense, or there is no further sense to be made. Either way, there is given being, finally in itself senseless and groundless. But what if there were a surd not absurd? Suppose the "that it is at all" is such a surd? Suppose God, as source of that surd happening, might also be a surd not absurd, and hyperbolic to the surd of finite happening as such? Of course, the language of the surd is deficient language, the language of a remainder, a residue. In fact, the "that it is" is no mere residue but given being as gloriously rich and enigmatic. It is this surplus of finite being that puts us in mind of the source of the given. What gives the surplus happening of the between? This cannot be defined in terms of any determinate being within the happening of the given between; the source is other, but not other such as to destroy intimacy with the gift of being itself.

The primal givenness of the "that it is" is not a matter of the "becoming" or "self-becoming" of beings. There is a "coming to be" prior to "becoming." The latter presupposes a prior "that it is," even granting that this "that it is" is given with an open promise, and not as a static and completed fact. Granted, there is the openness of (self-)becoming, but there is granted a "being opened" to be, prior to determinate becoming. This is idiotic, since all determinate sense presupposes it, and no determinate sense can exhaust it. This "being opened" is the primal giving of the porosity of being, the between as enabling an astonishing diversity of becomings, self-becomings, and together-becomings. There is an *ontological passio essendi* which gives beings to be before they can give themselves to themselves in their diverse self-becomings and together-becomings. The gift of being at all is more primordial than every endeavor to be: it may enable striving, but it is not strife. The idiocy of being points us towards an overdeterminate porosity of giving and being given, of creating and coming to be, of offering and receiving. When we are turned to it in the mode of marvel, there is intimated an overdeterminate generosity of being, giving before and beyond strife.

GOD AND THE BETWEEN:
SECOND HYPERBOLE — THE AESTHETICS OF HAPPENING

Our second turn is directed more towards the determinate character of the givenness: not the "that it is" but something of the "what it is." From the primal ontological promise of the givenness of being as given, we turn to something of the determinate promise of what is given, approaching the divine from the *aesthetics of happening*, the second hyperbole.

By "happening" I mean not only the idiocy of givenness but the fact that this givenness shines forth with its own intimate radiance, coming to manifest its own marvelous intricacy of order. Radiance: but we are not confined to sight only, for one might consider things musically, and speak of a resounding of givenness that sings in the hum of thereness. By "aesthetic" I mean the sensuous showing that (keeping to sight) shines from itself in the happening of being. The "aesthetic" signals a sensuous figuration or figuring forth of the ontological potencies of the primal ethos. This is not just relative to our perception, but communicates the self-showing of the given; self-showing as marked by radiance beyond fixation, by singularity, dynamic form, and ordered, open wholeness; self-showing also intimating a reserve of ontological promise, promise not shown in a completely determinate way in the reserved showing. The ethos of the between is charged with aesthetic effulgence that comes to be embodied both communally and singularly.

Aesthetic radiance shines from beings, passes in and through and between beings. Mostly, for humans, there is too much to this radiance, which, just as excessive to our complete intake, retreats into the background of showing. Within this more enveloping effulgence, the aesthetics of happening comes to showing in the singularity of things. This is consonant with the idiocy of being, but the bite of determinate existence manifests itself here. And while this singularity is determinate existence, it is at the edge of our determination in univocal or dialectical categories. The "that it is" becomes "it is *this*," and there is something excessive about, not only the "is," but the thisness of the "this." That beings should be given with this singularity resistant to univocal objectification and dialectical encapsulation strikes one into a wonder about the communicative character and source of such singularity. Does such a communicative character suggest a source supremely attentive to the singular as singular?

Beauty is revealed in the intimate order of immanent wholeness, but something hyperbolic to the immanent whole is also intimated. The stupendous prodigality of the between comes to pass in equivocal transience, but beauty is *fugitive*: it shows itself, it eludes us, and flies away; it is revealing and shy; wanton and concealing, forward and withdrawing, coming forth and reserved. There is a rich wholeness *there*—but something *beyond whole-ness* is intimated in the showing there. There is a *saturated* equivocity to the aesthetics of happening. This is something "meta": something crosses us, something carries us across. The fugitive nature of beauty invites us to the *boundary* of the sublime. On the boundary we pass more unreservedly into the movement towards the hyperbolic. The aesthetics of happening is metaxological: in beauty we behold a self-mediating wholeness, wholeness open and opening; in the sublime an intermediation of the transfinite, the overdetermined is communicated. The overdeterminate in the determinate and the self-determining whole calls us to the boundary, calls us beyond the boundary, between the sensible and supersensible, the visible and invisible, the hearing and the call.

In the fittingness of beauty there is something of the religiously fitting. In our shattering in undergoing the sublime, there is also something fitting in what does not quite fit our finite frame. Philosophy here requires more than system: it asks for the finesse of a religious poetics. With such finesse, one detects various expressions of the call of the beyond of self-contained immanence in some of the traditional proofs. One might consider Aquinas's fifth way from the governance of the universe, or Paley's argument from design, and its many variants, or Kant's discussion of the physico-theological proof. Here Kant focuses on determinate existence rather than the indeter-minate existence of the cosmological way. In Aquinas's case, providential order is at issue relative the unconscious teleology of nature. Paley's version most famously, or infamously, uses the analogy of the watch. This is not the best analogy, since it reductively configures the intermedium of being as a mechanism. Mechanical design is a sign, but as a configuration of the ethos this sign is designed to (re-)make the ethos as proportionate to our powers of making. This sign resigns the hyperbolic.

Suppose the aesthetics of happening is seen to suggest an origin figu-ratively to be likened to the artist. The art of this source would not just be the technical imposition of form upon matter, but a more radical bringing to be from which both the elemental good of matter and form are themselves derived. Its *poiesis* would originate a coming to be: not just a self-becoming or selving of beings, not a mechanical ordering, not just a "forming" or self-forming, not just an organismic self-organizing, not a work of art giv-ing birth to itself. Given this likening, this origination would be *unlike* any artistry we could adequately conceptualize, since our artistry always oper-ates in the context of the givenness of being. This other art is hyperbolic to our artistry. We make something; we do not create it in the hyperbolic sense of bringing beings to be. Yet we can have care for the singularity of the work, and this can show something of the hyperbolic. Great art has a singularity which resists an exhaustive univocal analysis or dialectical encapsulation. In it shines forth a freshness and inexhaustibility. Mostly we think of singulars in terms of their classification by generals: human beings, not this singular, for instance. To look at the world with this love of the singular, we would have to be the embodiment of agapeic mind: loving the singular for the sake of the singular. In its love of the singular, our art can show something of agapeic mindfulness and its hyperbolic import. Looked at this way, the aesthetics of singular happening puts us in mind of a source of agapeic origination.

GOD AND THE BETWEEN:
THIRD HYPERBOLE — THE EROTICS OF SELVING

In us the doubleness of the aesthetics of happening assumes an extraordinary urgency. The human being as self is idiot, then is unfolded in aesthetic selving, and further moved by erotic selving and agapeic communicating. These latter are decisive in making us mindful of the porosity of our being, participating intimately in the passion of being, and articulating the urgency of ultimacy. As forms of self-transcending they occasion different hyperboles of the ultimate as transcendence itself. We come to the third hyperbole of erotic selving when we turn to ourselves as media to surpass the equivocity of aesthetic happening.

And yet this hyperbole of self-being impels us further. The excesses of "objectivity" are never enough, and bring about a rebound on the "subject." There is no escape from selving, though there may be disciplines that transform its hyperbolic equivocity, and in this mark a pathway to the divine. In and through the inner excess something more is traced in this path than can be richly enough articulated relative to the idiotic and the aesthetic. I will offer first a general, then three more particular considerations.

Human desire is sourced in transience, but, in coming to mindfulness of the equivocities of becoming, something more and other is communicated. Our selving is rooted in, as well as roots incarnately in, the equivocities of aesthetic transience. Eros reveals an upsurge of selving from these carnal roots. What surges up in selving also exceeds selving. Though eros is more than sexual desire, we see the point with sexual desire, namely our dark intimacy with aesthetic transience and our surge beyond. We are drawn to sensuous beauty, but our sensibility of living is also our being sensible of death. Out of the equivocal transience the impulse to generation reveals a passing beyond self, a will to further life beyond oneself. Our endeavor to be wills life beyond death, even one's own death. And yet all this upsurging of selving is carried by those ontological energies given as the *passio essendi*. In given creation, the creature becomes generative, but in the case of the human being the creature becomes creative in a finite form. Thus *all human exceedings beyond finite determinability* are at issue in the hyperbole of erotic selving. The equivocities of aesthetic transience are not only sensible in our bodies; they come awake in the heart, the intimate in the carnal. They offer signs of the intimate universal in our carnal selving, in our bodies beside themselves.

Consider the transcending power of *reason itself* as one expression of the hyperbolics of selving. Reason is a self-transcending power to be beyond itself, in openness to what is other. It is not self-determining simply: there is a *passio* of reason, an erotics of reason. The Greeks knew this when granting the eros of philosophy itself. Yet reason's equivocity is the equivocity of the human being itself: its *conatus essendi* can seek to overcome its *passio essendi* and *assert itself hyperbolically* as absolutely self-determining. From a metaxological perspective, this is untrue to selving and reasoning, since it sends into recess what the *passio essendi* communicates: the being given to itself of thinking, and the excess of the enigmatic origin in the immanence of thought itself. The "Anselmian" ethos is truer to the human doubleness here important, and to the original patience of our reason. Prayer keeps open the elemental porosity and even can be like the advent of astonished thought: thought so astonished by what it thinks it seems to be laid asleep in reverence. Such thought is like prayer become perplexed at the mystery before it. What does perplexity here find unavoidable? The thought of that which nothing greater can be conceived. Thus Anselm's definition of God.

How see this way? We find ourselves before, or in, the incontrovertible call of the good. There is a sense in which the difference of good and evil is irreducibly given to us; we find ourselves in this difference; we do not first produce it. We may not originally know what it means, but it makes us to be the kinds of being we are, before we make ourselves into this kind of person or that. We may come to determine this to be good, or that, but our determination takes place in the space of a more original difference of good and evil. This more original difference is communicated in the porosity of our being to good, in our reception of the good of the "to be," indeed in our very being itself as received from and into the good of the "to be." Our original patience here to the goodness of being is spontaneously lived by us, in that our living at all is itself an affirming of the good of the "to be," a good prior to and more original than this good or that good, whether determined as such and such by us, or not. This more original difference points to a sense of good (and perhaps evil) in excess of determinacy, for it is not this good or that good, and in excess of our determination and self-determination, for these are empowered in the ethos of its original givenness. Communicated in an original porosity that endows the openness and exceeding of our self-transcending, it is in excess of our self-transcendence, even as it emerges to be minded in our self-transcendence. We are in the communication of the good, but not at all the ground of our being in the good. We are called to be good, and we are good, but we are not the good, the good that endows us and calls us to be good.

I try again. I do not say so much that morality leads to God as that the exigence of the ethical, in the unconditional requirement made, is hard to make sense of short of invoking God, and not just at the end but anonymously at work all along. How else make sense of the unconditional requirement? If we only think of the end, we will stress an erotic seeking of God as the goal of morality, and thus of morality as leading to a religion, perhaps like Kant. If we think the other way, we ponder an incognito agapeic effectiveness of the origin, as giving us our being as free, though free to revolt against the origin, and the good of given being, as well as our being as free to revolve back upon the origin as surging into its call, both in our freedom and the charge of the good that is effective in our freedom. Out of this second way, a different ethical eros emerges for us to be freely good, to be ourselves sources of agapeic origination towards the other. It is hard to make any intelligible sense of the hyperbolic dimensions of all this if our ethical being is entirely out of community with the nameless goodness of God.

Hell brings me to my third particular consideration. One might speak of the "proof" from evil, though there is no proof, only a way of metaxological mindfulness that shows us to be always in extremis and, so to say, tethered to God. For there is something hyperbolic about evil. The horror of evil floods into mindfulness, and we humans alone are devastated with this. Even if we do not do the evil, we are wasted by the evil power of humanity. It is a shame on us all, though that is not the present point, but rather a perplexed horror, suffered at the edge of despair relative to what we are. Normally, evil is said to be the great stumbling block to religious faith. The arguments are well known. How could a good God tolerate the evils that happen? If all powerful, God could prevent evil. If all good, God would prevent evil. Yet evil happens. Our choice seems to be: power without goodness, or goodness without power. And is it often not the seeming impotence of the good that drives many to despair about God, or to suspect malice? Is it not often that the same despair drives others to embrace power without goodness, and usurp the right of might in the world? The disjunction of power and the good states an equivocity that can engender the despair of faith or the revolt of defiance—itself a despair, continuing the first despair.

Can we finally make sense of the horror, the perplexity, the despair outside of the unavoidability of God? Is it only because God is, that evil is the monstrous perplexity it is? Were God not, would there be a problem of evil at all? If there is a determinate problem, the solution will be also determinate. Evil is not just a determinate "problem." Something about it exceeds determinacy and self-determination. Is this not why there is something hyperbolic about it? Here the hyperbolics of evil have everything to do with a *self-absolutizing* of the erotics of selving: a hyper-activation of the *conatus essendi* that absolutely revolts against any given patience of being. Instances of the extreme: Satan is sublime—Milton's Satan—sublime in revolt—and revolting, even if sublime. Satan: the sublime evil of the erotics of selving, in the usurped sovereignty that counterfeits God. Ahab is sublime—Melville's Ahab—erotics of selving bordering the infernal in Ahab's monomaniacal hatred of the hunted Moby Dick—Moby Dick, the white monster, the blank Leviathan, also hyperbolic and sublime, but whether in evil or innocence remains in mystery.

The horror is secreted in the *inward otherness* of our selving—here the excess in self of selving that turns to the infernal. Who doubts that human beings can be infernal, but can we make sense of the infernal outside of religion? Is being mindful of evil inseparable from being mindful of God: God as either violated, or horribly turned away, or withheld in the midst of being we otherwise would think of as good? This is sometimes secretly so, secret even to most determinate formations of selving. Evil is a spoiling and despoiling, but were there no good to be despoiled there would be no question of evil at all. It is said evil is a refutation of God, but it rather seems that without God there is no enigma of evil at all—evil certainly in the hyperproblematic, hyperbolic sense. One does not say God is, because evil is, but rather because evil is, one must say God is. One recalls Aquinas: *Si malum est, Deus est*. Said succinctly in reply to the pointed question of Boethius: *Si Deus est, unde malum?*

Further: even if God is, we cannot sidestep the question of the power of the good, or its impotence. Evil seems to show us the impotence of the good, or the indifference of the divine amounting almost to an evil itself. Should we then turn from this divine impotence and grow our own power, such that we willingly will to be power—without the good? That option has been taken up. The issue looks otherwise from an agapeic viewpoint and the letting of freedom that marks its giving? There is a freedom of the good that, from a certain point of view, looks like impotence—and yet such forbearance from force is not powerless. Highest power might not be unilateral self-assertion but an empowering of what is other: an agapeic letting be. The letting be might seem to look like an indifference, amounting to evil, in the sight of mortals. Yet the mystery of the letting be is of the same (hyperbolic) order as the enigma of evil itself.

Agapeic letting be creates a space of openness for finite freedom: finite freedom is empowered with the highest possibility of self-transcending, and so is itself the promise of being agapeic. That space of empowered openness

Porosity

witnesses to the porosity of the between and the allowance of both the
passio essendi and the *conatus essendi*. In that space the multiple possibilities of the equivocal germinate, including the being for itself of the finite.
As let be for itself, the finite being can stand over against the source that
lets it be as free and other. The finite human being can turn against finite
creation and will to be the mastering power over it, and out of the known
insecurity of its own equivocal finitude. Its *conatus essendi* overrides its *passio*, and it revolts against any patience to an ultimate other than itself. Its
very urgency of ultimacy can turn into the hubris *to be* God. Let be as free,
our freedom in the equivocal is potentially monstrous, indeed infernal. The
extremest freedom is the freedom to will to be God, and this freedom is
itself allowed or let be by the agapeic origin. This allowance is the highest daring: a hyperbolic endowment of the finite creature. It is a freedom
that always tempts us: as idiotic selves we taste the deepest intimacy with
our own being, and we would that our being were itself divine. It is, in a
derived way, already divine, but it is not God.

GOD AND THE BETWEEN:
FOURTH HYPERBOLE—THE AGAPEICS OF COMMUNICATION

In a general sense, the fourth hyperbole bears on the *metaxological relativity of community beyond immanent self-mediating totality*. The communicative
intermediation between self and other manifests an *excess in relativity* which
is irreducible to any ex post facto aggregation of a many or to any holism
of inclusive self-mediation through others. This excess in relativity means
that the intermediation between self-mediating beings cannot itself be just
a more inclusive self-mediation when these beings have the inexhaustible
promise of infinitude. The between as a togetherness of such beings is likewise inexhaustible because these beings are *communicative in excess of self-
mediation*. Granting such an exceeding community, beyond subjectification
and objectification, beyond any immanently self-determining totality, what
endows its possibility, what originates its promise? The overdetermination of
this communication of inexhaustibility also communicates to us something
of the primal ethos beyond our finite determinations and configurations,
beyond our self-determinations. We find ourselves here in the hyperbolic
dimension of absolving relativity. We are called not only to mindfulness
of this relativity but to what exceeds even its excess, its endowing origin.

First, the metaxological sense articulates being in the between as a
community of the plurality of open integrities of self-transcending being.
This community is not a formation, after the fact, of beings first given to
be as fully for themselves. They are given to be for themselves, but the first

giving is a communication of being, and from the first giving they are communicative beings, and hence in immediate rapport with beings other than themselves. Community is elemental, not a derivative. Even if it points to a further fullness to come, it is still elemental as given. If it were not so given, how could any further promise be redeemed? Beings are not monadic but communicative; their selvings are self-transcending and embody communicative power, more or less extensive and intensive, depending on ontological endowment. The togetherness of beings in the universal impermanence of creation and the inherent communicative being of the beings who are together, these do not create the elemental community. Rather they are created as and in the elemental community; this community is given with the being given of the beings to themselves. But if nothing finite in the between gives the elemental community, and the community is, who or what endows this community?

Second, I revisit the ontological way, but my point is not quite traditional. For it is just with respect to the meaning of *community* that this way might be understood otherwise. The traditional view often sees the ontological way as not really getting beyond a kind of subjectivity, albeit one engaged with an exalted concept of God within its conceptual thinking. This is not quite it. Before, I suggested we reconsider the thought of the excess of the "greatest"; now, and more importantly, we must reconsider it in relation to community. I mean that the power of the ontological way is just *its dwelling on a consummate relation, or an ultimate togetherness*: the ultimate togetherness of God with the mindfulness that comes to wakefulness in human selving. It is the being of the human to be communicative, but its communicative being finds itself in an inescapable community with ultimate communicative being. We come to the community in the ontological intimacy of human being, community given in the intimate soul but calling us beyond ourselves, above ourselves. Such a community is fitting for being religious as dwelling in the intimate universal, beyond merely isolated subjectivity and merely neutral, homogenous universality. The intimate universal is hyperbolic to self-enclosed subjectivity and any objectifying universality. The ontological way does not *establish* this community. Rather, it wakes up to mindfulness of community already always in play. That is why there is porosity and patience in this way: we awake to something excessive being given. (Something religiously analogous happens in the porosity of prayer.) In that regard, this way does not appeal to so-called empirical experience, for its truth is not pieced together after the fact, a posteriori. If there is "experience" here, it is a hyperbolic undergoing in the intimacy of immanent inwardness, and in virtue of what we are as given to be. In language not quite right, an ultimate a priori community is entailed by the mindful communicative being of the human being.

The ontological way is a way of immanence, but this immanence itself turns out to offer us an intimate symbol/hyperbole of transcendence as other to our own self-transcendence. The meaning of the most intimate imma- nence is just transcendence as communicative being. But this transcendence is communicated in excess of our self-transcendence. We do not think of God and then, after thinking, try to make up a community with God. The thinking is always and already in that community, though it may not know that, and even though it may not recognize that, or may indeed entirely reject the suggestion of being in that ultimate community. The ontological way is a waking up to the "yes" to disproportionate transcendence in the intimacy of immanence. Even more, perhaps it is our waking up to the "yes" of transcendence as other in the immanence of the intimate universal, and revealing there not the immanence of any isolated subjectivity, for there is no such isolation. That is the point: the deepest intimacy of subjectiv- ity reveals selving as essentially communicative being, in community with the sourcing original that communicates its being given to be. There is no "subjectivity." I am nothing—nothing if not in communication with the ultimate in community. The porosity of being is opened in an ultimate communication, and the passion of our being is our passion for God. This is perhaps what the mystic undergoes religiously. What this also might intimate is that thinking can be, as it were, a kind of sleeping praying. Praying is thought awakening to its original ground, waking in the intimate universal to its own most intimate being as a love of the endowing origin.

Third, how does this community relate to the *worth of being*? This ques- tion invites us to gather together the significances of the other hyperboles. To recur to the first hyperbole: does not the marvel of being astonish us with the given good of the "to be"? To recur to the second: do not the beautiful and sublime call us to a deeming of the fitting, and indeed the surprise of what we cannot quite fit in? To recur to the third: does not the erotics of selving passionately summon us to the inherently lovable, what for itself is worthy of being loved? Beings are in the between as a community, but a community can- not be thought apart from some notion of the worthwhile. Beings as together fit together; the being of community is a *fitting*: it is fit. Another way to say "it is fitting" is to affirm "it is good." Is there a certain fundamental rightness in the nature of things as being fitting? What would allow us to say that? We could say: community is the good for beings—but the community we here name is not any specific community of this or that; it is the togetherness of the finite creation in the universal impermanence in which each being par- ticipates. What, if anything, allows us to say that this community is somehow right, that somehow it and all that participates in it is good?

Fourth, what is the implication of hyperbolic community, not just in relation to the ontological community of beings, but to the ethical community of moral beings? I have touched already on the ethical, but without placing emphasis on community. The issue is evident with the hyperbolic erotics of selving, but now the stress falls on a hyperbole beyond erotic sovereignty: the community of agapeic service. It is not the erotics of selving that has the ultimate word but the agapeics of a service of the good as other. While the human being might be a kind of measure of things external to himself, and while he might attain the measure of some sovereignty of himself, he is not, and never will be, quite the same measure of himself as participant in the ethical community. The solicitation of something unconditional emerges immanently in ethical community, but there is also something hyperbolic to ethical community, pointing beyond moral and human measure. The ethical community of agapeic service makes us cross unconditionally the boundary of morality into the religious, where our love bears on the hyperbolic measure of the measureless good—God. The agapeics of community is intimately related to the other three hyperboles, but here there is also something more hyperbolic and most fully communicative of the divine overdeterminacy. We are what we are under the call of the good, porous to the surplus generosity of being good, but *we are so as participants* in an ethical community that is both elemental and ultimate.

This is the question that perplexes us: If there is this elemental community of ethical solidarity which is not constituted by us but which constitutes us within the communicative call of the good, how is this elemental community constituted (see *BB*, chapter 13; also *EB*)? How do we name the source in which and through which it is constituted? We cannot account for it through the human, nor through nature. Not the human, for we are given to be as ethical and become ethical in and through this ethos; we presuppose it; its character is such that clearly we do not make it. Not nature, since the sense of the ethical good here at stake is disproportionate to the sense of ontological value we find in nature—it exceeds the measure of that ontological value, which in any case, as we saw, does not account for itself in entirely immanent terms. Why not give to its originary ground the name "God"?

The gift of the elemental community summons us to realize the promise of the hyperbolic good. Our participation in ethical community is a call to the fullest realization of the agapeics of community. This is shown in the community of agapeic service (see especially *EB*, chapter 16; also *BB*, chapter 12). This involves not only a good elementally given, but a summons for us to give beyond ourselves: to be agapeic. Being agapeic is not just elementally given but freely comes to be in an elemental giving, in which the ultimate generosity of being is communicated. This may extend from *incognito* acts of everyday consideration all the way to sacrificial love, in which one lays down one's life for another. In excess of the erotics of immanent sovereignty, there is a community of agapeic service which enacts our being for the other in the most ultimate sense possible. The community of agapeic service is a hyperbolic sign of transcendent good. Our participation in agapeic transcending is our fullest self-transcendence: our love, in transcending self, transcends to transcendence itself. We find ourselves in a love that not only passes beyond self, but more ultimately passes *between* ourselves and transcendence itself.

GOD BEYOND THE WHOLE

From *God and the Between*

WHAT HAS PHILOSOPHY TO DO WITH CREATION?

Worries about the God of the whole make us wonder about a God beyond the whole. Need such a "beyond" be a dualistic beyond, fixed in a frozen spatiality, void of intimacy with the immanent whole? The metaxological response must be no. Agapeic origination is communicative giving to be, intimate to the being given to be, an intimacy that comes again in the woo of mystic love. Moreover, there is this striking singularity about God: God is God, and nothing but God is God. If this is so, we are addressing something absolutely singular that cannot be dealt with wholly in terms of any immanent holism. Are there any terms at all then? Does creation ex nihilo merit attention as addressing God's singular and hyperbolic transcendence? This singular God contests the primacy of the whole.

God as creator is central to the Western tradition, though now placed in question in a number of ways. For instance, in the wake of evolutionary science, "creation" seems a discredited scientific hypothesis about determinate cosmological beginnings. But surely creation is not a scientific hypothesis at all, with a claim to determinate scientific cognition. It has to do with astonishment and perplexity about the ultimate expressed in a metaphysical metaphor of origin that shapes our religious sense of the ontological ethos. We are dealing with the thought of something hyperbolic in excess of univocal, scientific determination. Some religious people can be as confused here by a univocal literalism as are their scientistic counterparts—and nemeses. Can we make any intelligible sense of this hyperbolic thought?

In many mythologies we find something like "creators," but it is within the monotheistic religions, stemming from biblical inspiration, that the hyperbolic notion develops. Our concern is philosophical, but this religious source is not irrelevant. An idea of religious provenance becomes the occasion of a more radical philosophical reconsideration. That "creation" has religious origins does not mean it is philosophically illegitimate to engage with it. You cannot put up "No Trespass" signs over religion and order

135

philosophy not to step across. Nor should philosophers themselves erect the "No Trespass" sign. Who is giving the orders here? Anything can become the occasion of philosophical thought; philosophy might have to revisit and revise its cherished ways under the impact of those others, like religion and art, which contest and challenge it. Some ideas are migrants without official passports. They wander extraterritorially from Jerusalem and shock into new astonishment the settled lucidities of Athenian minds.

Creation is said to be one such idea (by Gilson, among others). The claim is something like this: Since in the Greek view of cosmos, existence was eternal, the philosophical question concerns not *why anything is at all* but rather the *what* and *how* of things, as *already given* in being. Creation arises relative to our astonishment about the "that it is," not curiosity about the "what" of what is. Thus, by contrast with Aristotle, Aquinas is said to take seriously "that things are at all." While beings are intelligible, and intelligible perhaps in ways basically described by Aristotelian discourse, that they are at all is not simply an intelligibility; there is no unconditional necessity that they be at all; their being is not self-explanatory; their ontological character shows them as possible or contingent being. Hence the question, "Why being at all, why not nothing?" takes on momentous significance.

CREATION, COMING TO BE, AND BECOMING

Creation concerns the kind of beings we find in the between, insofar as they show themselves as *coming to be*. The most insistent showing of coming to be is intimated in the *becoming* of such beings, but it is very important to distinguish "coming to be" and "becoming." The becoming in the between is important, not because traditionally becoming was counterposed with being, as beyond all becoming, but because of the ontological dynamic of things. To think of origin by means of an escape from becoming risks depriving origin of that dynamic openness necessary for an origin to be an origin at all. Rather, the ontological dynamic shifts our attention to an *originative* source of dynamic being, an origin dynamic in a surplus sense to what is given in the between. The finitely dynamic does not arise from the static but from a more primordial *energeia*.

 Becoming puts us in mind of coming to be, but coming to be is not identical with becoming. For in becoming, one becomes a *determinate something*, out of a prior condition of determinate being and towards a further more realized or differently realized determination of one's being. Coming to be, by contrast, is prior to becoming this or that; for one must be, and have come to be, before one can become such and such. Becoming itself suggests something more primordial about coming to be. Creation is connected with this more primordial coming to be—a coming to be that makes finite becoming itself possible but that is not itself a finite becoming. In every finite being that becomes, which is all beings, there is intimated this prior coming to be which is not a finite becoming: "that is it at all" is here in question, and that it has come to be this at all.

The point is not a dualistic opposition that claims being is prior or antithetical to becoming. There is a "coming to be," an origination of the "that it is at all," presupposed in every being that becomes this or that. This prior coming to be is like becoming in its dynamic character, and yet it is other to becoming in that it exceeds finite determination or self-determination. Nor is it the finite realization of an initially unrealized potency. For the creative possibility of unrealized potency is also "power to be" that has come to be, and in a way prior to determinate becoming. Coming to be is hyperbolic happening. What is suggested is an overdetermined source of origination out of which coming to be unfolds. To speak of "creator" is a way of putting us in mind of this other source that is not a finite determinate source of beginning or becoming, for that would be to make determinate what exceeds determination. It is extremely difficult to think in this *huper* dimension on the other side of determinate beings. Our thinking is more convenient with finite things—convenient with this, that, and the other in *becoming*, less convenient even with the becoming of this, that, or the other, and even less again with the more primordial *coming to be* in becoming.

CREATION AND AGAPEIC ORIENTATION: DUALISM AND THE "NOT"

If we accept some sense of mystery, and say God is transcendent always, always other, can we avoid an unbridgeable *dualism* of the between and the beyond, and the equivocity of a sundering into difference beyond mediation? (A question for Levinas?) If the "not" of nothing defines an absolute difference between God and world does not this undermine divine mystery, in the long run?

I mean, we affirm one God, but absolutely other to the world, for the two are *not* each other, ever. Then the world is dedivinized; nothing in the world is God; without God, world is nothing, and has nothing to do with God. First consequence: war on polytheism, earthly traces of the divine are extirpated. Second consequence: earth appears as the godless place of our mastery: we image in the between the One outside who rules with absolute dominion. Third consequence: as the godless earth earns less respect, we are tempted to be its tyrants. Fourth consequence: creation is made our means, mere matter for exploitation; in itself nothing good, we impose our value on it. We are God's gift to the world, the world worthless until we give ourselves, but our gift is equivocal, mixing care with pillage. We become agents of the "not"—the little god of a thisworldly dualism—the otherworldly dualism turned upside down—dominating the "over against-ness" of things.

Is it fair to the hyperbolic thought of creation to accuse it of harboring such potential for (ecological) devastation? Equivocities in some formula-tions might suggest this possibility, but this is a warped parody of its deeper power. Creation need not generate oppositional dualism but a different sense of plurality, a communicative enabling of others as others. That the world is not God need not mean the "not" yields overwhelming negation. In creation as *agapeic origination* the "not" is defined in agapeic transcending, for it allows an arising of the other that is there for itself: origin is not the creation, but creation is not at all without the origin. Nor is world void of traces of the divine, as a work is not without signs of its originator or speech without some signature of its speaker. Transcendence is not nugatory, if the limit is with respect to the enigma of agapeic origination out of which the "It is good" is addressed to creation.

CREATION, HYPER-TRANSCENDENCE, AND DIVINE INTIMACY

Is all this too metaphysically abstract? What of more familiar emphases? For many religious people creation is associated with Genesis, but there we find no formula of creation from nothing. Nevertheless, the world is not God's self-extension. World is other, and good as other. God beholds that "It is good." To behold requires "standing back." This is a seeing that says "yes." The divine song of esteem is not a song of self, or even a self-congratulation on work well done. The work is well done, but it is the work that is good, deemed and esteemed so by the creator.

If the world is not God's self-doubling, God is not touched by the nothingness ontologically constitutive of the finite being. The origin is in excess of, over and above the most extreme negation, *huper* the absolute nothing. The creative act issues from the *nec plus ultra* of generously affirma-tive power. One might say: This power to give being from nothing is that greater than which none can be thought. Creation is not from something, hence it is not demiurgic making, limited by being as already given to be. Creating is sheer giving to be. It is heterogeneous to any human making which produces from something already existing. The power to create in this unique instance is absolute.

Why create at all? Because it is good. Creation is not arbitrary fiat, modeled on the capricious finger snap of some oriental despot. The metaphor of originative speaking is suggestive. God says, "Let there be . . . and there was . . ." Creation is an original speaking letting be. Speaking brings the word to existence. The word, speaking, lets being be. A word is not a roar. The roar would be more like the diktat of the despotic divinity. The word, spoken originatively, is the expression of communicative being. The originating word issues from the goodness of generosity. The word is the creative expression of being as agapeic and as communicative transcending. Word brings a world to be, word communicates a world, lets it issue into a space of sharing with others. Wording the between (*logos* of the *metaxu*): not thinking itself, not even thought thinking its other, but thought singing the other (see *PO*, chapter 6). Wording the between: a sung world—a song not only sung, but a song giving rise to new singers. The originative word would be the primordial "yes" that gives coming to be, a word that is also a blessing with being. We know this elementally in our own being given to be, lived as an affirmation of being that first lives us before we live it. The agapeic "yes" not only blesses with being, it blesses being: It is good to be.

If we say God's creating is not constrained by any principle of external limitation—be it matter, *Moira*, chaos, an evil god, *Ananke*—we aim to preserve God's *absoluteness*. If we say that this creation is continuing, we want to insist on God's ongoing *relativity* to the world. Creation names a tense doubleness in affirming *both* absoluteness and relatedness. How is this possible? It turns on the *absolved relativity* communicated by the origin as agapeic. This turns on the connection of absoluteness and the good, and this latter not simply at the end, but in the origin and the between. Agapeic origination is the communication of the good of being in the coming to be of beings. The origin as unconstrained creator is absolute in itself; as absolute good, it is communicative transcendence; as agapeic, it brings the world to being as other, and other as good for itself. Continuing creation points both to absoluteness and providential relatedness: the God of the origin is the God of the becoming of the between. The becoming of the between—reconfigured by some as "history," though it is more than that—is the interim between nothing and eternity, the interim we call time.

The metaxological double of absoluteness and relatedness suggests God as both radically *intimate* to beings and as *hypertranscendent*. Intimate as radical immanent origin of being's coming to be; hypertranscendent as beyond all finitized becoming. This hypertranscendence suggests an *asymmetrical* relation of God and world: world is God dependent; God is not world dependent. Is this asymmetry a dependence which diminishes the world? Not necessarily. In one light, one might say the holistic view diminishes the world more as a part of the divine. Here, given creation is not a part, but as apart, it is its own whole. It is not the absolute; it is a finite whole.

This hypertranscendence is connected with divine freedom. Nothing constrains the communication of true goodness—its free release is its free giving. It is also connected with divine power, but we have to be careful of the notion of external compulsion that often strikes us first when we reflect on power. Agapeic reserve will not quickly cross our minds as power. External compulsion is related to univocal determination of one thing by another: I order, you obey, and there is an incontrovertible line of command and effect from source to action. Some defenders of a transcendent creator love such power—unequivocal dominion of being. But there is no univocal line with agapeic origination: freedom is given in the between as a space of porosity, between origin and all creation. There is no ultimate univocalization of that porosity. Unequivocal dominion of a unilateral sort is not the point, in that the gift of free being is richer in promise, though more dangerous, than univocal determination.

If we are fixed on the magisterial God of despotic power, or the erotic sovereign who masters all he surveys, the agapeic God can look impotent, just because it lets be, lets freedom be. Hypertranscendence is releasing power, hence some will see no power here at all. That is not the fault or default of agapeic reserve. This reserve makes way, makes a way to allow the power of freedom of what is other to come into its own. Agapeic power is absolving power, releasing others beyond itself, without insistence on the return of the power of the others to itself. It does not bind but unbinds. And it binds by unbinding, in that the deeper bond of agapeic togetherness and service is only thus allowed. Absolute absolving power is agapeic as power that gives the power to give. Only if absolute power is an absolving agape, is the absoluteness of the divine together with the relativity of the finite.

GOD BEING OVER-BEING:
A METAPHYSICAL CANTO

From *God and the Between*

FIRST METAPHYSICAL CANTO: GOD BEING OVER-BEING

Is this the place to start: God as being, perhaps as over-being? I would visit the philosopher Paul Weiss in his old age, and coming in the door he would ask me, almost shouting: "How do you get from being to God?" A very good question, not an easy question, not one to be directly answered, as if there were an univocal path from one to the other.

We have to think in terms of the first hyperbole: the "that it is at all." Being is not a predicate, not a form; being is not a being, but refers us to original power to be. Is this what is the most original: the agapeic power to be, or give to be? But relative to finite being, origin as original can seem to be no-thing. We find ourselves in the fore-ground of the gift of being at all. We come to ask: What is being given to be at all? What is the original of coming to be that does not itself come to be but, as giving to be, makes coming to be possible and actual?

Is God, or is God not? If God is, what is this "is"? What is it to say: God is? Nothing, it seems, more than an indeterminacy. We seem to be told (almost) nothing. What (or who) is God who is? Immediately we run into the difficulty that our sense of "what" is determinate. The origin is not a determinate being but rather gives them to be as being at all. If there is something idiotic about being there at all, does this mean a kind of hyperidiocy to the "being" of God? It seems we cannot say what God is, if "what" is a determinate characterization or essence. Can we even ask then what God is?

The question generates different responses, but two are noteworthy. On the one hand, God is said to be Being Itself. Thus Aquinas: *verum ipsum esse*. The name "God" is said to give in Exodus is seen as religiously converging with what metaphysics reasons out of God as Being. On the other hand, it will be said God is no being, we must rethink God without

141

being. For instance, the Heideggerian ontological difference is appropriated and radicalized such that not only is Being different to beings, but God is neither Being itself nor a being (Marion?). This venerable response especially wants to take into account reverence for the excess of the origin: God will always be other, *epekeina tes ousias*, like Plato's Good, and perhaps even further beyond, like Plotinus's One *epekeina nous kai episteme*. *Hyperessential*: beyond essence, and the "to be."

The rationale is clear with both these options. God's difference is acknowledged, but as we must avoid univocity with the first, we risk equivocation with the second. In the first case, some community of God with the beings that are is at least implied in calling God Being itself, tempting one to enclose God and beings in one ontological totality, which then might seem to be the truer name for the ultimate. The difference of God would be compromised, and God as Being domesticated in terms of God's necessary place in the one totality which is the whole of beings. Of course, this univocity of being is not the only possibility; the analogical conception is obviously relevant, for this clearly wants to keep open the space of transcendence, even while not blocking some relativity to the immanence of creation. The doctrine of analogy complexly qualifies the "is" of being with the "as" of similitude, such that the temptations to univocal reduction or assimilation are noted, guarded against, and transcended. It calls attention to the participation of finite beings in being, a participation first made possible as a gift of the origin, a participation pointing to both the intimacy of the origin and also to an *asymmetry*, since the gift is exceeded by the giver. There is something absolute in the asymmetry: if God is as unconditional in self, God also is as absolving, in letting the finite creation be as irreducibly other. God is absolute in the intimacy of its own being for self, and absolving in the releasing of creation that is the love of finitude of agapeic origination. God's agapeic giving releases the creation into being its own open whole, and hence not just a part of a more inclusive totality. In this respect, the analogical "as" points us towards a metaxological understanding.

Relative to the second option, God's very otherness tempts us to see the Being of the divine as *not* Being, but other than Being. The reasoning has its points of persuasiveness. The origin cannot be reduced to what it originates, and hence is always over and above. It is no thing, and hence a name for God might be Nothing, and perhaps God has no proper name. The point is not a merely empty nothing, but an originative nothing that is creative of the finite beings. Since we cannot think this in terms proportionate to finite beings, it is better to exceed or transcend the language of beings.

The danger of equivocation here is that we vacillate between the full and the empty nothing. Perhaps we can hardly avoid talking in terms both full and empty. Univocal thinking will insist that a nothing that is absolutely empty is the only possibility. (Univocal thinking cannot think the porosity.) But how dare we talk about a full nothing? Will we not be seduced by negation, even in our affirmation of God, as we say again and again: God is not this being, not that being, not any being at all—and the "not" takes over, and we forget the fullness, and a space of emptiness opens between God and the world, and then once again an impenetrable veil of dualistic opposition descends. A new equivocal outcome emerges, namely, that God and world have absolutely nothing to do with each other. We say God is beyond being, but if so beyond, what can we say of God but nothing, and if nothing, then when we look at the world we see nothing of God there. It appears to us then as a Godless scene, and the religious reverence that would guard divine transcendence ends up atheist. God without being becomes being without God.

These equivocations turn us to pondering the nothing in less than empty ways. There must be senses of being which do not reduce God to a being, without making God a vacant nothing. I would connect such thoughts about the nothing to the *porosity of being*. Consider thus the porous space between the human and the divine in which communication passes. We are what we are in this porous between, and, in another sense, we ourselves are a porous between. We are an open space in which the divine communicates when we wake to ourselves in prayer—wake to ourselves as being woken to the divine beyond us. The porosity is *a kind of nothing*, but it is such as the en-abling milieu of communication, and indeed en-abling of the being of beings as a something created out of nothing. God is not this porosity, but primally possibilizes the porosity. God as creating is in kenotic and agapeic passage in this porosity. God is not the porosity, but the porosity is a kind of token of the kenotic agapeics of the God that creates. God, in creating from nothing, gives the porosity as the en-abling milieu of communication. And since it is through the porosity that God is communicated, we think that the God communicating is like the porosity—and it, of course, is (a kind of) nothing. If we were to talk about God as a full nothing, God would be like such an en-abling nothing, empowering all communicative being (for self and for the other), creating the porosity that allows the finite creativity of the creature.

There is a peculiar incontrovertibility about being, however we understand it. We deny it, and we have to affirm it; for denying it presupposes some sense of the "is," a point clear to philosophers since Parmenides, though its meaning remains difficult and obscure. This incontrovertibility suggests nothing outside being, but in such a wise that there seems to be no "outside." What could such an "outside" mean? Somehow being envelops all that it. Would this include God in an ontological totality, such that God is not ultimate, but the whole is, with God perhaps the highest being in the totality? We would have to give up God's radical originality, singular ultimacy, and absoluteness. If we wish to preserve these latter, some sense of the nothing has to be granted by our thinking, to ground essential differences, not only relative to the "outside" or "beyond" of being but within being itself. And there must be a truth more ultimate than the whole, the truth of God beyond the whole.

I suggest the following approach. We know this incontrovertibility in the between, for in the between we cannot think being away, for every thinking reveals a bond with being that is intimate to the thinking itself. This bond is ultimately metaxological, though it also has its univocal, equivocal, and dialectical modes. We cannot think being away, and yet (in the porosity of the between) we intimately know the finitude and possible nothingness of what is incontrovertible. What is incontrovertible is our bond with being, revealing a necessity that we cannot sidestep; and yet the being (and bond) so revealed is not absolutely necessary, since we also know that it once was not, that now it is ontologically frail, and that once again (to all appearances, given our mortality) it will not be anymore. The incontrovertibility is the immediacy of the "that it is," but when we mindfully meditate on the "that it is" and mediate a sense of "what" this "that it is" is, it is not absolutely necessary in itself, even if it does prove incontrovertible in relation to us. In fact, in that relation, we come to know that the incontrovertible "that it is" is passing into being and passing away. The porosity of being is the very between of passing. We come to know *ourselves* incontrovertibly, as having come to be, coming still to be, and still too passing away. Incontrovertible being in the between, as passing in the porosity, is not absolute, thus not God.

What then of God and being? Finite being, in its hyperbolic "that it is," points further than itself. Of God we might say, "That it is" but "what" the "that" is, we cannot say in the same way as we can say of beings in the between, or the between as such. For the "that it is" of finite being is, but also can not be: this is where the constitutive nothing of its finite becoming shows itself, and makes it contingent, not absolutely necessary. The "That it is" of God cannot not be. It is not a being in the between, it is not the totality of beings; its being is other. Hence the importance of speaking of the God beyond the whole. How "beyond," how other? I would say as the actualizing origin that is the actual possibilizing ground of all possible being. It is not itself possible being. It is beyond possibility and actuality, so far as this doublet defines the becoming of finite happening. It is itself the possibilizing actuality that is the source of finite possibility and actuality. It is not indefinite possibility but overdetermined original possibilizing. The difference of these illuminates something of the difference of the empty and the full nothing.

Porosity

But why move beyond the relative necessity of the contingent? Deep within us emerges the urgency of ultimacy, and deeper still, often more recessed than this urgency, the porosity of our middle being, overtly manifested in the openness of our questing being. As this porosity cannot be determined in terms of finite univocal limits, as this urgency articulates the open energy of our exceeding being, so they pose us as questionings calling for an answering that is radical, original, and ultimate. The answer(ing) must address the hyperbolic nature of our quest(ioning), for, short of the truly incontrovertible, there seems no proportionate response to our patience, openness, and hunger. The proportionate response must be disproportionate: it cannot be a finite response. Given our porosity, we cannot *secure* an answer through ourselves alone; our urgency of ultimacy must befriend again the *passio essendi* intimate with the porosity. This befriending returns us to ontological astonishment at being at all. What possibilizes being at all? It is the incontrovertibility of being, intimately known in our own being at all, that is in question. No univocal answer will unequivocally answer, for the true "answer" could not be that kind of answer, for this would be to assimilate the question to one of a finite problem. Being finite at all raises the question of its possibility: what makes it possible, indeed what makes its possibility actual? What possibilizes not only its actuality but its very possibility? It is not a question of moving from a possibility to the actuality, but of what possibilizes the possibility at all, and then what possibilizes the original movement from this possibility to the actuality of finite being and its "that it is at all."

This more primordial sense of possibilizing is not a determinate or finite possibility; its original actualizing cannot be a finite and determinate causing. It is not an indeterminate possibility and actualizing. This would be less than the finite "that it is," whereas it must be a more. I would speak of overdetermined origination, expressed in agapeic creation. Agapeic creation suggests the incontrovertible "that it is" of God, not absolutely in self but relative to the side of the origin turned towards the finite between, as ultimate ground(ing) of its possible being, "that it is at all."

The metaxological sense guides us towards the more intensive sense of the primal ethos of being, where the elemental porosity is more appreciated, and where the *passio essendi*, more primordial than the *conatus essendi*, is more given for mindfulness. There we are more mindful of giving qua giving of a more original energy of being—God as absolutely original "to be"—that originates the between as a porous medium of passing, and in which porosity and passage we know something of the nothingness of finitude, and of the divine energies as also a kind of creative "no-thing" in excess of finite fixation. The dialectical sense, *at best*, can point in the same direction: the communication of being shows a source of self-surpassing transcendence in which what is other to that source is not a dualistic opposite. There is a togetherness more fundamental than opposition, and hence neither source nor other is to be univocally fixed or equivocally opposed. The dialectical way to the overdetermined, in and through the determinate, can be likened to a *via negativa*. But negation does not lead us to nothing but to the porosity of being. The porosity is not a determinate negation. I am not saying God is a dialectical being but dialectical metaphors bring something to the fore that helps us think ecstatic being that remains at one with itself in being in relation to what is other. Such ecstatic being is surpassing: a transcending that is self-transcending; just so, in its being what it is, it is the ecstatic source of energy it itself is. If there is a "self" to it, its being is itself in being transcending transcendence. It is itself in its self-surpassing that is no self-surpassing, for this hyperbolic origin cannot be exceeded.

For such reasons we can justifiably speak of God as absolute being that mediates with itself, at home with itself in relation to all others, for the others are not antagonistic opposites that limit it. But we could not leave it at that, not least because of questionable erotic interpretations of what this means. It would only be *half right* to say that while dialectic as *via negativa* leads us towards the self-transcending "no-thing," the metaxological as *via eminentiae* leads us to the excess of the divine "more," finding an affirmative role for irreducible otherness. Half right, in that the meaning of the nothing is modified in the metaxological way in taking us towards the intimate ontological porosity of the primal ethos of being, and the intimate receptivity and opening of our being at all as *passio essendi*. These latter (porosity, primal ethos, and so on) point more robustly than dialectic to the transcendence of God's being as requiring an irreducible otherness and not just otherness comprehended within self-mediation. There is more than the "more" of the given between. This is communicated in metaxological intermediation *between* the between and the divine origin. We might call this "more" the surplus *huperousia* of God: surplus because in excess, *huperousia* because it is not being but above being, and, if nothing, then nothing in a manner beyond the opposition of being and nothing, or even their dialectical sublation. The being of the God of the *metaxu* is beyond the between, beyond becoming, beyond the being there at all of finite being, being beyond coming to be.

This second metaxological sense points us towards God as full, overfull being, but so full as to be as nothing for us, except insofar as its fullness is turned towards us in the between. We divine the "more" in what of it is turned towards us. What is turned to us is turned out of its own irreducible otherness, which is not a moment of the self-mediation of the immanent whole. The metaxological allows other-being to turn towards us in the between, out of its own otherness, and remaining in its otherness even in turning to us. What is more than this turning towards us is shrouded in enigma and is as nothing to us. But it is as nothing because the pluperfection of its inaccessible mystery is intimated in the fullness turned towards us. It is as nothing because it is too much for us. That it is too much for us is intimated in the way its turn is proportioned to what of it we can take in. It meets us in the measure of the hospitality of our being, but this meeting is its disproportionate hospitality, of which we cannot be the measure. We cannot take it in or be the measure of it: an excess both overfull and as nothing for us. But the overflow of the overfull passes for us agapeically in the porosity of the between, a porosity that is as if it were nothing, so quietly does the divine absolve finitude—indeed not just absolve it but rather love it.

We have to say both these things retain the doubleness at the end, as at the beginning. God is not a being and yet as origin of being is. God is thus Being itself and yet beyond Being, since Being itself is *huperousia*. God is Nothing and yet this Nothing is not nothing, in that the origin as no-thing is the inexhaustible creative source that brings to be any thing or being, abiding as more than any thing it originates. Nor is this Nothing the determinate negativity we find in the becoming of beings in the between; nor indeed the nothingness constitutive of originated beings (that have come to be), also more than determinate negation. The porosity as the enabling medium of (ontological) communication gives us a truer, more secretly agapeic sense of the Nothing. Just as one might say there is more to the being of a thing than its determinate presence, so one might say there is more to God than this "more" of the being and its determinate presence, as well as say that there is also a nothingness more (and less) than the determinate negation ingredient in defining things, and further again a divine Nothing that is more (and less) than both this nothingness and determinate negation. More and less? It is on another scale, in the dimension of the hyperbolic.

I summarize these different senses of the being of God and the nothing: *First*, God as the hyperbolic "more," exceeded by no thing, an exceeding no-thing that is absolute original power to be. *Second*, the *nihil* out of which God brings being(s) to be; this is not God's nothingness, since God is agapeic and not simply erotic, and hence can originate coming to be as a giving of being in excess of nothing, defining the character of the being that is brought to be; yet God's being is not defined by either the nothing from which beings are called into being, or by the beings so given to be. *Third*, the porosity of the given being of the between; this is the open milieu of the primal ethos of being; this enables all communicating, passing, and becoming. *Fourth*, there is something like the more derivative determinate negation that presupposes the more primal coming to be of beings, given by original creation, but that qualifies the various immanent processes of becoming as they unfold towards a more full self-becoming.

Agapeic being and the nothing might be seen together in light of how in everyday life we diversely say, "It is nothing." "It is nothing": this can be a gesture of nihilistic dismissal, but also one of release, of giving, even unto forgiving. See the agapeic being of God as more than nothing, hence creative, beyond nothing, calling finite being to be out of nothing. Finite being is nothing without this calling, this being gifted to be. But think of how a generous person gives and, when thanked, might give in reply: "It is nothing" (even though it is everything). For the point is to point away from the giver to the gift and the recipient: "It is nothing" accepts and returns the gratitude to the grateful recipient. And so there is not just a give and take, but a giving and regiving. Giving is amplified in being gratefully received. There is no limit to the "more" of agapeic amplification. (Owning nothing, the loaves and the fishes are miraculously multiplied.) "It is nothing" gives manifestation to the porosity of a love that gives generously for nothing, and returns generosity to generosity, and perhaps also to hatred and enmity. This "It is nothing" is the communication of good, of love, in the between. (Wandering with destitution, as if falling from the heavens at night, divine manna is given in the desert.)

Thus, also, there is an "It is nothing" of forgiveness. It is the willingness to set the evil "at naught": to offer again the promise of life, and so to restore primal faith and hope in being. "It is nothing": an unclogging of the porosity in which the good of the "to be" communicates itself and freely passes. "It is nothing": a relativization, an absolution of the relation from guilt and indebtedness that frees gratitude into a released modality: beyond obligation, beyond morality in that sense also, beyond the law, though it is not evil. "It is nothing": a kind of anarchic good, a mercy beyond the moral law. There is a transfiguration of the first hyperbole "It is" into "It is good": nothing but the communication of good being in and through the porosity of the between.

PART IV

AESTHETICS AND PHILOSOPHY OF ART

BEING AESTHETIC

From *Philosophy and Its Others*

In turning to being aesthetic, I intend no mere aestheticism but a crucial comportment towards being, a way of being with ontological weight. The poet may be its most concentrated configuration, but what he concentrates individually is continuous with a way of being that human beings, simply as human, reveal. Hence I use the term "aesthetic" in its widest traditional sense, that is, as relating to sensuous appearance (*to aisthetikon*) and the modes of mindfulness bound to sensuous appearance. I am concerned with being aesthetic as showing the appearance of mind within our sensuous placement in the metaxological community of being. There is no argument for the appearance of mind that does not itself presuppose mind, for every argument is a form of mind. But this circle is not malign; instead of a logicist deduction of mind from nonmind, it demands of us a phenomenological fidelity to appearing mind.

The aesthetic in this encompassing sense brings home to us an otherness that challenges philosophy to a different mindfulness of thereness in the middle. Being becomes drab prose when a merely utilitarian mentality neutralizes the thereness for purposes of exploitation. The aesthetic asks for our recovery of the poiesis of intermediate being. This cannot be confined to its artistic expressions, even granting these as frequently its most exemplary articulations. We are pointed to an origin of meaning as coming to articulation in sensuous being, in that this is more than mere neutral matter, in that we desire to transfigure any valueless thereness of bodily being, in that we cannot renege on the exigency to beautify being. Against art's idolization as in l'art pour l'art, against such cultural compartmentalizing, the aesthetic is not an insulated whole but an opening to the otherness of the whole.

In what follows we will look at the metaxological community between self and other in being aesthetic. We are immediate participants in the metaxological where we spontaneously live a certain intimacy with being.

The metaxological bond of self and other emerges in immediacy, but with its mediation we are allowed to stress, sometimes overstress, either the self or the other. In that the human self is dialectically self-mediating, it can inflate its own power to dominate the aesthetic middle. Thus, we may lose sight of the inherent community of self and other in aesthetic being. We can cease to participate properly in the metaxological, with aesthetic consequences such as we see in the so-called death of art. Despite this, the promise of the metaxological always persists. Art is essential to this promise and the recovery of a metaxological mindfulness of otherness at its richest.

BEING IMITATIVE, BEING CREATIVE

Imagination's original opening to otherness relates to the ideas of imitation and creation, two fundamental ideas in the tradition of reflection on art. The first corresponds to art's imaging of external otherness, the second to its imaging of internal otherness. The metaxological requires the togetherness of both. Imitation is a more complex relation than commonly held, but it risks a *dualism* of image and original; art as creation actually develops the mediation implicit in imitation, meeting the problem of dualism in a concept of art as a *dialectical* self-mediation of mind in sensuous expression. But when this dialectic tilts excessively towards subjectivity, as in modern notions of "creativity," we can subjectivistically distort the aesthetic middle as properly *metaxological*.

Imitation has been the dominant idea in Western aesthetics, if we understand dominance temporally. It has an old and noble line, and art has been seen as imitating nature or eternal form or ideal beauty. Appeal to creation is more common now, at times in debased form. All one has to do is boil a bowl of tripe, and one is credited with "creativity." Creativity has become a catchall for conceit. The accompanying denigration of imitation runs: be an original, don't be an imitation; imitation is second rate, only reproducing the old without producing the new; as mere copying, it just duplicates an original already complete in itself and so is only an *impoverished* version of that original; imitation is a mere parasite. So arises the dictate that we must cease "being like everyone else and be ourselves," cease being imitations and become originals. Imitation is merely reproductive imagination, while being creative shows the more primordial power of productive imagination. As Emerson famously said: imitation is suicide.

Yet if we look closer, imitation is a far more complex and fundamental aesthetic mediation and hardly deserves its bad name. I put it this way: without a foundation of being like everything else, we could never become ourselves, for the selves we would become would be vacuous. One can exhort someone to become himself until one is blue in the face, but unless one starts by imitating others, that is, by being open to otherness, one will never stir from the spot. "Being oneself" amounts to "being nothing," however much one panders to vanity and suggests that the person is an absolute original.

In fact, the opposition of imitation and creation—one passive and unfree, the other active and spontaneous—is entirely misleading. To be able to imitate is to possess the power of imaginatively identifying with the other, a power far more complex than simple reproductive imagination. An imitating being has the fundamental capacity to be other to itself. Consider. I am Peter, but I imitate Paul; if so, I am no longer plain Peter; that is, through imitation I have imaginatively put myself in the place of Paul, identified myself with an other self; yet in becoming Paul, I still remain myself, Peter. My identity has been *imaginatively doubled* through a creative appropriation of an other, a difference. Imitation is neither passive nor reactive nor identical with naturalistic copying; it is a form of imaginative acting, an opening to and mediation of otherness in which we become the other, giving ourselves up to its difference.

Some version of art as "creation" has dominated aesthetics since Kant, but the view was not unknown before this. Ancient peoples honored the poetic power, wondering about its perhaps divine source (the poet as shaman, magus, sage). They showed a hesitation here, a reluctance restrained by reverence. The power to create was the god's privilege; we must be content to be a creature—a result made, not a making source. Romanticism (concretizing Kant's productive imagination in the general culture) helped destroy the taboo on ascribing divine qualities to human beings and rushed over this ancient reverence. We are creators, it is claimed, even capable of rivaling God. Today we may be uneasy with the religious language, but one way or another we have slipped into the habit of thinking of ourselves as "creative."

In a reversal of the old opposition of image and original, creativity is again pitted against imitation. Where imitation asks submission to external norms, creativity insists that our activity contains its own norm. The view is: the self expresses itself in activity with its own intrinsic norms; hence it is not to be judged by external standards but provides its own justification. Thus are precipitated movements *like l'art pour l'art*. The self now becomes the center of concern, not, as before, the world of larger otherness; at the best, the self is seen as an *inner otherness*. Not surprisingly, some aesthetes, like Oscar Wilde, tried to make themselves their own greatest creation. Alternatively, art may seek to probe its own internal resources (as in "self-reflexive" art today), rather than render homage to anything beyond itself.

The undeniable truth here is that human activity does point to the self as an originative being whose activities come to be marked by immanent norms. Art, too, comes to exhibit such internal standards when, as a form of sensuous self-knowledge, the artist and, mediately, his audience know themselves in the creation. Thus, art is a dialectical *self-mediation*: the artist originates a work that is other to himself, but in that other, the self actualizes *its own* original power; hence in the artwork as other it comes to recognize itself. The work as other is its own creative power as self-othering. This is dialectical because there is a creative interplay of self and other; it is self-mediation because the self comes to mediate with itself, know itself in the work as a sensuous other.

This dialectical self-mediation has a significance wider than any individual self. It is a mark of civilization that it lives by such internal standards. With civilized selves, standards of excellence do not have to be enforced from without, for they constitute the innermost core of civilized life. The civilized self lives them effortlessly for they are the life blood of civilization. But civilization, like genuine creation, is born of tension. Dialectical self-mediation risks asserting that *only* the self mediates the relation of self and other; it risks the self dominating the other in a spurious self-sufficiency or autonomy that is actually closed to otherness. Creation tries to win our openness to otherness and the promise of wholeness despite the contrary seduction of closure and the forces of dissolution. Creation is not a matter of merely asserting one's originality but of being honest about recalcitrant otherness, grappling with the fluid original power of our being, turning it from amorphous force into forceful form.

This risk of closure to otherness is not always avoided in our notion of creativity. We now intone the term "creativity" like a sacred password to some Holy of Holies, but while we chant this mantra, the danger is that self-absorption gets substituted for self-knowledge, and we shirk the intermediated condition of creative tension. For originative power is not a private possession but something given to us. What is given, precisely as gift, preserves our link with the other as other. The creator betrays this original power if he encloses it within a shuttered selfhood. The nature of creative power is not just to commune with itself but to communicate itself. It does not realize itself in that swaggering self-assertion that sets itself against the rest of creation. Our opening of ourselves is our openness to what is other. Man is not "creative." Man cooperates in creation.

To avoid this closure of creativity, we must recall that the more perfect an imitation is, the more it presents itself as a creation; the richer the image, the more it is an original itself, an original image. If the artwork is such an original image, it can be said to seek the togetherness of these two sides: it articulates an original world of its own; it images, in complex mediations, the world of larger otherness. Between the work and the wider otherness there may be metaxological ebb and flow. This means that imitation and creation need not be radically opposed; imitation is an incipient form of creation; creation is imitation completing itself. One displays our ability to liken ourselves to things other; the other shows us to give expression to originative powers of our own. As a togetherness of imitation and creation, art testifies to our originative power and participation in the universe of otherness. It concretizes our self-relating openness to otherness, trying to hold together in the original image the inward otherness of the self and the otherness of being beyond the self. As an original image, the artwork is a creative double that aesthetically concretizes the actuality of metaxological being.

Thus also we avoid the extremes of passive representation, and sheer creativity from nothing. Where the first deflates art to an unoriginality below its real power, the second inflates it to an original power indistinguishable from God's. In the middle of these extremes, art's imaginative formation is double: a dealing with the vagueness of innerness, as well as the indifference of outerness. This aesthetically expresses the double mediation of metaxological being. We are often burdened with an inchoate sense of significance that asks to be expressed, but as long as this remains inward and private, it is all but insubstantial. To assume fully an articulated life it must be made concrete by being externalized. Imaginative formation shapes the inner formlessness through dialectical self-medition, such that our being comes to genuine expression, perhaps for the first time. What is inward may shine outward.

But imaginative formation is not just single self-formation but double formation: a mediation of both the self in its inward otherness and what is other as beyond the self. In its dialectical self-externalization, the self is gathered to this second otherness. This otherness may seem alien and opposed, but in the middle way we try to name this, the foreignness of being. A great work names being thus. We contend with the darkness to put a small cosmos where before for us was only a large chaos. What is outward now shines with inwardness. A reciprocal interplay occurs between inwardness and otherness in which neither side is reduced to the other, yet there may come to be a community of both in their very distinctness.

I stress that the artist need not be a dialectically dominating self stamping itself on otherness. The artist does not just superimpose a fixed form on sluggish matter, for at first neither he nor the matter is univocally fixed or fully defined. Both come to definition in the act of origination itself. The form of an artwork comes to emergence in the metaxological interplay of artist and his material. Imagination mediates a transition from formlessness to form, both in the inward self and in outer otherness. Indeed that the artist first has no fixed univocal self or form is at the source of views that couple art with inspiration, vision, intoxication, dream. Ordinary perception stabilizes the self, setting it apart from otherness, often in dualistic opposition to it, but imaginative formation returns our sensuously emergent mindfulness to a point prior to this fixed stabilization and dualization. Inspiration is just the breakdown of this stabilization and dualistic opposition. It is the unweaving of the fixed univocal self, the releasing of the inner otherness in the upsurge of an anterior, dynamic power that does not belong to the self like private property, for it is the original power of being emerging into articulation as the aesthetic self. Inspiration returns to the immediacy of the metaxological where the original power of being is "more"—"mine," yet not mine, intimate yet other. Against the dominating self, inspiration deconstructs the will to dominate otherness.

Thus, the similarity of madness and inspiration has been often noted, by Plato in antiquity, by Schopenhauer in post-Kantian aesthetics. Both relate to the breakdown or deconstruction of the self trying to dominate otherness and the upsurgence or breakthrough of the anterior, dynamic power of being that may possesss us but which none can possess. Madness is inspiration, but inspiration often without the redemption of imaginative formation; inspiration sucked back into chaos, the dark origin, not emergent from it. Imaginative formation, by contrast, harnesses the original power of being erupting in such moments of inspiration, and anchors in the artwork its otherwise overpowering energy.

AESTHETIC MINDFULNESS: ART'S TOLERANCE OF OTHERNESS

Art offers us a way to the metaxological community of self and other through an intermediated sense of wholeness, midway between the closure of "Hegelian" totality and the fragmentary incompleteness of "Wittgensteinian" plurality (cf. introduction). I will make two points, first concerning art's transcending of the instrumentalizing of being, and second, concerning its tolerance of otherness.

A strange obstacle to aesthetic mindfulness is that we seem *saturated* with art. Art today seems both remote and crowding. Remote: the divorce of artist and public makes the former seems careless of communication, except to the "art world," while the wider public takes refuge in the old, already canonized masterpieces. Crowding: everywhere we are surrounded, smothered even, with images plucked from art's realm, for example, in advertising that plunders art's treasury for the extraneous purpose of selling soda pop, jeans, and women's lingerie. Great music is packaged as "musak"—a vaguely present, tediously pleasant hum of background sound; great painting becomes insipid ornamentation, wallpapering we hardly perceive in passing; courtesy of technology, we seem surfeited with cultural decor.

But this very ubiquity produces a startling peripeteia: art vanishes in its surplus availability, becomes absent in its massive presence. As consumers we voraciously use up art like any other convenient commodity, a pleasantry

to palliate a void. Excess of stimulation produces defect of attention; satura-
tion of the senses produces our aesthetic enervation. Against this, aesthetic
mindfulness insists that we stop; attention must be arrested, brought to a
pause. We literally need to be brought back to our senses in their aesthetic
receptivity as opposed to susceptibility to stimulation. (This is one reason I
began with the aesthetic body.) Great art calls for silence, for slowness; it
must be taken in intervals. One cannot rush through its gallery and take in
what is there with a quick sweep of minimal seeing. It insists on quality of
attention, that we dwell with the rich thing itself. It claims concentration as
its right. It asks especially for *patience* in perception. When we solely crave
the sheer immediacy of the "happening," attention is quickly corrupted into
anxious, harried seeing, that is sightless seeing. Mindful intimacy is born
of patient perception. Art needs distance, respect, aloofness, in order to be
allowed to speak to us out of the quiet spaces of its otherness.

This means that aesthetic mindfulness must be freed from the instrumentalization of being. The instrumental mind attends to being only as a
means to satisfy its pragmatic aims, and must needs narrow its focus to what
it can handle from the inconstant, indefinite flux, to what can be bounded
and filtered to our use. But something escapes beyond. We label things,
handle them more efficiently, but they recede into a kind of invisibility. We
are not interested in their elemental thereness or otherness. We want to eat
them, barter them, secure our future; we want to dominate others through
them. What we use this way, we do not fully mind.

Consider: The apple in my hand disappears from sight; for I am hungry
and must consume it. I bring it into such closeness with my needs that it
must vanish in being consumed. I crush it with my mouth. And so it is not
an apple; it is mere food, a means to an end. Its being I make relative to
my desire. But now I am free and stand back, not driven by need. I push
this other apple away, place it at a distance. It is not food now; it is just an
apple. I have no interest in devouring it; I let it be. It exists, exists indeed
in its own right—its being in its otherness is not just relative to me. For
the first time I look at this apple because it exists simply for itself. The
direction of my mind ends there and does not glance away. Its being there
arrests me, stills the hurry of practical worry, releases a freer mindfulness. I
begin to contemplate what before I urgently consumed. I see more. I discern
something coming to appearance that before was unshown. It is there and
other, a strange suspended presence. It is other, yet intimate. I reach for my
brush and make the first stroke of a still life.

The instrumental mind specializes our sense of being, economizes the
imagination, prunes it of useless excess. But the truth is that great art is
rare and offers sparse consolation to the standardized perceptions of our
egalitarian age. Great art evidences a different economy of mind, one that

restores and enlarges imagination beyond utilitarian parsimony. It joys in sheer seeing, seeing for the sake of seeing, seeing freed from ulterior motivations. It baptizes what practical desire leaves nameless, and jolts us out of the rut of use. I mean something other than Oscar Wilde's dictum: "All art is quite useless." The dandy and utilitarian are not unalike; for both art is beyond utility, but in one case it is an amusement for relaxation, and in the other an entertainment for escape. Art's uselessness is rather a kind of metaphysical appreciation of the thereness of things just in the inexhaustibility of their being there and in the intimacy of their otherness. This we value for itself, letting it be with delight, surprised by joy in its otherness.

How does this relate to my claim about an intermediated wholeness? One can say that aesthetic mindfulness is a bounding of attention that is releasing rather than constraining. It is not that art is or could be formless; the point is rather the character of freedom that aesthetic form gives. An aesthetic whole is a paradoxical "open whole," for it marks the sensuous space of freedom. Much of experience is a muddy flux of happenings, a passing pandemonium, but one might claim that *all significant* experience partakes in some measure of artistic form. We are in the ebb and flow of happening, the streaming of being that mostly is not expressly gathered. Attention is needed to discriminate this elusive becoming, to make us singularly mindful of its appearing. In rising above the inarticulate immediacy of our being in the middle, imagination is aesthetic mindfulness, for it disrupts the homogeneous flux, congealing knots, eddies, patterns in the flux. As a synthetic power, it gathers a flux of immediacy into discernible, meaningful wholes. Such gatherings stud all significant experience, indeed testify to its poetic character. What we normally call art carries through in a heightened manner the quest for such unities, better communities, for they image a togetherness of self and other.

Thus, the artwork can offer an enclosure for aesthetic mindfulness without implying any totalizing violence. This relates to the fact that all perceiving, as Nietzsche among others saw, is perspectival. To occupy a perspective is to be somewhere *between* the absolute vision of a God that encompasses the totality and the scattered consciousness that is fragmented in the dissipating flux. Aesthetic framing may occupy this intermediate perspective. Framing is most evident in the painting within whose spatial borders attention is gathered. Music tends to frame in time; the ebb and flow of feeling concentrated and heightened in the rhythm of musical form. Likewise, the stage sets off an arena for the drama of human action. The cinema screen, by setting a limit to our wandering perception, focuses us, opens us. In all cases the frame gives space for mind, what Bullough called "psychical distance." (This distance from the anxiety of everyday desire was a point of metaphysical importance for Schopenhauer.) As subversive of instrumentalized framing, aesthetic framing is significantly different to what Heidegger called the *Gestell*. For it is akin to a contemplative concentration of mind, releasing wonder before the density of giveness, feeding a hope that all perception is not profane.

Aesthetic framing delineates a significant appearance, forms an emergent open whole, making it distinctively stand out against a background. Hegel and Nietzsche agree that some of the greatest of such appearing wholes are statues of the Greek gods. They repose within themselves, defining the surrounding space by their assured presence, charging that space with sacred presence, making it appear as "there" through their combined energy and equilibrium. But such wholes are not to be seen as falisfying univocal units, for the enclosing work of the frame need not lead to closure. Externally the frame is a boundary, but internally it may dissolve the psychic barriers repressing mindfulness. As a framed whole the artwork opens us out. The frame is a fenestration: at once an enclosed opening and an opening of mind beyond closure. (Recall that the artwork as original image is double: the aesthetic frame as intermediate whole facilitates both dialectical self-mediation and metaxological intermediation with otherness.) The whole into which we look is an opening to what is other. Like finally arriving at the seashore, we greet a limit, but the limit opens us, draws out the eye to a boundless horizon, to the space of free being.

I do not speak literally: the frame is not so much a physical limitation but metaphysically names a concentration of attention. True, modern art has often broken the frame literally. It does this sometimes to deny art's isolation from its others, sometimes to subvert the commercial packaging of artworks as commodities, sometimes to question the very ideal of wholeness. The literal frame deconstructs itself, but in so doing it serves metaphorical framing, namely, a different concentration of mindful attention.

Here deconstruction has recently attacked any quest for unity. As Adorno (a serious Left-Hegelian deconstructionist before post-Heideggerian deconstruction) says in parodic inversion of Hegel: the whole is the false. One can accept the disquiet with fragmentation, and especially the dismay with the totalitarian pretension of instrumentalized reason. But it makes no sense to deny our ineradicable exigency for significant "unity," which I read here not as "Hegelian" totality, but as our metaxological community with being in its otherness. The deconstruction of wholeness is itself parasitical on wholeness, and only makes sense if its external negativity secretly hides a dream of even truer wholeness. Otherwise our protestation against alienation becomes indistinguishable from acquiescence in the flat prose of the world. Instead of the functionary prose of the system we get the shrill prose of the protester; or worse, we get a parody of messianic fervor that likes to shout its negation in the ear of the others that it takes to be complacent.

Here the beautiful soul deidealizes itself into the ugly soul—the antiaesthetic vengeance of aesthetic homelessness. But in all this we still remain gripped in the vice of the utilitarian world, where everything seems to be only a means and nothing an intrinsic good, and where the recollected eye of contemplation earns no respect.

Hence, aesthetic wholeness as intermediate is not at all antithetical to openness to otherness, since the imaginative power that gathers becoming into significant "unities" is the same power that enables our identification with difference, our rapport with creation. In its quest of unities, art's resistance to instrumentalization (art as middle is not a mere means) follows from what I called its "tolerance of otherness." This tolerance calls to mind the doctrine of art's disinterestedness of Kant and Schopenhauer. But tolerance is more clearly freed from any implication of "indifference" or "neutrality." Tolerance of otherness is not negatively defined as noninterest; it is an active respect of the other, a courtesy to its being, an engagement with otherness that is not dominating.

Let me illustrate it through the difference of aesthetic and logical mindfulness. Logical mind prohibits contradiction in terms of the law of excluded middle: *either* A *or* not-A, but not both A and not-A. The result is a reduction of equivocity to univocity, a sundering into opposites, where to accept one position necessitates rejection of its other. From this intolerance of contradiction, art seems strangely exempt. But it is not simply equivocal; rather art allows a nonreductive mediation of the ambiguity of the middle. Though beauty and the ugly seem to be the logical opposites here, ugliness is not outside beauty's embrace, for in art the representation of the ugly may be marked by its own complex beauty. I do not mean bland harmony but beauty that includes the deepest pain. For instance, a depiction of Christ's agony seems to be excluded from beauty if we think in terms of a Greek god. But when great art depicts this grief, it includes within beauty what is beauty's negation. Beauty can be there, there even where death is.

Art is a tolerance of otherness precisely because its imaginative range allows of an openness to *all* possibility, including the terrible. It rejects nothing for the sake of abstract principle alone. Individual works will involve a definite selection or emphasis, but a great work strains to be inclusive of possibility; even possibility it cannot directly embrace, it may still let open, maybe suggest indirectly. It does not promulgate a dogmatic answer but rather articulates the shape of the deepest questions and concerns. Thus also one work need not contradict or negate another. The word "tolerance" (from "*tollo*" meaning to carry) indicates this willingness to bear all; nothing need be alien to it; rather the alien may be generously welcomed. True, tolerance can become frivolous in the dandy indulgence of the aesthete, or in the search for the merely shocking. Like the cult of novelty this vacuous tolerance soon stales into blankness. This explains why, at the opposite extreme, protest art, which is narrowly partisan, fails to remain fresh long but seres and yellows like the newspaper.

This tolerance evidences a vigilance to individuality as a thereness recalcitrant to complete encapsulation by the abstract logical universal. The general concept isolates a particular happening, say, of jealousy, but does not dwell on this particular happening as particular. It defines an example of jealousy as *one of a kind* and fits it into relation with other happenings of the same kind. From features common to all instances of the same kind, it generates a general concept to cover, hence to classify all examples of the same kind. The aesthetic mind is struck by the *that* rather than the *what* of a particular *thisness*. There is an otherness to the "this" that resists encapsulation in the abstract generality of the logical concept.

The jealousy is Othello's. To name the intimacy of its particularity, in its very inward thisness, we need something other than logical classification by abstract concept. Thus, in the work *Othello*, we meet something that stands on its own, something *sui generis*. From the point of view of generalities *Othello* deals with realities that are as common as dirt, yet it makes of them something completely its own, something not to be repeated. The work is tied to a unique image, and its tolerance of otherness respects this tie. It does not abstract from individualized difference, is not descriptive of generalized events, but is expressive of a particularity in its richness. It remains intimate with the happening in its textured aesthetic concreteness, nor does it seek to reduce its otherness.

Does this tolerance leave us with an aggregate of pointillistic particulars? Not necessarily. For tolerance is again evident in that art's *universalizing* power has been noted as often as its individualizing concern. Though Aristotle formulated the law of contradiction, and thus the intolerance of opposition marking logical universality, he also suggested an other universality in his famous words: poetry is more philosophical than history. Poetry discloses a universal import unencumbered by irrelevancy, while history is cluttered with contingency. History is sometimes an aborted effort to be intelligible, what Joyce called "a nightmare" from which he wanted to wake, what Eliot spoke of as an "immense panorama of futility and anarchy," what Hegel termed a "Schlachtbank." Time craves transfiguration.

By poetic universality is not here meant a controlling abstraction that is superimposed on thereness by instrumental rationality; it is emergent for the aesthetic as patiently mindful of the otherness of the concrete "this." If we look at a great painting, say, we see a particular "this," but we do not just stutter "this," "this," "this"—as if it were blank being and nothing more. In letting it be, we come to see more than indifferent presence. The more we dwell with it, the more mind is arrested, the more the "this" shimmers with an always other meaning. The painting is a rich "this," and as a double image it does two things, seemingly opposed: it gathers our gaze, concentrates our mindfulness; but when we are caught up in its frame, it radiates beyond as a beckoning to more. It is not an impoverished particular but a particular cosmos. Its universality precisely springs from its being just such an individual universe, full with a compacted meaning we cannot fix to this or that univocal meaning or set of class concepts. Something there is still not encapsulated. This compacted fullness chastens the logical impulse to analyze and abstract. It also compels us to ponder a universality other than the merely abstract, what Vico called "an imaginative universal," or an aesthetic embodiment of what Hegel termed the "concrete universal."

I am saying then that aesthetic tolerance, anchored in the particular artwork, metaxologically mediates a sense of being in its recalcitrant, inexhaustible otherness. The dynamic power of being comes to form in a particular work, and collects itself into an intermediate whole with more than individual significance. Or rather: the individual is not negated here, but its fullest meaning extends beyond closed individuality. The work as an aesthetic "this" both rests in itself yet radiates beyond itself (those who break open the frame want to stress the latter aspect, against a self-enclosed, smug aestheticism). Unlike Leibniz' monad, it is not windowless; but like the monad, it is an individual that in its intermediate being reflects the universe of otherness from its particular point of view. An imaginative cosmos shows forth a poetic universal in the Greek sense of *poiesis*: a coming into being, a coming to emergence in a work that stands there and embodies appearing mind. For instance, Rembrandt's great self-portraits show the aesthetic this-ness of an individual face. But this is no univocal identity but a pluralized, polyvocal presence. It is both a completely particularized presence and yet an other, universal face of suffering sympathy—a forgiveness that will not judge but by which we sense ourselves as judged.

The call of the community of being can itself be embodied in the pluralized identity of the ontologically rich individual. Art's tolerance of otherness is born in imagination's free play that opens up the space of the possible wherein we identify with the different, see with the many eyes of others, including suffering others. When Hegel called the artwork a "thousand-eyed Argus," he implied this concretion of plurality in the particular work. And when Aristotle defined mind (*nous poietikos*) as the power to become all things, he offerd us a way to think of the great artist's largess of imaginative mind. We might see the grand style as instancing this unified yet polyvocal tolerance, as incarnating an aesthetic version of what the Stoics called "*sumpatheia ton holon*." An artist in the grand style forces nothing of himself on his audience. As with Shakespeare, the creator is content to vanish into his creation. His voice is the community of the voices of otherness. The promise of plurivocity is realized in an aesthetic communivocity.

Thus great drama may make the whole of humanity its possible theme, including the contradictoriness inherent in being human. In the very unity of our being we are often opposition itself, but poetic universality embraces more than the abstract logical universal in embracing the human in the intermediated wholeness of its sometimes divided, contradictory being. Its yes is to the contrary, plurivocal fullness of concrete being and not to the logical, univocal consistency of abstract thought. In logic there are fallacies but negligible comedy; in art we have the cruel tolerance of the comic, its explosive yes to being, spanning scorn of the ridiculous and sympathetic derision of stupidity. The tragic, too, has its torn tolerance: compassion for the failure of greatness.

What I am calling poetic universality is beyond the dualistic opposition of univocal individuality and abstract universality, beyond the dualistic opposition of self-contained inwardness and estranging otherness that we found in inadequate views of imitation and creativity. It is also at odds with the unanchored selfhood and the impoverished sense of otherness that serves as the spur to its pretense of originality. As soliciting an emergent mindfulness, tolerant of otherness, it points us again to being aesthetic as itself the *poiesis* of being, which is neither the work of inwardness nor externality: in the middle, it is being itself that flowers in being aesthetic, that is, in the sensuous show of the overdetermined power of being given to us in the rich appearing of its thereness. The fundamental issue, as we now see it, is not at all the flowering of this power in the self, but the proper rerooting of this flowering in a recharged sense of being's otherness.

This rerooting requires renewed mindfulness of metaxological being. This reminds us that real creative power is the generosity of being. What ontological deracination yields is the void energy that fuels our talk about the end of philosophy, the death of art, the death of God. These "deaths" are related to the *Entzauberung der Welt* that some think is the destiny of modernity. Art must be reluctant to acquiesce in this supposed fate which, if welcomed, would signal its own slow suicide. Yet it too has sometimes fallen under the spell of disenchantment's evil eye. One is reminded of Kafka's Hunger Artist who draws attention to his own negative novelty by sterilely subsisting on a diet of nothing. The Hunger Artist takes no food from the other, but in fact he is absolutely dependent on the *notice* of others; when this notice is withdrawn, his hollow self-sufficiency becomes evident, and he wastes away. Faced with the deadened world, art first looses its disenchantment on otherness as transcendent and seeks refuge in inwardness. But when inwardness is hostile to otherness and ontologically ungrounded, it must inevitably become disenchanted with even itself and succumb to the neutralization of all being, the disenchantment of the whole in which art becomes antiart. As long as the worm of nihilism battens on its power, art will find itself debilitated in the struggle to regain a sense of otherness in its ultimacy. I now turn to being religious where we are forced to ponder just the mythic mindfulness of such ultimacy.

BEING AT A LOSS:

ON PHILOSOPHY AND THE TRAGIC

From *Perplexity and Ultimacy*

HOWL, HOWL, HOWL, HOWL! . . .

A violently reiterated Howl is not the usual way to initiate a philosophical meditation. Neither Aristotle's list of categories nor Kant's table makes mention of any Howl. Hegel's *Science of Logic* contains no concept corresponding to Howl. There is no Platonic *eidos* of Howl. Indeed the Howl seems to shout down, shout against all categories, drowning out the civilities of reason in its brute explosiveness. Perhaps we might think of the cynics, the dog-philosophers as not silencing the Howl. But Hegel saw nothing much in Diogenes, bastard offspring of Socrates. Nor did he take much notice of Diogenes' self-description: the watchdog of Zeus. And many philosophers are much more Hegelian than they realize, or care to know. We will shrug it off. With sweet reason on our side, we will say: Why have a bad conscience in turning from the Howl? Where can Howling find its place in the ideal speech situation? This Howl is no voice in the grand "conversation of mankind." The rest is philosophical silence.

Yet this Howl is different. A silence that merely shrugs it off betrays philosophy. For this Howl breaks forth as one of the great conceptless voices in the "conversation of mankind." Perhaps it would be better to say the Howl is a "transconceptual voice." Thus, we keep alive this ambiguity: Is the Howl other than conceptual, being empty of concepts, or is it more than every concept, hence full of a challenge philosophy must strain to think? For this reiterated Howl is the agonized voice of Lear, coming on stage with the dead body of Cordelia in his arms.

> Howl, howl, howl, howl! O, you are men of stones:
> Had I your tongues and eyes, I'd use them so
> That heaven's vault should crack. She's gone for ever.
> I know when one is dead and when one lives;
> She's dead as earth. (*King Lear* V, iii, 259–63)

165

The philosopher has no category of Howl. Who then are the men of stones? Is Spinoza a man of stones in describing his philosophical desire thus: Not to laugh, not to weep, not to detest, but only to understand? Is this what philosophy will do? Give us eyes and tongues, but eyes and tongues that are stones? We cannot, we will not speak about this Howl. We will be silent about heaven. Will we, like Anaxagoras, turn the sun into a god of stone? How then will we look on life and death? As if philosophical reason had nothing to do with life or death? And where then are our categories for that simple phrase that assaults the disarrayed mind: "For Ever"?

Lear's Howl is a transconceptual voice in the "conversation of mankind" that not only ruptures all logical systems but also threatens the very basis of that civilized conversation. It threatens, not because it will not hear the other, but rather from excess of hearing, from excess of exposure to an otherness that destroys every human self-sufficiency. Can philosophy listen to this Howl and not risk the ruin of thinking? For when one hears that Howl a crushing night descends wherein the mind is threatened with blacking out or going blank. The mind shudders, as if a dark abyss had opened and swallowed all sense. Rational mind undergoes a liquefaction in which all intelligibility seem to be reclaimed by a malign formlessness. There is anguish before this Howl.

The Howl is an outcry. It reminds us of the great outcry of Dostoevski, in the howl of Ivan Karamazov, against the suffering of innocent children. What is the source of this outcry? Why listen to it? Thinking too much on it—will it not make us mad? Like Lear's Howl, it issues forth from a depth of our exposed being that seems to elude conceptual encapsulation. The Psalm says it: *De profundis ad te Domine clamavi.* But what are those depths, what cries out from those depths? The Howl as an outcry is a cry from the heart. But what is a cry from the heart? What otherness has stirred the heart to this outcry? Must philosophy default here? Can there be a systematic science of such cries? Would not a systematic pretense be nonsense, a folly of logic? Such a cry, such an outcry, is elemental. If logic would that it were not heard, if it tried to stifle the outcry, would not logic prove itself to be metaphysical madness? Does the outcry need tragic saying? Can tragic art alone make us hear this Howl?

Our listening to the agony of Lear's outcry is not yet over. Have the men of stones the tongues and eyes for this savage saying:

> And my poor fool is hanged: no, no, no, life?
> Why should a dog, a horse, a rat, have life,
> And thou no breath at all? Thou'lt come no more,
> Never, never, never, never, never. (*King Lear* V, iii, 307–10)

This Never is an absolutely crushing word. Perhaps never has the word "Never" been uttered as crushingly as by Lear. Can philosophical dialectics take us into this Never, beyond this Never? Can the universal of logic or Hegel's world-history ever unharden the irrevocability of Lear's savage, reiterated Never? What can philosophy ever tell Lear, what alleviation give him in his elemental grief? What consolation could the Platonic *eidos*, or Husserl's *strenge Wissenschaft* ever offer? What, to reverse hearer and listener, does the conceptless voice of tragedy tell philosophy? What can we philosophers hear in this Howl, in this For Ever, in this Never? In their metaphysical horror is there incitement to think about essential and unavoidable enigmas—tragic enigmas forcing philosophy to its own extremes where its concepts begin to break down? Can philosophical mind break through to a deeper metaphysical thinking even in this breakdown?

I step back from the edge to approach these questions thus. First I will speak of philosophy and the tragic, most especially in relation to Plato, considered by many, Nietzsche not least, to be the archenemy of tragedy. I will say that this is too simplistic: philosophy has a complex, plurivocal identity, not reducible to scientific cognition, though not exclusive of rational cognition. Philosophy can be especially attentive to certain fundamental tensions between determinate knowing and significant indeterminacies of being beyond encapsulation in specific concepts. Subsequently, I will reflect on such tensions in relation to Lear's Never and the related notions it calls forth.

I am not primarily interested in tragedy as a problem in aesthetics. Modern aesthetics tends to be too much in the grip of an aestheticism that compartmentalizes art: in its excessive insistence that art is art, that art is for art's sake, that art is resistant to any intrusion from what is other to art, post-Kantian aesthetics ends up divorcing art from its origin in the fundamental creative and tragic powers of human existence. In elevating art into a false self-sufficiency, it ends up diminishing art's metaphysical power. This power interests me. I ask: What is it about *being* that is revealed by the tragic? More specifically, what does it mean to be in the guise of *being at a loss*? Tragedy reveals one of the ultimate forms of being at a loss. In a tragic situation we were faced with boundaries from which there is no escape. We are backed against a wall, as it were. We are pushed without easy recourse into a dead end of being. How we are, and what we do in this cut de sac, is revealing of what it is to be.

If my interest is metaphysical, I immediately add that metaphysics here escapes the stock Heideggerian charge of "metaphysics of presence." As is well known, Heideggerians accuse all of metaphysics, from Plato to Nietzsche, of being some form of the "metaphysics of presence." I say: If metaphysics can meditate on the tragic in the guise of being at a loss, then it-is ridiculous to see all this as "metaphysics of presence." Being at a loss shows tragic experience as already deconstructing the "metaphysics of presence." True, there is a philosophical tendency that would immediately want to convert being at a loss into some totally rational picture, see the loss as a mere prelude to a positive founding, a being refound, a new foundation, and so on.

I believe metaphysical reflection is capable of a more complex response. Being at a loss is not a mere absence, relative to which a dialectical interplay can be quickly initiated. Here an absence does not dialectically provoke its contrary presence, such that tragedy would be the play of absence and presence, with the presence more clearly grasped by the philosopher than by the tragic artist or the person undergoing the tragic. This again is too simple. Certain exposures to being at a loss seem to be unsurpassable in the direction of a positive finding that we can articulate on this side of going under into death. Or: a certain suffering knowing of being at a loss may itself be what is affirmative in tragic undergoing. Metaphysical meditation on that suffering knowing is solicited.

We begin to see the emergence of the crucial tension between philosophy and the tragic. Traditionally philosophy has presented itself as the quest for a rational account, indeed a rational account of being in the most comprehensive sense: a logos of the whole. The implicit presupposition of this entire quest is that being as a whole is ultimately intelligible. Should we think radically enough, should we take our logos, logic to the ultimate boundary, then being as a whole will reveal itself as available for intelligence, for reason. *To gar auto noein esti te kai einai*: to be and to think are one and the same. This utterance of Parmenides (frag. 3) seems to be the complete antipodes of Lear's Howl. Parmenides' saying is susceptible of a number of interpretations, but these are not the point here. The point is that philosophy seems driven by the conviction, should we say faith, that being is not ultimately tragic. True reason will never be at a loss; true reason will be the intelligent *finding* of the deep logical intelligibility that is inherent in the nature of things.

Philosophy does not deny that enigmatic and recalcitrant events do strike us, or that, to all appearances, we do experience being at a loss. But these are often seen as the ambiguous, perhaps duplicitous appearances that a more penetrating mindfulness will surpass. Parmenides says (frag. 6): the many wander like hordes that are double-headed, *dikranoi*: two headed, in two minds, at a loss what to think one way or the other. The many do not find being but are beings at a loss for logos—they cannot say what being means. Appearances appear tragic, but being in itself is not tragic. In being in itself there is no loss. Hence Parmenides' description of being (frag. 8)—a well-rounded sphere, neither more here nor less there, but homogeneous throughout, without gaps or ruptures. The description of beauty in itself in Plato's *Symposium* reiterates the apotheosis of such being without loss, beyond all lack. Time is the sphere of loss, for time is a perpetual perishing, time is decay, decrease, decease. Death is the ultimate loss of being, and the ultimate before which we experience being at a loss. Parmenidean pure being is deathless.

When philosophy sees itself as a complete rational finding, beyond being at a loss, it predominantly thinks of itself as a science. To be scientific is to be capable of giving a determinate account of things, a logos of a *tode ti*. Systematic science would be the apotheosis of never being at a loss. To every perplexity, every enigma, there would be a determinate response to be made. If philosophy were exclusively systematic science, it would ultimately be a systematic exclusion of the tragic. For in principle one should never be at a loss in systematic science. If one were radically at a loss, the suspicion would surface that the scientific claims for complete determinate intelligibility were questionable.

Suppose, by contrast, we think now of some great tragic heroes in relation to their *knowing*. Consider Oedipus' will to know: he refuses not to know the truth, but the truth was too much; in an excess of dark knowing, he must blind himself to continue. He may be personally guiltless, but his knowledge, self-knowledge, brings measureless suffering, not *eudaimonia*, as Socrates suggests knowing will bring. Consider Hamlet: he, too, is marked by a thirst for knowing that goes to the boundary of man's metaphysical predicaments; he knows and does not know that his father was murdered; he alone bears the burden of knowing/not knowing; he has to put an antic disposition on, use the mask of madness to deal with his wrenching situation; his knowing is not that the real is the rational *sub specie aeternitatis*; his is the cursed knowledge that "the time is out of joint." Where is the consolation in this knowing? His knowing essentially puts him at a loss what to believe as genuine, who to trust, what to do. All his knowledge brings is suffering. Yet both knowing and suffering are unavoidable.

Consider Lear again: the cushioned King has to become unsheltered to the extremities, stripped to his elemental humanity before the powerful elements, endure his passage through a madness more knowing than his regal sanity; and at the end there is the Howl and the Never that assault the calm of our philosophic faith in the basic intelligibility, indeed value of being. Lear's tragic knowing brings him to the condition of being utterly at a loss. The Howl says it all, namely, that Lear does not know what to say: the public communicability of discourse retracts before the horror, and all intelligible saying seems to founder. Tragedy brings a knowing that shatters every naive faith in the intelligibility and worth of being or saying. Is philosophical mind then at a loss? What can it think about such extremities of being at a loss?

No doubt about it, philosophy has a strong eros to overcome loss, not to be at a loss, to place reason where tragedy faces rupture. What then do we do with the devastation of losing, with being bewildered by loss? What does the philosopher do, for instance, with the erosion of being that time inexorably works? I say the philosopher because I want to underscore the singularity of the philosopher as a living thinker. A propensity of philosophers has been to displace reason's attention from the singularity of the philosopher to the putative universality of philosophy as such. The consolation of the logical universal usurps the idiocy of the singular as singular. Again I use the term "idiocy" in the Greek sense of *idios*: an intimacy of being at the edge of, if not outside, the system of public reality, an intimacy not indifferently available to anyone and everyone. (This idiocy will be important below in discussing the Never.) What of this idiocy of the particular philosopher as particular? The philosopher as a particular human being is washed away by the erosions of time. To be is to be bound to a process of genesis that not only brings into being but always brings about the demise of being. The erosion of the being of the particular, the loss of being for the particular is ontologically constitutive for every particular being. This cannot be denied.

Indeed I claim that we are marked as metaphysical beings, as well as tragic beings, only because this ontology of loss is intimately known by us. If we did not intimately know being at a loss, it is not clear we could fully raise the question of being in any other sense. Nor could we be characterized as beings who undergo or behold the tragic, or who bespeak the tragic in works of art and religion. Obviously the sense of the tragic is only possible in a human world; but it is not possible in a merely humanistic world, where what is radically other to the human is not given its proper due. Tragedy arises because we become mindful that there are rupturing others that inescapably disrupt, destroy any sense of ontological self-sufficiency that human beings might feel or claim on behalf of their own being. We are metaphysical beings in the measure that the tragic breaks through, in the measure that we know our being to be one that loses itself, that loses its way. We know that our way of being is unavoidably a way of loss. Being at a loss is a more deeply constitutive dimension to being human than might initially be suspected.

Wherever possible we try to stand our ground before being at a loss. Philosophy can be a mindfulness that tries to find its way in loss. It can be a finding of being in the losing of being, a mindfulness that thoughtfully tries to be at home with being in being at a loss. Here the identity of philosophy that emerges is other to its identity as systematic science. Losing, failure, breakdown, the eruption of the indeterminate are acknowledged as absolutely essential here. Logic offers no final answer with being at a loss. Nevertheless, one tries philosophically to speak of loss as essential, without reducing loss to the logical consolation of a conceptual essence.

So it would be very wrong to think that philosophy must always sim-plistically displace metaphysical concern from the rupture of loss towards the neutral logical universal. The situation has never been one of simple opposition or "either/or." In my remarks now to follow, with respect to the view that philosophy has no simple univocal identity, I will speak of Socrates and Plato, to a lesser extent Nietzsche and Hegel. Philosophy has a more complex plural identity which includes but is not exhausted by the will to systematic science. What is more than systematic science in philosophical mindfulness is related to the metaphysical meaning of being at a loss, and hence also to the tragic.

Thus, one way to read Plato is as a strongly Parmenidean thinker: the doubleheaded nature of the doxic many is not to be taken seriously, espe-cially if one has seen the circular self-sufficent plenitude of being in itself, absolute being without loss. Yet the doubleheadedness reappears in Platonic philosophy. Philosophy reduplicates a plurality that the Parmenidean ideal ostensibly leaves behind.

This is the tension. On the one hand, related to the Parmenidean ideal, we find a logicist concern with contradiction: contradiction is the doubleheadedness in thought that philosophy shuns. Hence, the allergy to equivocal language, double language that is potentially duplicitous. Logos will try to disarm or expose the duplicity of equivocity by formulating all questions of being in sheerly univocal terms: there is one meaning and one meaning only. But then, on the other hand, we must grant in Plato the articulation of *positive plurality* as constitutive of genuine philosophical dialogue. Nor is such dialogue just a smooth seamless exchange between a philosopher and others. It is born out of perplexity: someone is at a loss what to think and asks another for his views or response. The experience of being at a loss drives a philosophical dialogue, and needs the plurality of its constituent voices. Many voices, many heads are necessary to respond to the condition of being at a loss. Hence, the plurality of voices in difference or contradiction is not necessarily a merely negative thing. In response to being at a loss, plurivocity constitutively energizes the very dynamism of philosophical interplay and exchange.

But you will say: this is the negative dialectic that inevitably will subvert itself; the being at a loss drives beyond itself through the inherent momentum of logos as dialectically unfolding; the negativity of loss will negate itself and produce a positive finding. Thus, the faith in logos is preserved, and we always end up with a rational account beyond all loss. But if so, why do so many dialogues end in an impasse, an *aporia*: they end up at a loss. This is glaringly at odds with all those clichés of Plato as the "metaphysician of presence" par excellence, The dialogue drives logos to a new height of articulation, but also to a deeper acknowledgment of being

172 THE WILLIAM DESMOND READER

at a loss. Logos in *aporia*, logos at an impasse: these are constitutive for the Platonic sense of philosophical thinking. It is as if the wonder that is said to be the originating pathos of the philosopher reappears after he has done his best job in giving a determinate logos. The indeterminate perplexity *reappears*, wonder resurrects itself, in a different sense of being at a loss, now at the limit of logos iself (sic).

I find it peculiar that Aristotle is often honored as the philosopher of tragedy in the ancient world. His *philosophical practise* is antithetical to Plato's here. In a far more insistent way, Aristotle wants a determinate logos of a determinate somewhat, a *tode ti*. This is why he rejects the philosophical appeal to myth. This is why, when he reiterates Plato on wonder, one suspects that wonder has been dimmed into intellectual curiosity, the telos of which is not a deepening of metaphysical astonishment, but the dispelling of curiosity in a determinate answer to a determinate question. Aristotle significantly invokes geometry when claiming that the acquisition of knowledge issues in a *reversal* of wonder (see Meta., I, 983a15–25). (I will remark below on "geometry" and tragedy. It is significant that Husserl links philosophy and geometry, not only in *Ideas*, but even in the *Crisis*. He is only one of many sons of Aristotle respecting "geometry.") If Platonic wonder can be deepened but not dispelled, this is because being at a loss can be bespoken but never eradicated. Why? Because man as metaphysical is an *indeterminate question* to which no determinate answer will ever reply or correspond. If there is to be an answer, it must somehow include the truth of indeterminacy itself.

The greatness of being at a loss, of running into an *aporia*, is precisely its reminder that just this indeterminate openness is ontologically constitutive of the human being. A totally determinate science, in claiming to give a complete explanation, would actually be a falsification of this ontological truth of the being of the human. Its very success would be its most radical failure. All we have to do is become self-conscious of this, and the force of being at a loss reinserts itself into philosophical discourse again. This is always happening in philosophy. No sooner does it make some claim to knowing, but there begins the process of deconstructing the completeness or adequacy of this claim. In finding its way, philosophy immediately initiates a way of losing that thenceforth subverts its own provisional peace. Philosophical mind's true and enduring condition is one of metaphysical insomnia.

The antiphilosophical philosophy of deconstruction does some of its main business in bringing philosophy to *aporia*: making philosophy acknowledge that it, too, in the end, is brought to loss; that thought is being at a loss which sometimes hides its own loss in dialectical rationalizations. Of course, there is some truth in this. But I say: philosophy *has already* always

been at this point: always at a loss. This is the very perplexity that generates thought, that, in turn, is always deconstructing itself. This, too, reflects
the skeptical principle in all genuine thinking. Those least infected by the
skeptical principle are the minnows of the philosophical tradition. Hence,
deconstruction fishes best with the small fry of thinking, not the sharks.
To reduce Plato's sense of logos and *aporia* to the metaphysics of presence
is to draw in a net empty of Plato the philosophical shark. As a developed
philosophical strategy, skepticism is nothing but mind's alertness to its own
being at a loss before perplexities it finds intractible. Philosophical mind
comes to know itself in its own breakdown. It can also break through into
thought beyond breakdown. Skepticism, like deconstruction, tends to give
us breakdown without breakthrough.

When logos runs up against an *aporia*, different responses are possible. One might deny that the *aporia* is really an *aporia*, and redefine it
as a merely temporary block on reason; reason will eventually find a way
beyond, and in the end there will be no beyond; there will be no other to
reason. This is one typical philosophical strategy: there will be no others
to philosophy, since all reason has to do is continue, and the other will
no longer be other, because it will be conceptualized, will be thought. The
other of thought, in being thought, will be thought once again, and so it
will not be the other of thought. We end up back with Parmenides. And
so philosophy will meet itself again at the end of the road. The god of this
philosophy cannot include the tragic, because the ultimate picture will be
thought simply thinking itself; there will be no loss, no self-loss; all will be
embraced in the circle of self-thinking thought.

Another response is silence. The rest is silence, it says at the end of
Hamlet. Philosophers have known the power of silence. I name but two:
the younger Wittgenstein in the *Tractatus*; logic falls silent in the face of
the mystical; Aquinas at the end of his life when he refused to continue to
write and said of his work, "It seems to me as so much straw." Being philosophically at a loss and silence are intertwined. But silence, like being, like
being at a loss, can be "said" in many ways. There is the empty silence of
meaninglessness. There is the silence of an acknowledging, full of reverent
respect before the other. There is a silence of despair. There is a silence of
peace beyond measure. There is a tragic silence: this is a transconceptual
silence that rends the silence, all silences, the conceptless silence of Lear's
Howl.

It seems to me that the great systems of philosophy are encircled by a
silence that they do not, perhaps cannot name. The silence that circles the
system, the philosopher, turns his speech of clear concepts into the chiaroscuro of the tragic. But the philosopher as idiot can be haunted by this
silence; this can make him more than systematic scientist. The unsaid haunts

all saying; but some saying carries the silence of the unsaid in itself. This is most evident when the philosopher is also a poet. Plato and Nietzsche are the two great examples. Their thought is plurivocal; thinking is not the monologue of *noesis noeseos*, or Hegel's self-thinking Idea.

Thus tragedy raises the question of philosophical silence in philosophy's very lucid speech itself. We probe the philosopher when we ask about his silence: What does his speech avoid, what does his speech respect, what does his speech ignore, what does his speech dread to say? All such questions call for an awareness of the different modalities of philosophical silence. Consider Spinoza's motto *Caute!* his one word of command, or perhaps warning. Who is he commanding or warning? Of what is he afraid? What then does the motto mean? Many possible things, all beyond univocal logos. The tragic itself is always beyond univocal logic.

One thing we do not want at the limit of tragedy is the chatter of conceptual analysis that thinks it has the measure of an enigma when it makes a verbal distinction. At the opposite extreme to this analytical evasion, there is the possibility I develop in *Philosophy and Its Others*: not only thought trying to think its other; but thought trying to sing its other. To say how the Howl turns into song is too large a theme here, though I will offer a few hints at the end.

I return to Plato as a philosopher who thought in the shadow of the tragic. I do not simply mean the shadow of Greek tragedy, though this is true. He was concerned especially with tragedy as a religious drama in which appears the inscrutable will of the gods, even in the mask of their resistance to reason. The wrath of the god that mocks the pretensions of human reason was something deeply disturbing to the implicit faith of philosophy, namely that being, at its deepest and most ultimate, is intelligible. God is not envious is the refrain in the *Timaeus*, a refrain reiterated by Aristotle, by Aquinas, and significantly by Hegel himself. Hegel says it because he holds God to be self-disclosive: there will be no enigma in the ultimate which resists the approach of reason; God is simply reason, and the nature of reason is to manifest itself, reveal itself, make itself available to the philosophical mind. Likewise Plato was concerned to purify the gods of the masks of irrationality they seemed to wear in tragedy.

For the suffering in ancient tragedy has a sacred modulation; what is at stake is sacred suffering, and the tragic hero is not out of the ambit of the sacrificial victim of the gods. If one's basic faith is that being is transparently intelligible to mind, this sacred violence of the holy provokes shudders. Where is the *episteme* of this sacred violence? If the gods are infected with such an otherness to reason, an otherness violating to reason, we seem to peer into an ultimate arbitrariness in the nature of things. At bottom being does not appear completely intelligible to the tragic vision.

Moreover, there was the proximate tragedy of Socrates. The man who seems most rational meets a death that seems least reasonable, with respect to both justice and truth. Platonic philosophizing sought to penetrate Socrates' tragedy to the intelligibility, the life of reason at work in this philosophical life, in the loss of this life in a senseless death. If the life of reason cannot be found to be at work in this life here and now, then for Plato the loss is also the loss of the here and now. The work of reason will be said to transcend this life. And as the work of reason transcends this life, so in fact must it transcend this death. Again we see the desire to save philosophy's faith in intelligibility. The problem is that, if we anticipate ultimate reason and justice beyond this life and death, we then return, in some form, to the question of the ultimate light or darkness of the gods. Plato knew this too; else he would not have Socrates tell the myth of Er.

Plato wants to see the light. Nietzsche did not see this light. At the bottom of things he saw darkness. At its deepest the nature of things is such as to give rise to horror; in itself being is not intelligible. Still reflecting Schopenhauer, the bottom of things is a dark origin, in Nietzsche's case, a Dionysian origin that erupts and is given shape in the tragic drama, but which in itself exceeds all form, for it is the forming power which in itself is formless. That is, the ground of being for Nietzsche, what he calls das *Ureine* in the *Birth of Tragedy*, is not intelligible in itself. Intelligibility is a consoling construction of concepts that we and philosophers like Socrates create as a shield from too violent an encounter with the Dioysian will to power behind it all.

A major point here is: Schopenhauer says the Will is on *the other side* of the principle of sufficient reason; so in a sense there is no sufficient reason for the ultimate Will. Nietzsche runs swiftly with this insight in relation to philosophy and the tragic: the ultimate origin is beyond the principle of sufficient reason; and hence to the extent that philosophy is contained by this principle, it cannot properly think the tragic. There is a suffering that comes through in the tragic that exceeds the ministration of the principle of sufficient reason. In face of this suffering we need art more fundamentally than philosophy.

Who, for Nietzsche, embodies the principle of sufficient reason? Socrates, of course. Socrates wants to disarm the a-rationality of the tragic, neutralize in universals the sacred suffering that springs from the dark Dionysian origin and that the tragic drama makes present, that tragic drama celebrates. Philosophy fakes its own being at a loss, disguising its conceptual consolations as "truth." Tragedy looks into this fearful darkness, yet it bespeaks this darkness with a certain celebrating joy. This joy is our brief salvation from despair and meaningless suffering. It is our encounter with death and our unreserved yes to being, despite the destruction and the terrible. Deep down life is inexpressibly joyful: this is what the tragic says to Nietzsche. Philosophy is treasonous to this suffering and this joy; it turns away from both towards the abstraction and the concept; Socrates offers in dialectics his therapy for the darkness of life. For Nietzsche this is the epitome of philosophy's impotence, its ineptitude before the tragic.

This is not Nietzsche's last word about philosophy and the tragic. If this is Nietzsche's judgment on traditional philosophy, it is not his judgment on the promise of philosophy. He himself clearly wanted to be the first Dionysian philosopher, the first philosopher of the tragic, the first tragic philosopher. Philosophy in the tragic age of the Greeks was already marked by this promise, only to be aborted, nipped in the bud by Socrates and Plato. But even Socrates was a masked Dionysian: he, too, suffered from life; he, too, wanted a saying of being that would enable the transfiguration of being, in a manner analogous to the transfiguration of life and death that the sacred suffering of the tragedy enacts. The antithesis of tragedy and philosophy is not an ultimate antithesis, though clearly the way to transcend this antithesis cannot lead us back to Socrates and Plato and their heirs—so Nietzsche thinks.

Once again the relation of philosophy and the tragic raises the question about the very identity of philosophy, and indeed, after Nietzsche, its future identity. Can philosophy honestly name the otherness of the tragic without disarming its horror or neutralizing its challenge by means of its conceptualizing appropriation? If philosophy can try to think the tragic, must it redefine its modes of thinking, such that it opens itself to what may resist its categories, perhaps ever cause their breakdown? Would not this also demand a rethinking of the relation of the poet and philosopher, and in a form that finds the Platonic view unsatisfactory? Or must we also be cautious with Plato here too? Is not Plato's philosophizing also a mask of the tragic poet?

Nietzsche's views force us to make a more general remark in line with earlier points about systematic science, namely: if the scientific view were completely applicable to the whole of being, there would be no room for the tragic. Scientific mind treats being as valueless in itself. The question of the worth of what is, the very worthiness of being, does not directly arise for it. This question points to a convergence of metaphysics (as asking about the meaning and truth of being) and ethics (as asking about the goodness of being). [In Nietzsche's case, metaphysics and ethics are subsumed into aesthetics.] The tragic exposes mind to a radical experience of being at a loss. Ingredient in this loss is the possible loss of the worth of being: the horrifying possibility is brought before us, not only that being lacks an ultimate intelligibility, but that at bottom it is worthless, it is valueless.

Tragic experience seems to suffer being as drained of any value. Being is, but is as nothing. Better not to be at all, perhaps: a saying Nietzsche repeated after Schopenhauer, who himself repeated the Greek Silenus, companion of Dionysus, and the figure to whom the drunken Alcibiades compares the enigmatic Socrates. Metaphysics tries to be mindful of such issues; science does not. Science is itself a mode of mind that devalues being, drains being of value: the being there of the world is taken for granted as a given fact; the being there of what is arouses no ontological astonishment, or metaphysical nausea, or aesthetic jubilation, or religious celebration, Scientism—in claiming that science will answer for the whole—is thus identical with nihilism: the assertion of the valuelessness of being. Nietzsche himself understood this, and blamed philosophy for being the remote source of this nihilistic scientism, which paradoxically is driven by hatred of the tragic, that is, epistemological dread of its suffering knowing. The paradox is that the scientistic impulse presents itself as beyond love and hate. In fact its "love of truth" hides a hatred of the tragic for its recalcitrance to conceptual encapsulation.

The silence of science returns philosophy to the saying of art. The metaphysical question does arise in art, and painfully in tragic art: a great hero comes to nothing, his being is shown to come to nothing. In this loss of being what then is the worth of being? What is worthy being when all being, even the greatest, seems inexorably to come to nothing? Science has nothing to say about such questions. There can never be a science of the tragic, and were the scientific mentality to try to impose its norms on the totality, the result would have to be a blindness to, a denial of, perhaps a repression of tragic experience. The irony here is that this repression embodies a metaphysical violence that has its own implicitly tragic dimension. We normally do not couple Spinoza and metaphysical violence, the noble Spinoza who in austere purity of mind philosophizes *sub specie aeternitatis*. Yet there is such violence in Spinoza's claim to treat human beings and their emotions like he would treat solids, planes, and circles. This sounds high-minded, since the philosopher seems willing to sacrifice the pettiness of his restricted ego purely for disinterested truth. But such a putative will to truth is potentially a violent repression of the truth of the tragic. There is no geometry of the tragic. When philosophy thinks it is the geometry of the tragic, this is tragic for philosophy.

I think Plato knew this. Over the entrance to his Academy is said to have hung the saying: Let no one enter who has not studied geometry! Yes, but this does not say, *only* geometry; nor that once having entered, all modes of mindfulness will be reduced to geometry. Again I reiterate that the philosopher's self-identity can be forged in a deep awareness of being at a loss. This is relevant here. A crucial place where the limits of logos come up in Plato's dialogues is the *Phaedo*. Socrates is in prison on the eve of death. He accepts that there is no escape, no way out for him. Is this death tragic? Is the philosopher at a loss in the face of it? Will geometry help one through the portal of dying? Where is the geometry of death?

I am within traditional respectability in raising the issue of philosophy and the tragic here. Certainly Hegel, even panlogist Hegel, thought of Socrates' death in tragic terms. Dialectical reason is at work even in tragic death. For Hegel there is a clash of two justified principles or powers. Socrates embodies the new principle of subjectivity: inward thought makes claim to absoluteness over against the social substance. Against this thinking stands the social substance itself, whose unreflective ethical *Sittlichkeit* was the fundamental ethical embodiment of the people's *Geist* at its most ultimate—religiously and aesthetically, as well as ethically. Both those powers have their justification, but the emergence of the first from the second produces an inevitable clash between the two and the downfall of both. The unreflective ethical *Sittlichkeit* was at a loss what to do with Socrates as embodying the radical freedom of thought; Socrates himself was at a loss in asking ethical questions in a form to which traditional *Sittlichkeit* could not answer. This double being at a loss necessitates for Hegel the loss of both as distinct opposites and their falling to the ground. Socrates was guilty for Hegel; but Athens itself was infected with the spirit it condemned in Socrates and so in this sense was condemning itself. It was already unknowingly in the spiral of dissolution that the Socratic spirit represented—the dissolving powers of thought before which nothing seems to stand. Thinking brings us a loss of unreflective tradition, shows what is hitherto accepted and lived as coming to nothing.

Hegel's view is very illuminating in its dialectical sense of the togetherness of opposites. But I am not interested in displacing the tragic issue onto a neutral universal, not interested in displacing the issue from the particular philosopher to the stage of world-history or to philosophy as systematic science. Ultimately, for Hegel, the particularity of Socrates and his death is *world-historically redeemed* as preparing a more thoroughgoing victory for reason in history. Hegel displays the philosopher's faith in the final ascendency of rational intelligibility. Universal spirit as world-historical is the victor. But what of the tragedy of Socrates as *this* philosopher? What redeems the death of this particular self as idiot?

Plato is deeper here and more revealing for our purposes. He presents Socrates as a particular human thinker. Socrates explicitly says in the Apology (32a) that to survive as a philosopher it was necessary for him to live as an idiot (*idioteuein*). He would have been dead earlier if he had not lived as an idiot. Thus he outlived "the sects and packs of great ones that ebb and flow by the moon," as Lear—about to be imprisoned and become "God's spy"—calls the factions of feverish politics, the world-historical mighty. Plato's Socrates does not give us systematic science or a world-historical account in exoneration of his philosophy, his life. We are given an apology for an *individual life*. Though that life involved the search for the universal, the life itself was the mindful existing of a *this*. Only a *this* can apologize; a universal does not apologize, nor does it live the inviolable inwardness of an ethical life. This latter is part of Socrates' tragedy. There is no way to make sense of the enigma of Socrates if we think that his life was exhausted by a logicist obsession with the ideality of universal definition. One does not live or die for such a definition. The ideal sought must be different to a definition encapsulated in any logical category.

Socrates' death makes us reconsider the enigma of his life as philosophical. We begin to sense that there was something ineradicably *Once* about this life. Death revealed to us, to Plato, the Once of this life, in confronting us with its Never: once Socrates was but now never more. Why was Plato too sick to attend the dying Socrates? What was this sickness before death? Is there any "geometry" to heal it? Can we imagine Plato howling: Why should a rat, a horse, a dog have life, and Socrates no life at all? Will Socrates ever come again? The answer is: Never, never, never! Hegel will say to this: No, no, no! Socrates will always come again. But he will not come as *this* Socrates, but as universal thought. But Plato knew: that is not Socrates. It is Socrates as a this that concerns us; it is Socrates as a this that apologizes for philosophy; it is not the universal using Socrates as an instrument that apologizes; it is not the Socratic spirit. Socrates says: I, I, I, and the I is ineradicably singular, irreplaceable. There was only one Socrates, one and one only, even though this unique singular claims to speak on behalf of the universal.

It is for this I, not for philosophy as such, that we cry at the end of the *Phaedo*. At the end, we weep for an *other*; it is the death of the *other*, Socrates, the beloved other that had his friends and Plato at a loss. (Below we will see that it is the death of the beloved other, Cordelia, that pushes Lear to the most extreme loss.) The tragic issue is not just concern with my death a la Heidegger, but with the death of the other—Marcel and Levinas would agree. But perhaps the deepest moment in the *Phaedo* is when Socrates covers his face after taking the poison, and his body began to mortify, petrify with the advancing poison, as if becoming stone. The universal has no face; the universal Socratic spirit has no eyes wherein terror or fear or exhaltation or consent might appear. But Socrates as idiot, as an irreplaceable this, has a face, has eyes.

Why must those eyes be veiled? What was in those eyes of the dying Socrates? Composure? Terror? Did Socrates crack in the face of the Never, all his previous arguments about immortality notwithstanding? Did the impersonal universal lose its power in this final moment? Or do the eyes have to be covered up because the eyes reveal the absolute singularity of the person, the absolute particularity of the philosopher? The death of the singular philosopher, the veiling of the eyes in the final moment, is completely enigmatic to philosophy as systematic science. There are no concepts within any system that can tell us about those eyes looking on death, looking out of death, on life.

The I as idiotic is in the eye in a manner that is evident nowhere else. The idiocy of the I is its ontological intimacy, and this intimacy of being appears in the eye. In the face of death, the eye is the place where the face may manifest the person's yes or no to being, to death, to the Never, to the Once—if indeed this yes or no come to manifestation at all. Socrates' eyes are covered because there is no public universal that can encapsulate what might have appeared in them. You might say: terror appeared, and then imply that terror is public; we all share terror; terror before death is universal. True. But this is beside the point in relation to the intimacy of the eyes, their idiocy from the point of view of the universal, its stony eyes.

Consider how, regardless entirely of death, we find it extremely difficult to hold a person's eyes; there is a dangerous ambiguity about eye to eye contact. How much more powerful is the dangerous ambiguity when the living survivor is making contact with the eye of the dying one. What passes from eye to eye, what metaphysical terror is there in this communication, what metaphysical consent? What passes between the eyes is an intimacy of being which no impersonal universal can ever bespeak. This is why Plato, the poet-philosopher, gives us an image here, not an impersonal universal. The manner in which Plato covers the eyes is a stroke of philosophical genius. There is nothing to compare to it in all philosophical literature. Plato says nothing; but the writing of this silent gesture before death, witnesses what cannot be said.

I note here how visitors to Nietzsche after his breakdown frequently commented on his eyes. The visitors seemed to see in Nietzsche's eyes a *knowing beyond sanity*, that invariably shook them in a brief disruptive revelation. The terrible eyes struck them in every sense, as if the dead eyes, the mad eyes were the eyes of tragic wisdom; and then just as quickly the veil would be redrawn and the vacant face of idiocy would look out at them. I note, too, the prominence of the theme of eyes in King Lear: sight and blindness, "reason in madness." We recoil at the horror of Gloucester's plucked eyes, empty sockets like Oedipus' gouged eyes—gouged with the malignant cry, "Out vile jelly where is thy lustre now?" Is this all that the eyes and the ontological intimacy of the I are: vile jelly? Were Socrates' eyes, Nietzsche's eyes just vile jelly—where is their lustre now?

Lear advises Gloucester: "Get thee glass eyes." Gloucester already knows: "I have no way and therefore want no eyes; I stumbled when I saw" (*King Lear* IV, i, 18–19). Death opens the eyes of weeping. Weeping eyes cannot be understood in terms of Sartre's Look; the actuality of weeping is totally inexplicable in Sartre's reduction of the promise of the eye to the Look. The Look is the apotheosis of the eyes of stones, the Gorgon's eyes that turn to stone. But stones do not weep. Nor does "geometry." Only flesh weeps. Only flesh knows the tragic.

By contrast with Hegel's *Aufhebung* of Socrates' particularity into the world-historical universal, Plato offers us the singularity of an apology, even though the life apologized for may include the search for a universal more than personal. The philosopher is often between these extremes, tempted to sacrifice the first to the second. The artist is also between these extremes, but his temptation is perhaps the reverse, the sacrifice of the promise of the universal for the singular. Both need each other to allow the epiphany of universality in singularity, as well as a nonreductive acknowledgment of the singular as singular: to name the singular without reduction, and to grant the universal without dessication. In trying to find the middle, the lure of the extremes will be differently modulated by the artist and the philosopher.

If Plato does not offer a Hegelian *Aufhebung*, this does not mean we lose all faith in logos. Death is the place/noplace where the philosopher's extreme being at a loss is manifest. In the thought of death we try to think what cannot be thought, for to think the thought of one's death is to think oneself as being. Logically, we are caught in an *aporia*. Existentially, we are faced with the temptation to give up on logos. Hence, it is here that we find Socrates' warning in the *Phaedo* against misology. This is extremely significant. I see it as Plato's/Socrates' gesture that philosophical logos must not simply give up before the ultimate experience of loss. Being at a loss before the loss of being—this is impending death. The philosopher's response cannot be a question of conceptual chatter continuing. What does one do at this point, if anything? What can one say?

Socrates' gesture of philosophical *faith* is to continue talking. I stress that the talking is not logically univocal but irreducibly plurivocal. Philosophical speaking has more than one mode, more than the argumentative statement of thesis and evidence. Apart from the significant fact that the Platonic dialogue itself is more than a logicist monologue, within this dialogue Socrates suggests the possible need of philosophical song or music. He himself blends with the swan of death, the songbird of Apollo. This again evidences a view of philosophy very different to systematic science. Song and system cannot collapse into one totality. It is true that Socrates offers different "logical" arguments with regard to immortality. But these are logically easy to trouble, as Socrates himself grants. On being logically troubled, and in the face of the consternation of his interlocutors, Socrates goes so far as to compare his philosophical speech to incantations and charms. Finally, Socrates offers a myth.

Songs, charms, arguments, myths—different voices of a plurivocal philosopher. There is no one voice in the face of death, in the face of being. Why this plurality of different voices? Because Plato is a plurivocal philosopher, responding to the living/dying philosopher as a plurivocal this. Socrates was like a father to his friends who, bereft of him, would be as orphans the rest of their life (*Phaedo*, 116a). Nor can we forget the weeping of Xantippe. And then the silence—"best to die in silence," Socrates suggests (*Phaedo*, 117e)—and the masterful gesture of covering the eyes, as death creeps over the body. The covered eyes: Are they the eyes of death? Are they the extra eyes of posthumous mind (see below), mind looking on being from beyond the ultimate loss? Are they the eyes of a Never that crushes all hope of a beyond? Socrates is dead, dead as earth. Then the eyes *uncovered*: staring, fixed, immobilized, stones; their once vibrant presence extinguished, never to come, never; dead as earth.

This is not logic; this is not system; this is not the abstract universal. All of this is an image, a philosophical icon. At one level the image says: Philosophy must go on. But at another level it cautions: It can only go on if it is honest about loss, if it keeps before its thinking the image of death, the memory of the dead.

ART AND TRANSCENDENCE

From *Art, Origins, Otherness:*
Between Philosophy and Art

THE END OF ART: ASKING TOO MUCH, ASKING TOO LITTLE

The "end of art" puts Hegel immediately in mind, and his well-known proclamation: for us art, on the side of its highest destiny, is now a thing of the past. What exactly he means is still disputed. One reason the thesis is controversial, I think, is that in modernity art has been asked to bear a special burden different to other epochs. I will point to a paradoxical position: Too too much has been asked of art, with the result that too little, or almost nothing, is now being asked of art. And too little is now asked, because too much was asked—asked in the wrong way.

My title also echoes, while altering, another thinker's words for whom the end of art was important. My original here is Heidegger: the end of philosophy and the task of thinking. Heidegger claimed that the end of metaphysics is in cybernetics, and looked to another beginning in which the thinker would be in dialogue with the poet. The renewal of thinking is bound up with the continued life of art, in the figure of the poet. I find difficulties with Heidegger's claims about the end of metaphysics, and, as we say, ambiguities in the high place offered by him to art.

There seem to be a plurality of ends, or if you prefer, different "deaths" at stake: the end of art, the death of God, the end of philosophy. We are more familiar with the Hegelian claim of the end of art, and the Nietzschean death of God, but of late the end of philosophy has returned to haunt us. I say returned since, of course, the theme haunted Hegel's time and his aftermath. Our century is not original regarding this provocative theme. For instance, we might see Marx and Kierkegaard as claiming this end: Kierkegaard to make way for religious faith; Marx to clear the path for revolutionary praxis which also will pierce the heart of religion with another stake, the stake of dialectical subversion. It is significant that the death of one is followed or accompanied by the death of another, as if for one to continue the others must continue also, or for one to be reborn the

183

others must also come to life in a new way. Or perhaps each must be rooted in a shared milieu, rich enough in metaphysical and spiritual resources, to nourish the extreme demands each, at its best, makes of the human being. We now seem to lack such a milieu, and the wings of creative venturing which can be birthed there.

Heidegger's proclamation of the poet's task in the wake of the alleged completion of metaphysics can be seen to ask for a *being born again*: metaphysics may die into cybernetics, but thinking asks to be reborn beyond calculative mind, and in dialogue with the naming of the holy, said to be the poet's vocation. Heidegger's poet is not a post-Kantian aesthete, a specialist of aesthetic experience. The poet is sacerdotal. If the thinker thinks being, the poet names the holy. One might say: the poet serves to mediate the blessing of being; the thinker remains attentive to the communication of being. Heidegger sees himself as freeing thought from the prison-house of "theory," but his invocation of the poet as the namer of the holy places us back in the neighborhood of the religious festival, hence closer to the meaning resonating in the ancient word, "*theoria.*" Heidegger may be right to recall us to this different sense of thinking; but I find questionable the implication that the history of metaphysics is the stifling of this thinking. There is an unmistakable rupture between the premodern and the modern sense of "theory," which tells against any monolinear totalizing of the history of metaphysics.

My point takes shape: something *extraordinary* is being asked of the poet. He is to partner the thinker in one of the most ultimate of enterprises. Heidegger is not original in placing on the artist such a weight of metaphysical destiny. Nietzsche also makes a hyperbolic demand. The end of philosophy in the guise of Socratism might promise a new beginning: the higher artistry of tragic philosophizing. Nietzsche offers a radicalization and transposition of the metaphysical status Schopenhauer attributes to the artist, namely, redeeming us from the bondage to the futile wheel of will, releasing us into the freedom of contemplative, will-less knowing. And of course, the lineage of such ideas goes further back to Schelling's elevation of genius to metaphysical status. This elevation reflects, as well as consolidates, the apotheosis of the great artist in the Romantic reaction to Enlightenment scientism. It is important to makes sense of this apotheosis, not least because we still think in light of it, even though we have grown more acid with suspicion than was common in the youth of romanticism. In the form it has taken in post-Enlightenment modernity, this role of the artist is all but impossible to maintain. That is, the artist is to be the voice and exemplary manifestation of transcendence. Given the history of the last two centuries, I believe such a role is impossible to sustain outside of some religious representation of the meaning of transcendence. Cut off from this, the claim is not just impossible to sustain, but may produce deformations of the meaning of transcendence, and indeed a kind of violence of human self-transcendence against itself.

Not only is the relation of philosophy to art and religion in question; so also is the relation of the religious and artistic. This relation is deeply equivocal in post-Hegelian culture. That culture often either lacks or rejects the resources of Hegel's dialectical way to deal with this relation. I have argued elsewhere that because Hegel is not lacking a sense for this relation, he might offer better means than many of his successors to shed some light on the paradox I stated above: too much has been asked of art with the result that little or nothing is now asked of art. But Hegel also contributed to that paradox. Why? Because of equivocities in dialectic's relation to religious transcendence and art's otherness. Sometimes overtly, sometimes implicitly, post-Hegelian thought takes a stand in relation to these equivocities. But it is enmeshed in them too, since it exhibits a decidedly equivocal relation to the religious, and to transcendence in religious form. Very differently to Hegel, art is asked to bear the burden of transcendence but within a cultural ethos wherein reference to the energies of the religious remains either muted or transposed or stifled. Art does not die into the religious, there to be sublated; rather the religious "dies" and the nameless afterlife of its transposed transcendence is ambiguously resurrected in art.

I hesitate to speak of our *postmodern* condition, since the word can mean everything and so can also mean nothing. Nevertheless, my point has continuing relevance. Enlightenment critique, Marxist demystification, Nietzschean suspicion, and so forth have their postmodern *afterlives*. We remain at best diffident about the religious. While we are less gushing than the romantics about genius, still a kind of "saving" role is often assigned to art: not religion—only art can "save" us now. While our "comfort levels" with the religious are very low, the same cannot be said for the aesthetic. Could one say that the most impressive of "post"-religious art is, as it were, prayer without praying? Do we not find here too the afterlife of a religion of art, a *masked* religion of art, one that sometimes has to squint through the mask, or wink: one eye open, one eye shut?

ART AND THE "END" OF METAPHYSICS

What here of this so-called "end of metaphysics"? Despite the bad name metaphysics has had of late, the need for metaphysics has not ceased. Sometimes it takes forms that do not officially present themselves with the calling card marked "metaphysics." One of those incognitos is connected to "art."

In modernity we often find a kind of allergy to transcendence. I do not mean human self-transcendence. Clearly the powers of human self-transcendence have been asserted, glorified, divinized, debunked, but never treated with any less than ultimate respect. We take ourselves very seriously, even when we deconstruct ourselves. We have to account for ourselves in every sense: we are mature, autonomous, self-determining beings, and so on and on. We are self-surpassing, self-overcoming beings. Transcendence? I am transcendence!

Whence then the allergy to transcendence as other (T3)? Self-transcendence has been yoked to a model of autonomous self-determination: the self is the law of itself, self-regulating, self-legislating, not only in morality a là Kant, but indeed in aesthetics where the genius is frequently proclaimed as the legislative power who gives, directly or indirectly, the rule to art. But such autonomous determination is dialectically equivocal concerning the place of the other. The other disturbs every effort to make this self-determining autonomy absolute, *ab-solo*. The song of self-transcendence sings to itself over the murmurings of an equivocal attitude to transcendence as other to self.

The equivocity is evident in modern philosophy itself: metaphysics must be absolutely self-determining knowing, justifying itself purely through itself; and if it makes any forays into transcendence as other, it must do so from the standpoint of its own secured and guaranteed autonomy. Traditional metaphysics of transcendent being must fall, if this is the ideal of knowing one sets before oneself. Transcendence as other must be subordinated to self-transcendence, but such a subordination signs the death warrant of transcendence as other, whose real meaning becomes just its meaning for me, not for itself as other. It must submit to me, I do not submit to it, or indeed to anything. I am the Lord.

Kantianism is clearly hamstrung by this requirement it sets itself. Kant had his own desire to open thought to transcendence, but the overriding ideal of self-determining knowing (albeit not fully realized for Kant in knowing, but claimed in practical reason) makes him at best equivocal about transcendence as other. This hamstringing of transcendence as other in no way destroys the need for it, as Kant also clearly saw, if again with a divided mind, indeed a bit of a bad conscience, with respect to the ineradicable metaphysical exigencies of the human being.

Of course, Kant is an extraordinary thinker, and some of the nuances of his views are easily flattened. Hegel is also an extraordinary thinker, but he is representative of this project of autonomous or self-determining knowing. He is dialectically complex, and his philosophy is deeply qualified by gestures towards some conceptually strategic acknowledgment of transcendence and otherness. Yet when it comes down to it, in the end, he is entirely a modern thinker, in that self-determining knowing supplies the meaning of the whole. Where the other is acknowledged, it will be included as a necessary moment of a more encompassing process of self-mediating knowing. This is evident in regard to art, since art always has a residue of otherness, namely, the sensuous otherness of the medium of artistic expression; this is not conquered in art itself. Only in philosophy is this externality entirely overcome, Hegel believes. Even where religious transcendence is noted, it too is yoked to a long and complex dialectic in which finally transcendence is reduced to immanence, and the traces of divine enigma conceptually conquered.

The whole scientistic impulse of Enlightenment did not help here. Any reference to transcendence is seen as the continued residue of a properly outmoded obscurantism. Comte's triadic unfolding from religion to metaphysics to positive science is representative: progressively the signs of transcendence must be transformed into the immanences of determinate positive science, entirely at home with its own conceptualizations of being, and cleverly free from any homesickness for religion or metaphysics. Does the exigence of transcendence vanish? Not at all. Scientism is itself a surrogate project of transcendence: it is human self-transcendence, attempting to divinize its own scientific powers, as the light that the world will recognize as properly its own, and there will be no mystery here, and no mystery beyond this proper light. All will be light.

And yet there is only too much darkness to all this light. We have become more tired of these proclamations of light, when we remember the monsters this light has spawned, and will no doubt continue to spawn. The sweats come in many forms. As the project of modernity unfolds, we find again and again systematic tendencies leading to the devaluation of transcendence as other. The tendencies are to be seen in philosophy, in religion itself (Kant's religion within the limits of reason is exemplary), in hostility to religion (Marx, Nietzsche, Freud), in ethics (utilitarianism and Kantianism, emotivism, relativism), and indeed in art. Nevertheless, it is with respect to art that a *different light* begins to glow. As the light of Enlightenment congratulates itself, a howl of protest arises from the blindness of the human spirit that this light produces. The romantic protest may have its problems, but we still bob in its backwash, if only because we still bob in the dark backwash of Enlightenment.

There is the problem too that transcendence as other seemed to have been conceived in very dualistic fashion. Transcendence as other was up there, or over there, or beyond, all in opposition to down here, and the here and now, and the present. I think this is a flattened way to describe the thinking of transcendence by premodern thinkers; yet there is no doubt that it can easily lend itself to the kind of dualistic opposition that, in turn, can easily lead to the redundancy of transcendence. For if transcendence is so other as opposite, it seems we can finally say nothing of it, and its relevance to life here and now becomes open to critique. There is the added factor that the language of transcendence was often used to buttress the legitimacy of political orders that seem restrictive of genuine freedom; hence religion seems to provide a mere ideological rationalization of the will to power of the rulers. The fuller and more enlightened release of the powers of human autonomy demand the destruction of transcendence. Hence for Marx, the critique of religion is the basis of all critique, the indispensable step to foster a proper revolutionary attitude. Others like Feuerbach, Nietzsche, Freud, Sartre, to name only some, suggest that the destruction of transcendence as other is necessary to release our own powers of self-transcendence, our autonomous creativity. Art will come to share in the same project, in that nothing other than art will be allowed from outside to interfere with the proper fulfillment of its own immanent creativity. The hint of an other will be greeted with irritation, or alarm, as a threat to aesthetic purity and autonomy.

BORN AGAIN BEYOND AESTHETICISM: ART AND BEING RELIGIOUS?

I come back to the three "deaths" mentioned at the outset. If there is a death of one, it is symptomatic of sickness in the community of them all. Hope of resurrection of one calls for hope of resurrection of the others. Is there any one that has greater power? After long consideration, I see that religion has power that neither art nor philosophy has: it is most intimate with the primal porosity, the *passio essendi*, and the urgency of ultimacy; it serves to move transcending for the many and not just the few, and hence it is more crucial to the culture of a community, and its pervasive spiritual well-being or feebleness. The religious is the more democratic art of the ultimate, imaging a culture's divination of original being, sustaining publicly this divination by ritual practices, even while rooted secretly in often unarticulated intimations of transcendence as other. And while in the intimacy of the soul it keeps open the porosity between the human and the divine, yet it also issues in ethical life that publicly enacts its most secret love of what is ultimate.

The matter does not proximately concern any sectarian, or ecclesiastical or institutional form of the religious. Institutional form is not unimportant, since it concretizes the communal shape of a religious inspiration. This last is the issue, though again there may be an intimacy more primal than this proximity. One might ask: Is not inspiration inseparable from the primal porosity and the *passio essendi*? Is it not perhaps the artistic counterpart to what in religion is the showing of the divine or revelation? Do not eros and mania, and their shaping of our original self-transcending, reveal something of our utmost promise in the between, but as moving from the finitude of the middle to the boundaries of the between, between what is human and transhuman? On that boundary the intermediating powers of being aesthetic and being religious join, but as facing beyond themselves, and by being addressed by what exceeds them. The greatness of art always renews our astonishment and perplexity about the original and the ultimate. What are the ultimate sources of origination? Can we fully vouch for them in terms of human originality? Is not human originality itself a created originality? We are *passio essendi* before we are *conatus essendi*, passion of being before striving to be. We are first created, before we create. If so, what is the more ultimate source of originality? The issue at bottom is the interpretation of originality and ultimacy in terms of human self-transcendence or in terms of transcendence as other, or the communication between these two.

I would say this last: great art intimates something of this communication. It keeps unclogged the primal porosity of our being in the between. But the most overt name for the worldly form of this communication is religion. At its most fundamental and intimate this communication has everything to do with the *passio essendi* out of which the urgency of ultimacy springs. Religion in that sense is closer to the womb of origination: there is an ontological immediacy of the communication of ultimacy, felt as urgent in the human to whom it is shown. This, of course, has to be mediated: religious communities and their art, and indeed human art, can shape the form of this showing. Art is religious to the degree it is inspired, and this even though the divine be silent in a deep incognito. Inspired art is prophetic in more senses than one: it images what is and what is to be; and in this, it also images what has been aborted in the given promise of original being. Truthful to what is, it seeks fidelity to what is to be; in this it may know also the grief of the stillborn beauty, in what was and what is.

If there is an intimacy with the origin, this origin is excessive to our self-transcendence. So far the intuitions of the post-Hegelians are not wrong. Origin is not the abstract indeterminacy of the Hegelian beginning, driven then forward in its own self-becoming. It is agapeic origin. This is a name with many religious resonances. It is not defined by a metaphysics of dualistic opposition, nor the dialectical logic of a progressive teleology, nor finally the a/logic of a deconstructive a/teleology. The latter too has not seen deeply enough into the difference of the erotic and agapeic origin (as we saw with Nietzsche, and Heidegger). Great art offers an imagistic concretion of agapeic origination.

If the religious is the most intimate, closest to the origin, as taking on worldly form, it is the most universal in potential—and this despite the particularisms of sects that would arrogate this universal promise primarily to themselves. The incognito of the religious today is revealed in the felt pull of this promise of the universal. The promise remains relatively *indefinite*, and the universal struggles to show itself in the forms of determinate community. A sign of this: diffidence about the institutional, a diffidence often motivated by religious scruples. And yet the communal, hence mediately the institutional, is ingredient in the fuller communication of the ultimate.

We live in a culture of autonomy in which the religious as naming transcendence as other is made one lobby among other, or driven to the margins, or sent underground. By contrast, I suggest the religious porosity between human and divine is the grounding happening in the most intensive and extensive sense: grounding happening, in which occurs the communication between original human self-transcendence and ultimate transcendence as the other origin. Most intensive, in that it is most intimate to the unfathomed being of the human being. Most extensive, in offering the most embracing largesse to human creativity: the enabling gift out of which our own powers are allowed to be shaped and to shape themselves. A culture which acknowledges such ultimate gift is a religious culture. All culture is religious in that regard of being impossible without the ethos of the primal gift of being as original. This is given to the human, but not initially given by the human, but given as enabling the self-becoming of human powers to the utmost of their creative promise.

This matter is primarily one of ethos: not of this or that specialized activity within the ethos (art, religion, philosophy as specialities). I mean ethos relative to our sense of the ontological milieu of ultimate value. Our current reconfiguration of the ethos is dominated by objectification, subjectification, instrumental mind, freedom as autonomy that has difficulty with the other, and so forth. The "end" of art is not due simply to a "reflective" culture. While there are many factors, what is dominant in the ethos of a culture is crucial. In this instance, if a certain objectifying orientation degrades the soil on which wonder flourishes, the debilitating effects on art, religion, and philosophy will not be far behind. "Thought," of course, can play a part in all of this, especially a certain univocalizing instrumentalism that wills to eradicate the equivocities of being. Dialectical thinking is not immune from this temptation; not all practices of philosophy are. Such practices of philosophy are complicit with degrading the ontological milieu which, though equivocal, is yet full of promise. Not surprisingly also, such philosophies often turn out to be enemies of religion. By contrast, the full ontological weight of great art brings us back to the ethos: arrests us to the mystery of what it is to be; and is hence a happening of original religious astonishment and perplexity before the ultimate. In the desert of instrumentalized being (itself produced by our reconfiguration of the ethos), it guards a reverence that is metaphysical. It images an agapeic mindfulness that listens to voices that speak beyond the dry raspings of devalued being, voices that sing of the secrets of the always sacramental earth.

Some of the above thinkers might be seen in this light, though they do not see themselves so. Are they always helpful enough in attending to the incognito of the divine? The way some of them name art adds another layer of possible misidentification, when the religious is left to languish in the equivocity of its post-Enlightenment feebleness. What of Hegel? The fact that he names all three, art, religion, and philosophy, as forms of absolute spirit is important, given the subsequent equivocations, especially in relation to art and religion. Nevertheless, I would reformulate his way of treating this triad. The otherness of the origin (T3) is not to be reduced to the dialectical holism of transcendence made immanence. In Hegel, human self-transcendence and transcendence as other are symmetrically mediated with each other, such that each becomes a moment of a more encompassing, total process of self-transcendence, which is no transcendence finally, since the transcending finds itself again in what initially seems other. Transcendence as other is entirely mediated in the total process of thought's self-determination in which self-transcendence is total self-mediation through its own others: T3 is modeled on a dialectical variation of T2; and so the irreducibility of the otherness of the origin is slighted.

In that respect, my sympathies are with some of the post-Hegelians who divine this otherness of the origin to total self-mediation. The powerful nature of the Hegelian self-mediation of the whole often occludes this sense of original transcendence beyond the whole; and yet this otherness erupts in different guises, say the inward otherness of the inspiration of genius, the astonishment before the "that it is at all" of nature (T1) in experiences of the sublime, or in religious joy, or fear and trembling, or the sweats, before the unmastered and unmasterable originality of God. That said, though Hegel's more forthright naming of the religious makes him an ally in bringing the issue into the open, his dialectical equivocation on divine transcendence as other always risks an extraordinary *counterfeiting of God*. The equivocities of post-Hegelian culture on the religious, and its request that art bear the burden of transcendence, finally help less than one might have initially expected.

There is a pluralism of manifestations of ultimacy. The agapeic origin sources the pluralism of creation. There is no determination to one form of manifestation to the exclusion of many; or indeed to the inclusion of many within one and one only form. That the origin is agapeic enables the happening of communication which is inherently pluralistic: to create is to glorify the pluralism of creation, not to reduce its manyness to one essential form. Art, religion, and philosophy are articulations which approach ultimacy in its originality. Instead of the *Aufhebung* of art into religion and religion into philosophy, I would stress the space between each, as the place each is enabled to be, by the origin, each in its difference and communication with the others, and with the origin. The origin enables the spaces of the between and possibilizes sameness and otherness in an open community. This open community, relative to transcendence/difference, cannot be described in terms of dualistic opposition; relative to sameness, cannot be captured in univocal monism, nor either the dialectical self-mediation of One, understood in a kind of Hegelian sense; nor again is it a deconstructive equivocal many—for difference thus totalized is indistinguishable from total identity. It involves what I call a metaxological intermediation of different sources of transcendence; even though the ultimate transcendence (T3) is the hyperoriginal that hyperbolically possibilizes, without univocally determining, the promise of the other transcendences (T1, T2).

Religion *lived* is our being in the porous happening of communication between ultimate transcendence (T3) and finite transcendences (T1, T2). Religion *reflected* in its truth is (metaxological) philosophy which understands that *to be is to be religious*, namely, to have one's being in the happening of the between by virtue of the ultimate giving of the agapeic origin. Among the tasks of metaphysics, after the "end" of art, is to search this truth of the *metaxu*. Being true to that task asks us to be mindful of how art matters metaphysically. Can this task be faithfully discharged without constant honesty concerning the truth of being religious?

Our revels are not now ended: not now, perhaps never. The dream is not over. There are dreams that drowse, half waking, half lost, in the sleep of finitude. But there are dreams of art, religion, and philosophy that call to waking beyond such sleep, waking again to an absolved porosity of being in which we hear a guardian calling: no more a dissembling amen to being; no feigned Sabbath of thought; no more counterfeit doubles of God. Vexed and balmed, we are searched and asked: Are we no more than a gust of nothing? Or more, much more than an extravagance of empty?

PART V

RETROSPECTIONS AND REFLECTIONS

WORDING THE BETWEEN

BEING PHILOSOPHICAL:
ON METAPHYSICS AS METAXOLOGICAL

In the following I offer a reflection on some of the recurrent themes of my work, not dwelling at too great length on any theme, hence omitting much, and occasionally referring, if need be, to writings where these themes are amplified. In a broad sense I follow the structure of the current book. First I will speak of being philosophical as inseparable from metaphysical thinking that seeks a *logos* of the *metaxu* (between). Then I will outline some crucial considerations involved in crossing the between along both a vertical and horizontal axis. I turn then respectively to our being aesthetic, our being ethical, and finally to our being religious, each as diversely traversing the between. All of these movements I will view in metaxological terms, where the wording of the between stands central.

The word "metaphysics" is not in good standing today, especially in continental thought. One might sympathize with this attitude were it confined to *certain* practices of philosophy but when it is extended to the entirety of philosophy one demurs. In all our thinking, and living, certain fundamental senses of being are already at work, and continue to be at work, even when we claim to be "postmetaphysical." We must become mindful of these senses. We awake in being, in the midst of beings, and there is an intimate strangeness to being at all. There is something astonishing about this. Metaphysics asks about the fundamental meanings of this being given to be, and our mindfulness of it. This is not a matter of designating being as "substance," nor simply of juxtaposing "becoming" and "being." We find ourselves in a dynamic world and must acknowledge the tumultuous happening of "becoming." But there is also a "coming to be" which is not just a "becoming" of this or that, but a coming to be at all. Even then, the difference of "being" and "becoming," indeed of "becoming" and "coming to be," is not the most original. The most ultimate difference is that of the origin as the primal source of both "coming to be" and "becoming," whether more determinate or self-determinate.

To say these things is already to move much too fast, I admit. I hold that a metaphysical exploration of our being in the midst of things will point towards this most ultimate origin, but to begin, I would plead for a practice of philosophical thinking that does not float above the ethos of being in abstraction, but comes to itself in the midst of things. There the astonishing being given of being(s) opens us for thought, and cries out against any form of Laputan abstraction. We start in the midst of things, and we are open to things. We are open because we are already opened. Before we come to ourselves as more reflectively thoughtful, we already are in a porosity of being, and are ourselves as this porosity of being become mindful of itself.

This ethos of being I call "the between," and for me metaphysics is not an abstraction from this but a more deeply mindful engagement with it. We are already enabled to be within the between. What all this means is not in question at the outset, for we live out of enabling powers of being before we come to ourselves more expressly. Thus starting in the midst, we do not aim for Laputan thought hovering above the between, but from the middle we try to think to what is most original and most enabling in the between. Mindfulness emerges from our being in the midst and, to be true, it must remain in fidelity to this given beginning. Of course, human liv-ing is not abstract theory but also practical and ethical. Our being in the midst extends to a mindful way of life and a life of mindfulness. There is something before the contrast of theory and practice, or the subordination of one to the other. Original mindfulness is not so much an act as a passion. It is a patience before it is an endeavor, a receiving before it is an activity. But if it is so as patient to receiving, it is so in a mode that itself enables our more constructive, indeed our creative powers. All these are *endowed* powers. In themselves they refer back to sources of power not produced by the exercise or the enactment of the power itself.

It helps here to remember a double sense to the word "*meta*"—*meta* can mean both "in the midst" but also "over and above," "beyond." This double sense defines our humanity—inside and outside, immanent and transcen-dent, immanently self-surpassing yet surpassed by what is not determined purely immanently. The *metaxu* as immanence is a given porosity of being, already in relation to what is beyond itself in being in relation to itself. If the between is porous it means that it is impossible to fixate univocally a "this side" and a "that side." What is most important is the happening of passage between—of passing. And this in an ontological sense—coming to be, passing into being, passing, passing away. All the pathos of life and death is contained in passing, passage in and through the between. Passing itself suggests a between since it cannot be fixed to any one moment or phase. Passing is as passing—just as a between is nothing without the enabling milieu of relatedness that sustains and goes beyond the beings upheld as existents in the relatively stabilized middle.

This double sense of "*meta*" can be taken to correspond to the difference of *ontology* and *metaphysics*: ontology as an exploration of being given as immanent; metaphysics as open to a self-surpassing movement of thought that points us to the porous boundary between immanence and what cannot be determined entirely in immanent terms. This double sense of the "*meta*" means that there is a tense togetherness of immanence and transcendence, or better, an intense twinning of the two, in a metaxological metaphysics. While premodern metaphysics is sometimes said to opt for the *meta* as "above," modern philosophy generally has opted from the *meta* as immanent. A metaxological metaphysics cannot be easily fitted into this perhaps too simple contrast. It is willing to bring a more generous hermeneutic to the premodern metaphysics, while demurring in the face of repeated modern and postmodern efforts to stipulate finite immanence as the absolute horizon of significance, greater than which none can be thought. The doubleness of the "*meta*" points to a porous boundary between immanence and what is not determined entirely in immanent terms.[1]

To return to a more elemental sense of being: we moderns have early on lost ourselves in rational systems and now in the postmodern revolt against such systems we also have not found ourselves. One has to admire the Greeks for having their feet on the ground of the ordinary, while striving to look up and indeed audaciously to venture thought that is more soaring than slouching. I think of Socratic dialogue as witnessing to an honesty to where we find ourselves, an honesty also willing to confess that in the midst of the ordinary something beyond comes to make a call on us. We can receive the call(er), or we can turn away from the invitation. True, all of this might not sound like "metaphysics," because often we think of this as the *produced system* rather than the *practice* of a kind of thinking. The latter should be emphasized as struck by certain elemental perplexities, our response to which may have a systematic side but is not necessarily exhausted in a system. If there is something systematic, there is also something that exceeds system, and indeed something that precedes system to which we must attend.[2] This too reflects the double condition.

Granting the concretely existential embeddedness of any thinking of the between, I will briefly summarize what I take to be four basic senses of being. Recurrently in my work I speak of being as plurivocal—against the univocal reductions of modernity, the equivocations of postmodernity, and the dialectical sovereigns of modern idealism. And yet the plurivocity is diversely voiced in the univocal, equivocal, dialectical, and properly metaxological senses of being. The univocal sense tends to emphasize determinate sameness and identity; the equivocal tends to emphasize difference that escapes univocal sameness, sometimes even to the point of indeterminacy, and the loss of any mediation between sameness and difference, identity and otherness. The dialectical sense seeks to mediate differences, differences sometimes equivocal, but not by reduction to univocal sameness, but by transition to a more inclusive unity which, it is claimed by some, contains and even reconciles the differences. The metaxological sense, properly speaking, stresses the between and deals with the interplay of sameness and difference, identity and otherness, not by mediating a more inclusive whole but by intermediating a community of open wholes, allowing recurrence to the rich ambiguities of the middle, and with due respect for forms of otherness that are dubiously claimed to be included in the immanence of a dialectical whole.[3]

Where dialectic, especially in Hegelian form, tends to move from the indeterminate to the determinate to the self-determining, the metaxological is shaped by a fourfold sense, namely, the overdeterminate, the indeterminate, the determinate, and the self-determining. In the tradition of philosophy, many thinkers have thought of intelligibility in terms of determinacy and oscillated between the determinate and the indeterminate. Dialectical philosophy in modern form claims to plot a movement of intelligibility from the indeterminate, through the determinate, to the self-determinate. Metaxological philosophy grants the justified place of indeterminacy, determinacy, and self-determination, but these are enabled and exceeded by the overdeterminate, not only in the beginning and end, but in the middle also, where they tend to place it into the wrong kind of recess. Metaxological metaphysics asks a fidelity to the overdeterminate. The overdeterminate, as not less than determinate like the indeterminate, and as exceeding all determinates and self-determinings, is centrally important for addressing the surplus givenness of finitude and the signs of what transcends finitude.

A danger here is of conceiving these four senses of being in too fixed determinate terms. The point is not at all to dispose of the univocal, equivocal, and dialectical senses of being but rather to realign them more truly with the fullness of the *metaxu*. Remember we are dealing with passages between identity and difference, and of the relatively provisional stabilization of these which is never absolute. Wording the between in such passages is what is important metaxologically. The stabilizations that come to be could be called *constances* rather than substances: what stands with (*con-stans*), rather than what stands under (*sub-stans*). Remember standing is not a "stasis" simply. To stand at all is to embody an equipoise of energy. A metaphysics of constance would have to do with the relative stabilizations of the energy of the "to be" as "standing with," or "being stood with." What is at issue is a kind of ontological fidelity in passing itself.

Evidently, then, wording the between must stress the importance of *relationality*. It is necessary to explore the plurality of possible forms of relation—these might be unidirectional, reciprocal, symmetrical, asymmetrical, to name some of the many forms of togetherness there are. Part of the task of a metaphysics of the between is to explore these relations, both in the nature of things given, in the nature of our knowing of these things, and in the original source or sources that enable relativity at all to be. Moreover, there may be an original source whose relation to finite relations may not itself be simply another finite relation or being. There is the danger of hypostatizing the between, as if it were some "big thing," though it is not anything at all. The particularity of different forms of relativity is thus important, and above all a kind of relationality that exceeds finitude, if the boundary of immanence is porous to what exceeds immanence.

CROSSINGS IN THE BETWEEN

There are two forms of the relational *metaxu* I will mention as important: the relation of inner and outer; the relation of down and up. This is here baldly put, but we will see something of the ontological and metaphysical intricacy that can attend these relations. Together they constitute horizontal and vertical axes, and much passing in the between is defined along these axes. If the *metaxu* has to do with a space between inner and outer, this need not be determined in terms of a modern fixation of subject and object or maligned in the terms of postmodern deconstructions of dualistic oppositions. We are dealing with passings in the between; hence one might recuperate the power of dialectic as already more than an "either/or" between these two, and thus as relatively true to the relationality of the between. Of course, we cannot forget the modern tendency to give a primary stress to self-relation. In passing in the between I think it will not do to deny an inner self-relation over against a confronting other. One might say there is in innerness also an inward otherness, as there is in outerness an excess that cannot be exhausted by fixed determinations. The between cannot then be a matter of any dualism of inner and outer or its deconstruction.

The outer other is not just other as opposite, but is other as in community with the one facing it. Whether we consider selving or othering, the between is unavoidable. Selving is exceeding by its own immanent othering; the other is exceeded by what cannot be determined in terms of its own determination. Othering is other than the determinate other, even as selving itself is in excess of self. This means the *redoubling* of the excess of the middle—the "too muchness" of overdeterminacy. This is one of the reasons why wording the between metaxologically is not only more than dualism and its deconstruction, but more than the modern form of dialectical self-mediation, no matter how inclusively conceived. Othering is a communication or in communication, so what comes to us from the other is always more than dualism. And while self-mediating dialectic, in the emphasis it puts on immanence, is more than dualism, it does not do true metaxological justice to the inward otherness, or the excess of communication to the othering of the other.

To turn to the relation of up and down, the vertical axis, the between is a space of transcending: passing is transcending, if we think of "trans" as in transit. The transitory is in transit, but "trans" is always a referring to a moving beyond. The transcending moving can be back and forth, a point explored by modern philosophy on the horizontal plane in trying to surpass the dualism of subject and object. But it can be up and down, so we often think of transcending in connection with the transcendent. I would not reject this, as is too often done in modern metaphysics as a mere "*Jenseits.*" The latter is a questionable fixation of the transcendent, as if it were a kind of super thing or super being. Nevertheless, the "super," the *Über*, the above, the *huper*, remains in question. There is a transcending to the "above," but if there is a between of relativity, it is not a matter of passing from the moving to the static but of plural energies in communication. The transcendent, the above is to be seen as marked by a hyperbolic energy of communicative being. If the transition is a movement up, it is not to an unmovable summit. One should rather say, the light comes down from above. One thinks of Plato's sun, for example. It enables the between to be, it shines on the between, enabling the beings in it to be and grow and to know. The good makes all things to be as good, though none is the good. The sun is above but it also communicates all around us, being even below us and seeping into cracks in the darker recessions of the underground.

Passing up and passing down in the between has some likeness to passing along a Jacob's ladder. We can be visited in the between with a dream of angels ascending and descending. Up and down also mean that the between opens into a space that takes us below the surface of the earth. The cave is a between, strongly marked by equivocity, and we lie in the underground much of the time, without univocity. How deal with the equivocity? This is a question for the practice of philosophy. Too often we have thought of the between as a space from which we go up, but what about going down into its deeper darkness? Modern idealism has blithely thought its reason was immune from this going down, so relentlessly did it insist on going up to its own absolute knowing. After Hegel, we can now see the between as also demanding the going down: down below the ground of the underground, deeper into the darkness before what the rationalist perhaps too callowly called the principle of sufficient reason. Schopenhauer and Nietzsche are philosophical spelunkers here, though I do not think they fully comprehended what the passage in the between up and down, down and up, fully portends. They were in reaction to the rationalistic callowness of the idealistic going up, and hence do not fully understand what might be demanded by a metaxological passage from below up, as well as above down. They are not alone in their reaction to the sun of Plato, or the God of monotheism, wooed away by what they take to be a more primordial dark-ness, finally disgusting to Schopenhauer, desperately affirmed by Nietzsche. A metaxological metaphysics wonders if God is in hell too—by not being hell. If there is only going down, there is no going up. For suppose we were to insist that the truer way is going down. Then this truer passage would itself be a kind of going up, even though older, honorable ways of going up seem to have been blocked or denied. A doubleness comes back. Going down, I would say, can be a clotting of our porosity to what is above us, or it can be a purgation and hence release of a new patience to what is more than ourselves.

I would not quite put it exactly as Heraclitus did when he said that the way up and the way down are one and the same (Fr. 60). He also said: Dionysus is Hades (Fr. 15). There are ways of going down which are ways of going up. Sometimes to go up we have to go down. The vine and its fruit come up out of the dark earth. The grain must perish before it begins its fragile unfolding towards harvest. Christ harrows hell, and perhaps we all have to spend our season in the hole. If the cave is Hades, one of the deepest questions for philosophy is how we return to life—how we return to the surface of the earth. It will not do to insist that everyday life is enough, or that science will solve all the problems, or that an engaged and respon-sible pragmatics is good enough for finite mortals like us. I would defend the robust rightness of much of the ordinary, or the intelligibilities revealed gloriously in things by science, and the worthy ameliorations of life enabled by responsible pragmatics.[4] But here on the vertical axis of the between we are talking about passings that are sur-passings to the sometimes tormenting extremes of the human condition, sur-passings not the less human for the fact that they are oriented to the more than human. To deny hell, to deny heaven, is to flatten the earth, and a philosophy of the between is not for flat-earthers. Like Dante we have to descend into the inferno, hopefully to come to the mountain of purgatory and try again to climb, or be lifted, above ourselves, to be what we truly are to be in the light of the true.

The between then is not a neutral space between fixed univocal points but a field of movement. It is a milieu of passing and transiting—a milieu of motion: of remotion and promotion, of submotion and supermotion. I speak of this between in terms of an *original porosity of being*, neither objective nor subjective, but enabling both, while being more than both. The porosity is a between space where there is no fixation of the difference of minding and things, where our mindfulness wakes to itself by being woken up by the communication of being in its emphatic otherness. Already before we more reflectively come to ourselves, in the original porosity of being there is the more primal opening in astonishment. There is no fixed boundary between there and here, between outside and inside, between below and above. There is a passage from what is into the awakening of mindfulness as, before its own self-determination, opened to what communicates to it from beyond itself. We do not open ourselves; being opened, we are as an opening. Astonishment awakens the porosity of mindfulness to being, in the communication of being to mindfulness, before mind comes to itself in more determinate form(s). In that respect also, this astonishment correlates with a more original "coming to be" prior to the formation of different processes of determinate becoming, and prior to the more settled arrival of relatively determinate beings and processes. Very important here are differences between wonder in the modalities of astonishment, perplexity, and curiosity.[5]

The difficulty of thinking this more original porosity is due to the fact that all thinking already presupposes it as already having been offered. All determinate knowing is made possible by it, but it is not yet determinate knowing. I come to be awakened, and come to an awakening to myself, in a more primal porosity, where the intimate strangeness of being has found its way into the intimate between-space of my receiving attendance. The porosity is not a vector of intentionality that goes from subject to object. It is not determined by a univocally fixed objectivity stamping its determinacies on a *tabula rasa*. If it is not determinate objectivity, neither is it indeterminate or self-determining subjectivity. There is fluidity and passing—a liquid matrix. The porosity is prior to univocal objectivity, and it is prior to intentionality. In and through it we are given to be in a patience of being more primal than any cognitive or pragmatic endeavour to be. The univocalizing mind desiring to understand this or that thing or process presupposes this porosity, even while it fixes determinations. It presupposes our being awoken in a not yet determinate minding that is not full with itself or fulfilled with objects but filled with an openness to what is beyond itself. Strange wording: filled with openness. For such a porosity looks like nothing determinate and hence seems almost nothing, even entirely empty. We cannot avoid what looks like the paradoxical conjunction of fullness and emptiness: being filled with openness and yet being empty. This is what makes possible all our determinate relations to determinate beings and processes, whether these relations be knowing ones or unknowing.

One way to bring out the significance of this is to say that metaphysical thinking also participates in a kind of ontological surprise that is given to us in virtue of this original porosity of being. There is no absolute divide between being human and being metaphysical. We humans are what we are in virtue of this ontological surprise at what is there at all and, in a sense, as "too much" for us. We could not anticipate this, so surprising is the pure gift of the porosity granted and what is granted in the porosity. This surprise is not only before the being there of being, as transobjective, as more than any determinate being. There is the surprising event of *being surprised at all*. Once awoken, we are surprised at being surprised. There is something transsubjective about this surprise. One might say that the first astonishment is a mindful joy in this redoubled surprise of being.

A more primal porosity of first given minding is at the origin of all modalities of mind, but as intimate with the giving of the first opening, it can be passed over, covered over. It enables the passage of mindfulness, but the endowed passing can be passed over, since we come to ourselves in this passing. First a happening, it is only subsequently gathered to itself in an express self-relation. In this being gathered to itself, there is the risk of a contraction of what the first opening communicates. The gathering concretizes us as determinate, and as thus ontologically concentrated, we can contract the opening of the porosity to just what *we* will grant as given. This happens when first astonishment becomes perplexity and then curiosity, and our mindfulness becomes contracted to modes of minding that are determinate and self-determining. Nevertheless, we do not produce the porosity; we do not determine it; it communicates from beyond our self-determination. Prior to the more determinate and determining selving of mindfulness the porosity, that is neither of selving or othering, happens as the between-space in which, and out of which, a variety of determinate and self-determining forms of minding come to be. These latter are derived, not original. What is more original is the between of porosity.

I would underscore the ontological/metaphysical character of this. The porosity of *being* is like a no-thing. It is not an indeterminate nothing, for from this nothing comes to be. It is not determinate negation, for this presupposes beings as already in being and in process of becoming. If one were to call it an overdeterminate nothing, this would be to refer to its irreducibility to indeterminacy, determination, or self-determination. Such a no-thing is inseparable from surplus creative power out of which beings come to be beings, and hence there is a patience in their being received into being, but they are relatively for themselves, and as such embody a conjunction of the passion to be and the endeavour to be. We are the porosity of being become mindful.

In this context I talk about the human being as a *passio essendi*—a passion of being presupposed by every endeavor to be—*conatus essendi*. These are always twinned, and while the passion is not originally our willing, the endeavor becomes our willing; because of its source in the porosity willing is always mingled with the possibility of nulling. My general sense is that the latter is always tempted to take over the former—the active self-assertion overtakes the receiving of being, and to a degree tries even to null it. Nevertheless, the receiving is more primordial. Metaphysical thinking must find its way back to openness to this patience of being. Metaxological metaphysics must remain true to the original porosity. Even the *conatus* is to be given its full significance as a being "born with"—"*co-natus.*" The endeavor to be is self-affirming, but self-affirming itself is witness to the double condition of twinned self-relation and relation to the other—in the *co-natus* itself. One is with oneself because one is "born with." Selving is not just self, but is a being endowed by virtue of a constitutive relativity to an other enabling source that is not oneself alone. When our selving loses any porosity to the more primal patience, its seeming self-affirmation mutates really into a kind of self-hatred. For this endeavor to be is in flight from itself, from what it is, from the patience of being that gives it to be at all in the first instance. The conditions that make possible its being at all are refused.

I will now develop some of these reflections in relation to being aesthetic, being ethical, and being religious. In the first we will pass along the axes of the between from the inner otherness of the elemental flesh to the communal liturgies of tragic and comic art. In the second, we will look at the community of selving and othering, from the intimacy of the passion of being to the agapeics of community. The immanent porosity of the human being to being opens to what is good and worthy in itself to be affirmed. Porosity to what transcends us makes us potentially liable to attack from hostile others, human or nonhuman, but it also constitutes the promise of our community with others beyond hostility. In the third, the twinning of the vertical and horizontal axes of the between concerns the communication of, our communication with, the superior otherness of the divine. Being religious places us in the space of porosity between the human and the divine. Being surprised by prayer supervenes on our astonishment before being.

BEING AESTHETIC: PASSING FROM
ELEMENTAL FLESH TO SACRED FOLLY

The aesthetic happening of being must also be understood in terms of crossings of the between. I am referring to what is first a happening manifest in the sensuous being there of beings. Relative to us, the happening is also communicated to the sensible incarnation of mindfulness that is the embodied human being. Aesthetic happening is the passing of communication in sensuous form. *Ta aisthētika*—the aesthetic things: and yet there is both an expressed and a recessed side to all of the aesthetic things. The aesthetic between is not only out there between us and the external world. It has a more recessed side in what I call the idiocy of being. We come to know that idiocy in intimate mindfulness, but it is not confined to us. The idiotic is a field of happening which is presubjective and preobjective. In using the word "idiot" I refer to something not to be reduced to more neutral public universals, and yet not something entirely autistic. We live and participate in this intimate field of being, but it lives us, in the energy of the "to be" that is in affirming life before we affirm our own life. The life we later come to own, and even claim as our own, emerges for expression from this more primal and idiotic affirming of the field of between-being.

We know this intimately in the elemental flesh. When I talk of aesthetics here I do not mean to refer to aesthetics as a theory of art.[6] It has to do with aesthetics of happening, and this is to be understood ontologically, indeed metaxologically. The sensuous givenness of being as there is a great glory. We are in the midst of it as incarnate beings, in a world itself manifest sensuously. There is an aesthetic between; we are as between-beings in that aesthetic between. Our own flesh is a between: a porous passage between more recessed intimacies and the externalities of a saturated immediacy out there. The aesthetics of happening is a living refutation of the dualism of "in-here" and "out-there." There is the surplus immediacy of given being out there—and this is not the neutral valueless thereness so sought after by the modern scientific reduction. The given world is saturated with qualitative value and texture. Qualitative texture is not due to our projection, though what we appreciate of it is communicated in the interplay between us and its givenness. We are the bees of the invisible, Rilke says. But the bees fly to and fro and make no honey without the flowers of the earth. Our bodies already fly to and fro in the glory of the visible before we think at all. The flowers of the field send forth their aroma and beckon us to gather the nectar. In this aesthetic happening of the between, all is in communication in a kind of sensuous swell.

It is the artist who is the great servant of this surplus immediacy, but we are all unknowing guests at this feast in our being embodied. Think of the to and fro in terms of the breathing warm body. To breathe is to inhale and to exhale, to take in and to let loose, to incorporate and to free. Stop this rhythm of passing in and passing out, and death soon comes. If we are warm flesh, there is also a sweating, a porosity in the flesh itself. Close the pores, and the body overheats and closes down just through its own lack of access or openness to what is other to itself. We are in this breathing between all the time.

Art has to remain faithful to this elemental flesh—that is to say, to embodied being, to the body itself as a porosity, as a *passio* of being. It must open into what is in excess self-determination—to remain the living and warm and breathing between it is. Of course, the aesthetic between opens inward as well as outward. Hence one might say that the idiocy is like a well or reserve—an abyss in inwardness itself. The bees of the invisible fly in the air and gather from the flowers of the earth, but they make honey in the secret places, places where the honeycombs are the hidden stores of the invisible. In its recession into the storing abyss the idiocy goes infinitely deep—into nothing—and yet it is not nothing but endowed original power to be.

The elemental flesh begins to wake to itself in us with the power of imagination, a power we must not take too subjectivistically. If you like, the nothing is more like a creative voice than a mere empty absence. This is why (aesthetic) imagination can be seen as a *threshold power* and why it is so important in the process of aesthetic articulation. There is the traditional view of treating the image as a mere sensuous aftereffect of some fixed external state of affairs—this is a univocalization where imagination is said to be straightforwardly reproductive. There is something more original about imagination. We sometimes associate this with the productive imagination of Kant and the romantics, among others. I would say that this threshold power is not self-activating—there is again a more primal patience, a receiving before there is an activating, a passion before there is an endeavor. On the boundary between the *passio* and the *conatus*, imagination opens us again to the original porosity and in the opening is given access to originating power. This intimacy with the *passio* and porosity is reflected in the traditional trope of our needing to woo the muse. Wooing, a liturgy of courting, is prior to and beyond all self-activating or self-determination. It awaits in the right readiness for the enabling source that is intimate to what is our own, though most intimately the source is not our own simply. The enabling source is doubly idiotic in this sense: it belongs to the intimacy of our being, but it does not belong to our being. I take this again as reflecting the double character of the metaxological: being in the midst and yet beyond—being of an immanence that in its immanence opens to what is more of transcendence.

Imagination might be seen as threshold between the *passio* and the first free(d) articulation of the *conatus*. Our body is like a dark soil, and there are seeds sown in its intimacy that we do not know are even germinating until a sprout breaks through and crosses the threshold, and thenceforth we know there is more sown in us than we could ever cultivate through ourselves alone. We are servants of a harvest planted in a ground we must both cultivate and gather, though we do not own the seeds or the harvest, and yet they both are signs of what is most deeply intimate to our being. There is here a turning back down into the darkness of the inward otherness. Something of the hidden reserve comes up to the surface and is given the sensuous outering of what otherwise remains mute in the inward idiocy.

Of course, for some idiocy is a word for silence. But we could just as well speak of the creative silence as the porous nothing out of which the word comes—the word first as fleshed—as all words in the end are—as all words share in the word becoming flesh. If the word takes flesh in the porosity it is analogous to something coming to be in the nothing, though the originating power is not nothing but is more than the entire process and reserved in the mystery of that "more." Overtly or incognito, there is a communal dimension to this: words are inheritances from others, carriers over time of the revealed and secret significances of a people. Our own words are not our own. They are endowed with a plurivocal heritage. The true poetic voice is not owned. One's own most idiotic voice voices the idioms of the plurivocal people. Without the others there is no voicing. Because we have been spoken to we speak.

One might say that wording the idiocy is the aesthetic outing that not only deals outward what indoors dwells in us, to adapt a line by Gerard Manley Hopkins. It deals outdoors what dwells in the intimacy of being in what is other to us. The aesthetic things of the given outward middle shine with surplus immediacy and have reserves of a secret mysteriousness on which the suggestiveness of great art attends and for which it somehow finds itself gifted with the right words. By word, I do not mean just the vocalized human word. The song is a word, or wording; the shimmy of a gesture is a word; strutting and fretting on the stage an hour is wording. What we call words are wordings of the between. Wordings are neither subjective nor objective, though some are more objective, some more subjective. As communicative they are always both between self and other and more than self and other. Some wordings are more transsubjective, transobjective—when they are the words of love, for instance, or the wordless words of praying.

For instance, it is only an excessive univocity that would say the objective is to paint an "exact" copy. Metaxologically, it is to communicate with the "trans" in the objective—the "trans" that communicates into the middle—the "trans" that is not just of the subject, though it is "trans" even in the subject—"trans" in that the threshold on which imagination turns is both inward as well as outward, downward as well as upward—an aesthetic crossing of the *metaxu*.

Something of this between character of imagination has been noted in the past, though the emphasis has been directed to the way the sensuous is formed and transformed by something transsensuous, say, the spiritual. Thus we have classic definitions of the beautiful as the Ideal, as with Hegel: the Idea in sensuous shape, entailing the spiritualization of the sensuous, the sensualization of the spiritual.[7] This is not wrong, nor is it wrong to stress, as Kant does, how imagination is midway between sense and understanding. Yet it is not true enough to the between, since it is one-sided in stressing too much the side of subjectivity. Nor is it a question of restoring the objective. For a metaxology of between being, it is more a matter of finesse for the transsubjective and transobjective. Once again we are called to, called out by, the ontological reserves that enable determinate being but which exceed determination and self-determination. This is the overdetermination appearing and receding in the determinate and the self determining: because appearing communicated, because receding elusive, and yet always suggestive of more than every determination and our self-determination. Aesthetic happening points us back to the recessed ontological intimacy of the between that yet is communicated, and whose recess is not just a failure of communication. It is the intimation not just of wholeness but of what is surplus to wholeness. It is not just the finite glory but the reminder of the transfinite in that glory. It is a recall to the love of the finite that itself is lifted in the passage of that mysterious glory—the mysterious glory of passing being—of transience as the "trans" of the fleshed "to be" as it passes.

All of this secretly passes into our embodied being and is communicated in an immediate way in it. But it is also communicated in a mediated way, when we begin to wake up to the passage as passage and the forming as forming, and the coming to be as becoming. The way we adorn our own bodies is an elemental example of this. This is not wallowing narcissism. Adorning occurs always within the envisaged companionship of others. Adorning the body is a second "yes" to the first "yes" of the givenness of the body. It is a "yes" to the beauty of the body not in brute factualities simply but in terms of reserved promises. Adorning brings something of that reserve to outing. True, we can mutilate ourselves also, but this too shows the original release in the elemental embodiment.

Art completes nature, the ancients put it, and they were not wrong. What nature means is perhaps as mysterious now as in ancient times, perhaps even more mysterious now, paradoxically so since scientifically we know more and more about it. The intimacy of being is recessed in the reductive objectification. The service of true art is needed more than ever amidst the dearth of ontological wonder. Art, I would venture, is the servant of the energy of the "to be" that passes and takes form in the aesthetic becoming of the between. Without the wooing of this true energy there is only the crude imposition on it of a clunky self-wrought form. There is no true fit. There is nothing truly fitting. We are fitting it up, thinking we are "creating" the set up. But the "set up" is a derogation from the promise of the aesthetics of happening. It is forcing the given. A tyrannical *conatus* cannot wait, does not want to woo what might come to it in the readier *passio*. It lacks the deeper creative power of this more intimate ontological patience.

The gift of beauty comes to us in that patience. I would stress gift: we cannot project beauty. The surprise of beauty takes our breath away. It refreshes, before our voluntary assent to it, or later refusal, the ontological passion of being. We are moved before we move ourselves. I do think the passion of beauty is bound up with the erotics of being, and we sometime know the tyranny of that eros. There can be a tyranny of a love that will not leave us be—but this is a tyranny that can take us to limits where the finite faces what exceeds it. The erotics of beauty calls forth the movement up; the mania of overtaking love comes down into the between with companioning despotism.

As one cannot project surprise, so one cannot project sublimity. Something comes upon us, comes over us. There is something "over" here—and there. This is a crossing of the between where the horizontal axis is pierced by a communication from the vertical: something more than us enters the intimate recesses of the soul, and seeds it with an initially unchosen terror and a dawning, disturbing affection. The piercing on the vertical axis can, of course, go deep down as well as high up. It is so that we cannot usually separate what is high up from what is deep down, and indeed since the communication has come in the intimacy of being we cannot quite say what is of our inner selves and what is of the outer other and what is of the superior other. Again all is passage, and the passing in and out, up and down, is surplus with overdeterminate significance. If there is a patience in this passage, still art is not an unresponsive passivity, and it shows also an active figuration, configuration, even transfiguration of what passes. Art can create fresh figures of the ethos, figures that refresh our elemental porosity, opening new eyes and new ears, new senses, a newly refreshed body. Art can be the wording of a "becoming incarnate," passing towards fresh figurations of what is hyperbolic to us, indeed of the hyperboles of being (to which I will return below).

One might think of the tendency of beauty to enclose itself in finished form, and how finished form is broken open by the rupture of the sublime. This was known in previous ages, but it has been made of special interest in our postmodern times. I would connect it, at least in part, with the desire to be reopened to othernesses short-changed by the modern Enlightenment culture of self-determination and autonomy. The sublime communicates the beyond of autonomy. Surprise is beyond anything we could (pre-)conceive, but it is sometimes shown with a violence in what exceeds us. There is something idiotic at the other extreme of an estrangement that is beyond our rationalization and instrumentalization, and yet it is also strangely intimate. It is idiotic in these two senses.

Here art finds itself on the threshold of the sacred. Even if we want to stress the horror or the monstrous, this too is in the space of the sacred. Desecration is a sacred act, even if it acts in hatred against everything sacred. The abjectness of some contemporary art strikes one as trying to desecrate a sacredness that should not be there at all, but the desecration is parasitical on what it abjures, so it pays its withheld complement to the sacred. There is an extremity, some of whose greatness is seen in the exposure to the idiocy that we find differently accented in great tragedy and comedy. We are on a porous boundary where finitude cannot close itself off from an exposure to horror and compassion. The exposure is idiotic because it is radically intimate, idiotic because while communicated it cannot be communicated in neutral concepts. It is intimately universal, but instead of enclosing finitude in its own immanence, it renews the primal porosity of immanence to transcendence as other. This sacred space is a frontier of the ultimate between.

Think of King Lear: Stripped of regal sovereignty, he passes through madness and learns the wisdom of being nothing. He learns painfully a patience on the boundary and becomes porous to those who are as nothing. He learns compassion. The idiotic passion of being touches on the agapeics. At the end, he is said to have outlived himself: he assumes something of what I have called posthumous mindfulness. He becomes, with Cordelia, one of "God's spies," who take upon themselves "the mystery of things," who "bless and ask forgiveness," and "live, and pray, and sing, and tell old tales, and laugh at gilded butterflies . . . and wear out, in a walled prison, packs and sets of great ones that ebb and flow by the moon" (see King Lear, 5.3.9–19). There is almost nothing of what we normally call consolation in this. The consolation is in truthfulness to the extremities of exposure. Racked on the between, a life beyond life and death opens. There is the empty space of an otherness that more properly should be called sacred than simply aesthetic—the transaesthetic in the aesthetic itself. If this is the view from nowhere, the look involved is not one of spectatorial neutrality but one of a love. This love lives in outliving life and death.

In comedy the idiocy comes back, and its irrepressible resurrection can have a sacred significance, though often this is deeply incognito. Comedy, it is true, can be overtaken by the violence of a mockery that does not love, and yet there is comic laughter more in the mode of a forgiving release. There is a debunking power that laughs at the pretensions of false finitude, but there is the festive energy of laughter that releases again, even in absurdity, something of the intimate joy in being at all. In the music of comedy sings the festivity of the living. Even the crude noise of comedy is the applause of life. This idiot wisdom can be the earthy double of divine comedy.

Notice again that we are dealing with a between that is, so to say, a daimonic middle between mortals and divinities, as eros was said to be for Socrates. The daimonic between is attested in other ways too. We return to the metaxological axis of going up and going down. It is not just going to and fro, or going round and round. The latter is too circular, whereas the between is cruciform, or quadratic—though like Celtic crosses the circular, hugely present, becomes a maze on the crossing. With the daimonic between there is flying up and falling down, uplift and crashing, heaven and hell. The old masters were rarely wrong, and Icarus is still our companion, as is Orpheus. And perhaps this is the secret of the fascination of Orpheus: seeking the threshold, he would stand on the surface of the earth with his beloved Euridyce. But when coming to the surface of the earth out of the nether world, if we turn back with a too direct look, even out of love, the result can be vanishing and loss. The indirection is needed for the song. We need to be patient in traversing the between. Trying too directly to conquer the gap between oneself and the beloved is to collapse the between, and we end up deprived of the beloved. The threshold of the sacred is the most dangerous verge.

BEING ETHICAL: PASSING FROM THE GIVEN ETHOS TO AGAPEIC GIVING

I now turn to the *metaxu* as the field where ethical communities, communities of selving and othering are constituted. Here more explicitly there is passage from the idiotic passion of being to the agapeics of community. Given what I have said above, it is impossible to segregate the aesthetic from the ethical and the religious. Each is a wording of the between. In being ethical the stress is more on the between as enabling communities between self and other. To be in the between is to be in communication, but there are different forms of communication, and hence also different kinds of community. One reason I affirm the continuity of the ethical with the aesthetics of happening is the following. One of the major trends in modernity is a certain devaluation of being. Due in part to the objectification of modern science and its technological exploitation, we find the reduction of nature to a valueless thereness, stripped of the qualitative aesthetic characteristics which are manifest in the surplus immediacy. This coexists with a corresponding stress on the human being as the autonomous subject, but in the background is always this devaluation of the ethos of being. A rethinking of the latter also means a rethinking of the former. A true metaxological ethics must add its voice in favor of a fitting ecological aesthetics, one respectful of givenness in both an ontological and an ethical manner.

Important here is to see that the issue is not just a matter of offering another particular ethical system. The first issue is not, say, Nietzscheanism versus Platonism or Christianity, or Kantianism versus consquentialism. None of this precludes discrimination of ethical formations that are more faithful to the fullness of the between, or a metaxological ethics with well articulated contours. But first the *metaxu* calls our attention to the more primal ethos of being wherein to be is also to be good, and for humans to be good. We need to take a "step back" out of specific ethical systems towards this ethos, there to attend to what I call the potencies of the ethical, which I will briefly name below. I have attempted something like this in *Ethics and the Between*. This "step back" is in ethics a little like Heidegger's purported "step back" out of metaphysics. In my case, a metaxology explores the enabling sources and powers that give being to be as it is, and give it to be as good.

If Heidegger seems to give us being without good, and Levinas good without being, I pursue new thinking concerning the hospitality of being and good. There is not alone a forgetfulness of being; there is a forgetfulness of the good of the "to be." Metaxological ethics asks an anamnesis of the worthiness of the "to be" as such. This sense of ontological worth shows itself in the rich surplus of aesthetic happening. This worth is first more onto-logical vis-à-vis the ethos of being, but we reconfigure the givenness in the light of what we consider most important and ultimate. Our reconfiguration forms a second ethos, but this can be a repression or mutilation rather than redemption of the resources of worth in the givenness of being. In general, we have stressed a *conatus essendi* that is not true to its own *passio essendi*, and to the porosity of being wherein is communicated the fact that our own freedom is originally not univocally our own but an endowed freedom.

The modern neutralization of the ethos of being leads to, indeed expresses a divorce of "to be" and "to be good." Being in the between gives the lie to that divorce. An objectification that reduces what is there to valueless happening is untrue to the between, even if it is produced by between-beings like us. Being is in interplay, being is *inter-esse*. This is not grabbing appropriation of the otherness of what is given. It is participation and involvement where coimplication between selving and othering is of the essence. Even grabbing presupposes a more original porosity to the other we grab. Thus too even the objectifying project of neutering the world is itself the expression of something not neutral. Making nature worthless in itself is an *inter-esse*, though bent in the direction of a rendition which makes it easier for our overtaking of it in our projects. The objectification is a project of the subject, deemed worthy as such, though the subject here is hiddenly secreting the ontological poison of its own tyrannical will to power. Its own ontological treason is masked, and the resulting subjection of being is presented as the true relation. The otherness of the ethos as such is silenced. The between is not allowed to utter its own wording. We speak for all, but the all is silent in this speaking. The result is a monologue of the subject with itself in the project of devalued objectification.

Return to the between as an ethos means new eyes for the "to be" as good. The surplus immediacy of the aesthetics of happening already hints that in the givenness of being, the "to be" is as promising of an agape of being. This promise is to be redeemed, but there is a community of being already at work, not only between humans, but between humans and the hospitable ethos. This hospitality is evident in the immanent porosity of the human being to being as it is, and to what is good and worthy in itself to be affirmed. Of course, equivocity is not entirely absent. Porosity to what transcends us exposes us to the potential for hostility from others, human or nonhuman. This porosity also constitutes the promise of our community beyond hostility with others. Our own being ethical has much to do with negotiating the porous boundary between hospitality and hostility.

We have already betrayed that boundary when we so moralize the good that we invest the human being alone with being the source of all value. We say that nature in itself is valueless—as Nietzsche does; though then, impossibly, he wants to say "yes" to all, but why say "yes" to what is so worthless? When we reduce the rich between to valueless happening, instead of elevating the human, we cast ourselves under the shadow of nihilism. If we make the whole other to us thus valueless, all our putative constructions of value take place within this valueless whole, and hence, in the end, they too partake of the same valuelessness. They too come to nothing. Humanistic moralizing ends up autistic. Thinking beyond that nihilism and humanistic autism is at stake in the question of the "to be" as good.

This moralization of the between is bound up with a view of ethical autonomy which places what is other in a very equivocal position. Otherness becomes that heteronomy in freedom from which autonomy claims self-legislating power. A priority is given to one side of the relationality between us and what is other. Autonomy lies between us and ourselves. No doubt the other will be brought back in—for instance, in Kant's kingdom of ends—but on the terms of an autonomy that already has seceded from the ethical richness of the between. If we say the other is an end in itself, and moral community is *between* oneself and these other, the form of ethical intermediation governing it cannot be a matter of *self*-legislation. We have to invoke a freedom beyond *self*-determination. There is a rich between already sustaining every selving; hence autonomy is always derivative from the promise of the between. If this is a freedom, it is an endowed freedom; hence it is never simply autonomy. There are different forms of freedom, and we should guard against identifying freedom with autonomy, as we often do in modernity. There are freedoms before autonomy; there are freedoms that exceed autonomy. These are especially of interest to an ethical wording of the between.

I add that this stress on autonomy is not fully faithful to the original porosity of being. It is not faithful to the meaning of the *passio essendi*. It is a form of the *conatus essendi*, in the sense of the will that wills itself, that does not pay proper attention to the *co-* of the *conatus* in which it is already birthed. The double relativity is there already in the birth of endowed freedom, and hence the bond with what is other to itself. This freedom before autonomy is not self-determination, but a being given to be as the power to be relatively self-determining. In the between ethical selving and othering are always twinned together. The strong tendency in modernity is to let the *conatus* take more and more self-determining form, to the clotting on self of the porosity, and the recession of the *passio*. It can take individual rational form in Kant, more than individual form in the social self-determination of Hegel's idea of freedom, futile form in the self-striving of the will in Schopenhauer, desperately affirming of itself in the will to power that wills itself in Nietzsche. The autistic afflatus of all that now has deflated in postmodernity, and the recessed twinning with othering comes back some more into focus. Too often now it is the abjectness of autonomy that we see, rather than released freedom beyond autonomy. We must be ready for released freedom if our purpose is to word the ethical between.

Our freedom is freed into its own being for itself, and as freed it refers back to endowing sources which are other to its own self-production. As freed it is relatively for itself but its being for itself can be so stressed that the relativity to the other sources is hidden or rejected. Then an autonomy that occludes its own more original sources comes to think of itself simply as freedom. This autonomy makes a circle of itself, and in so encircling itself hinders itself from being freed beyond itself, since freedom to be beyond itself is immediately retrenched into its own self-circling. What it needs is a selving released from itself into the community of the between wherein it becomes porous again to the intimacy of the "to be" as good and its plurivocal unfolding in what I call the potencies of the ethical. These are endowed powers that are self-enabling but not autonomous in the above sense. They are enabling of ethical selving, but because they are endowed they are not self-produced as such. They enable us to produce ourselves in a derivative sense to shape ourselves in communication in different ethical communities. Here is a brief summary of these potencies.

First, there is the *idiocy* of the "to be" as good: our elemental intimacy with the surplus worth of being: we taste the sweetness of the "to be," in a predeterminate sense that is intimate and other at once. Second, the *aesthetic* potency: this bears on our rapport with the incarnate worth of the world—embodiment is embedded in an aesthetic ethos of saturated sensuousness. Third, the *dianoetic* potency: we seek law-like regularity to the ambiguities of the aesthetics of happening, and what I call ethical constancies are emergent in the between. We must be on guard against false fixations, for the point is not to secure ourselves with spurious certainties but to discern and follow reliable directions in passage in and through the between. Fourth, the *transcendental* potency: certain constancies occupy a special position in this sense that without them determinate ethical living would not be possible. The metaxological relation between self and other is transcendental, as is the agapeic origin as enabling good. I mean "transcendental" in a more Platonic than Kantian sense: the being of the good and the relativity of the metaxological are original sources of enabling, presupposed by determinate approaches to the ethos and specific human formations of the ethical. Fifth, the *eudaimonistic* potency: in the fullness of our flourishing there is a primordial "being pleased" with the fulfillment of powers. What is unknowingly loved in the idiocy comes more into its own, comes into a fullness in its neighboring with the good of other-being. Eudaimonistic rejoicing is not without its own travail in the chiaroscuro of the ethos, for as Aristotle, echoing Sophocles, said: count no man happy till he is dead. Sixth, the *transcending* potency: in the determinate human being as exceeding itself an overdetermined energy of self-surpassing comes to expression. This transcending potency cannot be fully understood in univocal, equivocal, or dialectical terms. The inward source of this transcending is a strange otherness in innerness itself, and we cannot mediate with ourselves entirely through ourselves alone. There is the surpassing mystery of self-surpassing itself—this is ever more than we can fix in our moving to something more. To what "more" are we moving? Here, and seventh, I speak of *transcendence itself*, not just our self-transcendence. The transcendent good is no particular good; it is good as no good, for it is good beyond goods. It has been diversely named, but perhaps the best word in ordinary language for it is the extraordinary word "God."

Metaxological ethics names the ethos as the space wherein the ultimate good intimates itself in the idiotic, aesthetic, dianoetic, transcendental, eudaimonistic, and transcending concretions of life. This good is communicated into the between, opening its finite otherness, and through this, opening to the self-becomings of different beings, each becoming towards what is good for it. We are pointed to a community of the good beyond determinate goods, and beyond self-determination, a community offering its promise from the start. A plurality of possibilities is enabled in the between. I would stress both horizontal and vertical axes which cross each other in such a way that in the middle they are also found in overlapping and intertwined forms. The togetherness of the plurivocity of potencies can be sometimes a buzz of many, sometimes a confusion, sometimes symphonic, sometimes cacaphonic.

As I said above, what is at issue is not simply Platonism versus Nietzscheanism, say, each as more determinate orientations, but the potencies as enabling a plurality of different configurations of the ethical. Through them we participate and interact with the primal ethos and reconfigure it into a second ethos under the sign of the worthy. Different configurations can show one potency or a constellation of potencies in the ascendant, but a determinate configuration does not exhaust the ethical promise at play in the between. For instance, Nietzsche will stress the aesthetic and transcending potency, Plato and Augustine the transcending and the transcendent, Aristotle the eudaimonistic, and Kant the transcendental. Each is a configuration in the ethos of the between, but the "step back" out of specific systems allows us to look at each differently, and not simply as antagonistic "systems." Undoubtedly configurations can clash, and some are more faithful to the full promise of the ethical between. For the "step back" is also with the aim of renewed porosity to being good in the ethos of being, and in the plurality of possibilities a vision comes forth of the enabling powers as marked by the promise of being agapeic—redeemed in the community of agapeic service.

In *Ethics and the Between* all this is more extensively developed. In addition, I explore different forms of ethical selving in the light of the plurivocity of freedom—that is to say, with reference to freedoms before and beyond autonomy. I will round off this reflection on the ethical between with a brief glance at different forms of its communal intermediation.[8] All of these pass between the intimate and the universal. Communities in the between range from the more intimate, to the more instrumental, through more erotic forms, to touch on the agapeic. Four forms of community seem to me crucial: first, the ethical community of the family, where the intimacy of being is more important; second, the network of utility, where economical and instrumental values often dominate, and where today we find too much of what I call a reconfigured ethos of serviceable disposability—things must be serviceable for us, but once they have served their use, they are disposable (persons too are often treated as items of serviceable disposability); third, the community of what I call erotic sovereignty, where the intermediation of social and political power is to the fore; fourth, and finally, what I call the community of agapeic service, where our ethical and religious service to our neighbors and fellow humans is most important.

I focus especially on these last two, since they highlight the extremities of height and depth in our ethical crossings of the between. Erotic sovereignty deals with immanent excellences, and these can be very deep, while agapeic service is oriented by transcendent good above will to power, and it points us beyond immanence to a good higher than ourselves. We might think of Nietzsche's provocative phrase, "A Roman Caesar with the soul of Christ," and suggest that the relation of the erotic sovereign and the agapeic servant is at issue. I would say that the community of agapeic service points to a Christ beyond Caesar and, indeed, beyond the grand inquisitor. In crossing the between, especially with respect to its ethical depths and height, there is the extreme exposure of our being and the appeal of a willingness beyond will to power. We are to be beyond ourselves, willing beyond ourselves, willing beyond willing itself, freed beyond the will that wills itself into the ethical community of agapeic service.

What do we *ultimately* trust in crossing the between? This is an issue for released freedom beyond autonomy. In all forms of community there is a trust between selving and othering, though it is often betrayed. In the intimate community of the family, the idiotic bond of trust is elemental. In the instrumental community of serviceable disposability, there is trust in our own exploitative power, but it often overtakes a more released trust in others. In the erotic community beyond use, intermediated by sovereignty, immanent power often trusts in its own promise of mastery. But there is an ethical community beyond sovereign power and its immanent excellences, and beyond politics. This is the community of agapeic service, where we pass into the ultimate exposure. In porosity to the divine, there seems to be nothing there, yet the emptiness rings with appeal, appeal for nothing but trust, appeal that is the apotheosis of the bond of trust. Passing between extremes, the appeal intermediates trust in good in an ultimate sense, in relation to the extremes of life: birth and death, and the ordeal of suffering in between. In the face of our coming to nothing, agapeic communication is trust in the good, by love of those who are as nothing, in facing their nothingness. It is community seeking to live in absolute service of the good.

There is overlap and divergence and a certain doubleness here. Both the sovereign and the ethical servant are moved by the self-surpassing energy of transcending. Both ambiguously move on the border between human transcending and the good as transcendent. In the sovereign there is more of self-transcending than transcendence itself; in the ethical servant there is more of transcendence itself than self-transcending. In the middle between transcending and the transcendent, the sovereign inclines to the former, the ethical servant to the latter. In the middle ethos, as always, there is no complete eradication of ambiguity. A sovereign may be a secret servant of the transcendent good, though perceived as a peremptory exploiter of will to power. An ethical servant may struggle to purge his or her great devotion to the transcendent good of human-all-too-human self-insistence, and never completely succeed.

The appeal of the ultimate trust asks for a kenosis of the will that wills itself—an emptying out of the self-insistence that clogs our porosity to what is beyond us. What is beyond us is in ourselves and in the other also, and the kenosis of willingness dissolves the clot of self-encirclement, letting an energy of affirming life pass into and through the purged porosity. Our void, our being voided, becomes newly free and fertile for passage beyond self—passing into more and more intimate recesses of the idiocy—passing into more and more dangerous territories of hostile otherness. Kenosis and generosity are twinned, for the point in being nothing is to be an everything of welcome for the other, and indeed to be more fully selving in not being for self alone. The doubleness of the *meta* comes again: in the midst and beyond, and beyond in the midst. One is not possessed of the good; what is good is nothing to be possessed; allowance of the passage of generous giving is all.

This struggle with the doubleness of transcending and the transcendent good is intermediated in the community of agapeic service. It is not always struggle, for there are graced communications when self-transcending is freed from self-circling and an energy of generosity is released towards the otherness of the between, into the givenness of creation as good, into the neighborhood of others as good. A godsend of generosity visits us in the between. The communication is graced, becoming in turn a community that bestows good on others still estranged. A communal way of life may be formed wherein is intermediated this struggle and this release. Being ethical becomes porous to being religious. For such a consummate community of agapeic service might be called the religious *kononia* or the commons of the divine. There is a suffering in this as well as a doing, there is an opening to the other as well as a self-forming. Being ethical in the between is to be on an edge, and on edge, alert to what comes to us from beyond ourselves.

BEING RELIGIOUS: PASSING FROM IDIOTIC MYSTERY TO HOLY AGAPE

If the humanistic moralization of ethical worth raises questions, even more so does the moralization of religion. There are extremities of the between that exceed the human measure and are both more and less than our self-determination. It is our being to be religious, and this is a passage between the human and the more than human. There is an intimate communication involved that reaches back into the abysses of intimate idiocy and upwards into the highest heights. Being religious stresses most intensively the crossing as between inner and outer, and between up and down. In the outer, there is the glory of aesthetic happening, insinuating signs of the more than human. In the inner, something of the inward otherness opens back into the more original porosity where the otherness touches on the source enabling us to be at all. In movements up we come to boundaries which perplex us about a transcendence that is other to our self-transcendence. In movements down into the depth beneath us, we come to a dead zone of desolation, and *ex profundis* we cry out in horror and plea. In our time we seem to have more taste for the groundless ground under the ground of the underground but we can be entirely too blithe about this. The cave of everyday life, as one layer above hell, might seem to be all that stands between us and horror. I would say being religious reaches into hell. There the primal porosity is frozen into a snarl of self that is less the love of the "to be" as the fixated love of its own being, so fixed on itself that its self-affirmation as absolute becomes the counterfeit double of the absolute, and of the affirmation that releases selving into the between.

Here too our reconfiguration of the primal ethos of being has led to a loss of taste for the divine, and part of our task is to understand again something of this primal ethos in and through the reconfigured ethos. This means also being freed from idolatrous fixations of the promise of the between. Here I will emphasize what is so evaded in our time of antimetaphysical equalizations: *superior* otherness. Finesse for superior otherness has been largely lost by Western intellectuals, and since around Kant's time, atheism has become a kind of default position. It is not that there is much thought going on, but we have lost the savor of these momentous matters, and there is a kind of irritated impatience with any "beyond." There was a time when it was part of the philosophical vocation to venture some words of its own, wording its own sense of the divine communicated in the between. The falling silence of this voice I connect with our being arrested by certain fixations in the foreground of the reconfigured ethos, an arrest that is coupled with the loss of religious porosity that itself might just enable release from the fixations. When philosophy pursues its radical autonomy every heteronomy must be disturbing to it. When it pursues the self-activation of thought against every passion of being it must be on guard. Being surprised by prayer can supervene on our astonishment before being, but this supervening is the intervening and subvention of what is prevenient and has precedence. A radically self-insistent practice of autonomous thought cannot abide that precedence. It will pitch its tent in the foreground of the reconfigured ethos and hinder the entry of mindfulness into the deeper resources of the primal ethos that the reconfiguration risks covering over.

There is an antinomy of autonomy and transcendence deserving of attention here. Autonomy refers to our self-relation in its immanence, transcending refers to a going across ("trans") or being beyond. We have stressed autonomy in modernity to the detriment of transcendence as beyond. Absolutize autonomy and one must relativize transcendence; but if there is a transcendence that is absolute we must rather relativize autonomy. Metaxological philosophy points in the latter direction. It tries to rethink the relation of the exterior transcendence of given creation, of the inner self-transcendence of human beings as infinitely self-surpassing, and the superior transcendence of the divine that is still more than these. Wording the between points to this third transcendence—against the absolutizing of autonomy, though with reference to the *meta* as both in the midst and also beyond. Some postmodern thinkers have wanted to deconstruct autonomy, but have they gotten free enough to rethink this third transcendence? I think of seafarers trying to get into open water and always being beaten back by waves of modern autonomy, beyond which they cannot fully get into the clear water out beyond. The true between is there out beyond. It is also preparing breakfast on the shore. The true out beyond is right where we are—here.

I refuse to genuflect before the crude shadows of a dualistic "either/or" between immanence and transcendence that have haunted philosophy since Kant. If we take seriously the double sense of the *meta*, any univocal "either/or" between immanence and transcendence cannot be finessed enough. Intellectually threadbare repudiations of any "beyond" reveal only a fixation, and a fixated version of the "beyond." They are void of imagination. No fixation is compatible with the porosity of passage in the between. There is no way to fix an ultimate "either/or." It is in passage itself that the turn is made. A turn is a turning, and in going this way one does not go that way. But this is not a fixed "either/or." It is a matter of navigating the equivocal, steering a passage by finesse for the signs of communication.

Our reconfiguration of the ethos of being has come to mean that the signs communicating of divine transcendence are whited out. There is a loss of reverence for being received into being. There is a loss of the patience of being which knows its being to be endowed. There is loss of the co- of *conatus*, which in turn reinvents itself as a self-affirming will to power that will have no superior other over it—except perhaps its own superiority bootstrapped into the false heights. Of course, a new sense of immanent transcendence insinuates itself then, most famously with the "over" of the Overman. The more than human turns out to be more of the human, and hence not more in the more radical sense of the superior otherness.

Neither the self-sublating infinitism of Hegel nor the postulatory finitism of many of his anti-idealistic successors is true to this superior otherness.[9] These options offer philosophies of unremitting immanence, and whether in holistic or deconstructive form, the "beyond" is henceforth banished. A metaxological philosophy navigates differently the fluid boundary between finitude and infinity. The double sense of the *meta* as in the midst and yet beyond challenges us again. The difficulty for metaxological thought is of moving on the porous boundary that joins these two together, of attending the vein of intimacy that marks the communication between them, and not just in the extraordinary, but in the ordinary events of everyday life. There is no space of a privileged above. The above is below; the above is within; the above faces outwards; the above surfaces in the night dew of desert places. It is the most fluid of the enigmas that pass in and through the between. It is the most reserved of sources that gives it to be—more original than "becoming" and "coming to be," and more intimate to them than they are to themselves. Intimate to "coming to be" and "becoming," they are not it; though the derived energy of their "to be" helps us figure some sense of its being beyond, in its being in the midst.

God is not a "beyond" that is hiding from us. It is more we who are in hiding. Like Adam and Eve hiding in the garden, we do not want to be "seen." Seeing but unseen, we think we can shutter the porosity, close it down, close it in, and believe we are impermeable, untouchable. We hate to be known, so we say we do not know. The great Psalm 139 voices it in an extraordinary way: We flee God, we hate to be searched; but to where can we go, to where can we flee? If we ascend into the heavens, God is there; if we make our bed in Sheol, God is there. If we fly with the wings of the dawn, God is there, and if the darkness falls on us, even the darkness will be a light and will not hide us from God, for the night shines like the day and both darkness and light are alike to God. It is extraordinary to think that this light is not like light, and this darkness is not dark, and that beyond what we call dark and light is a light that darkens and a darkness that lightens.

Some autonomous philosophers will squirm in affront at the religious directness of agreeing with the psalmist. If I had quoted a poem, would they squirm at the aesthetic directness of it? The point is that crossings of the between are crucial. It does not matter if you go out or go in, go up or go down. God is there, and even on the boundary of nothing which is not nothing, God is there too. In the idiotic roots we are not just bound to self; nor in the outer immensity; nor in the dark abysses of our own hell are we self-being; nor on the exposed heights we are not self-binding. Up down, in out we find ourselves bound to the more than ourselves.

Even in hell, wherever hell is, if hell is at all, the divine is there. Hell is not beneath the between, or above it, but is the undoing of the between in the attempted closure on itself of the given porosity of being. Hell is being impervious. It is willing in the porosity that is nilling of the porosity. Being religious turns hell away from its imperviousness, in keeping unclogged the most intimate porosity of the human and divine. There was a time when I spoke of being religious more as marked by an urgency of ultimacy. The urgency is not just our urge but a power that is urgent in us, in the way that a call to be can be urgent. It comes from more than ourselves and yet intimately calls us to be more than ourselves. The urgency of ultimacy is perhaps is too redolent of the *conatus essendi* as endeavor to be. Being religious restores us to the most intimate passion of being that is prior to our endeavor to be. The *passio essendi* returns us to the most naked porosity—to our being as nothing—nothing without being given to be by the ultimate origin of coming to be.

Being nothing we are given to be as something, existing in a space between nothing and something. Our being something is itself constitutively defined by a nothing, for it would not be were it not received in being by virtue of the gift of the origin. This is an endowed being at all, an endowed being for self, a being for self endowed with the extraordinary power to be beyond self. This is to be as gifted with the promise of an agapeic transcending. Our being is not just a lack seeking itself—it is that and more, it is a hidden gift of surplus promise and power which energizes even the lack that knows its suffering for want of what is more than itself. Hell is hatred of our being as nothing, hatred of our being something as endowed. Hell, hating all porosity, would endow itself, but it can create nothing through itself alone. Its creating can only be an uncreating, and its "no" to the nothing becomes itself a more voiding nothing, for it cannot consent to the something that is its own being as endowed. Hell as nilling is a counterfeit double of the original porosity, but it is a sterile porosity rather than a fertile one.

Finally there is no wording of hell, but the between is worded. There we partake of a *reverence* that constitutes us as the porous beings we are in the company of the divine. I would speak of a primal reverence that is before determinate respect, before this or that form of honoring. The attenuation of reverence in modernity again goes with the apotheosis of a certain autonomy. Reverence is always before an otherness that exceeds one's autonomy. It shows true finitude that bows in love before what is superior. I would also speak of a *confidence* that has something of this primal character. Confidence is a "*fides* with"—something it confided to us in our being. We might seem to be self-affirming and hence expressing something of self-confidence. But this is later than a more primal ontological confidence. Hence despite error and evil, there is an ever reborn trust in the intelligibility and goodness of being. We live this, and only because this primal confidence has been confided to us. If it were not, we would not be the seekers we are. As we search the between the seeking becomes a mixture of confidence and uncertainty. The uncertainty is the reflux of mystery back on a more primal confidence, which when it wakes up to self and world is made to wonder about what is there, and also our relation to what is there.

In a way, only after the fall do we awake to ourselves both in the mode of lacking confidence and in the mode of an overconfidence that insists on itself as the measure of all that is. There is a metaxology of true confidence: not the abjectness of fallenness, not the self-inflation of hubris. Already there is a trust *with*—the "con" of con-*fides*—faith with—calling us to a form of fidelity—and not just fidelity to self but the incognito other with whom we are what we are. The incognito companion is more than us, before us, above us, beneath us, enabling us, restoring us, redeeming us. Religion is this confidence understanding itself in relation to the divine source, and the call to fidelity beyond despair. This is the call to the ultimate communion—the community of agapeic service. In our over self-confidence we have ended up abject—master of everything we end up subject to powers beneath us. Flying up we end being thrown down. This is not a true patience to the heights but a despair on the flat.

How approach God from the between, or be approached? For the philosophical thinker one risks being too religious, and for the religious person one risks being too philosophical. It is not easy to find a way between these, and indeed to find a voice poised between humility and audacity. While speaking philosophically one needs to do some justice to the plurivocity of being religious. Nor is it impossible to speak theologically. We can glean from the immanent *metaxu* something of God's own metaxology.[10] Finite immanence itself is a between: it is not an absolute whole, and what wholeness marks it might be called an "open wholeness." This is part of the meaning of its ontological porosity. Given its ontological porosity we can speak of another "between": between given being and what ultimately enables it to be. This is a space between the finite between and the God of the between who is not the finite between. We might look on creation as God's metaxology—God's wording of the finite between.

The agapeic nature of divine metaxology, as I understand it, brings us closest to Christianity, but this is so in an essentially ecumenical sense. The many religions are communicated in the between, and clandestinely at work there is what I call the intimate universal.[11] The intimate universal is ecumenical, both with regard to the many mansions of Christianity itself and its family bonds with its sibling monotheisms. Indeed I have offered my own praise of paganism whose glory has always been its song of signs of the divine on the earth itself, its horror of our evacuation of creation of these signs. As above I demurred with respect to being without good, and good without being, so also I demur about being without God, or God without being. The between as sacredly worded tells against these "either/ors." Pagan celebration of the immanent gifts of the earth can be a sacred gratitude in its own way. This gratitude is part of our wording the between—wording the divine.

Paul Weiss once said to me about *Being and the Between* that he thought it did the impossible: redoing Hegel from a Kierkegaardian inside. I do not think of myself as redoing Hegel and would rather describe metaxological thought as transdialectical. The intimate universal is neither the concrete universal of idealism nor the existential singular uncontained by system. The God of monotheism allows the universal and the singular to be reconciled in the intimate universal. This, in a way, confirms Weiss's point, though I would still hesitate along these lines. There is a different relation of being aesthetic, ethical, religious in my work than Kierkegaard's, as there is a different understanding of the community of art, religion, and philosophy than in Hegel's doctrine of absolute spirit. I am at one with Kierkegaard in the sense of superior transcendence, though Kierkegaard and Hegel have something in common as sons of Lutheran Protestantism. Perhaps I am too Catholic and pagan in the sacramental sense of the given creation. I am not sure my sense of inwardness is anguished with the same stress as Kierkegaard's. I sense that superior transcendence has more of the sun of the south in it than the vanishing wintry light of northern climes allows. A metaxological philosophy must have something of the mediterranean about it, and the sun of the middle earth.

Within the between of finite immanence and bringing us to its porous boundary, there are what I call the hyperboles of being, and I will finish with these, though in fact they are passages, and understanding them is bound up with a religious crossing of the between. The *figurative* character of wording the between in relation to God is here important. I have spoken of metaphor, analogy, and symbol, as well as hyperbole, though one can discern the significance of the watchword of each of these figures: the "is" of metaphor, the "as" of analogy, the "with" of symbol, the "above" of hyperbole. The passages of these figures go in, go out, go down, go up. The hyperboles communicate more than the terms of immanence can circumscribe, for they are happenings of opening to ultimate transcendence as other to the immanent between.

I do not think we can fully appreciate these hyperboles without genuine metaphysical mindfulness of the primal ethos of being. I am talking as a philosopher, though I think nonphilosophers live these hyperboles, live in and out of them, though they do not always understand their significance, and sometimes misunderstand or betray their promise. I hold that the astonishing perplexity of God is best approached philosophically on the basis of the fullest senses of being thus given in the between, and what this fullness communicates. To divine the togetherness of God and given finite being, with reverent heed for their difference, and holy hesitation for the reserve of divine transcendence, we need a transdialectical *logos* of the *metaxu*. The community of God and the between is not captured in any whole claiming absoluteness by its immanent closure on itself. The "trans" of the metaxological is carried to the "above" of the *meta* by these surpluses of being, the hyperboles, manifest in the immanent whole. The very word "hyperbole" calls attention to this "throwing above," or "being thrown above": *hyper-ballein* in Greek. In the between we are thrown, but also thrown above, above the between.

First hyperbole—*the idiocy of being*: given finite being shows a sheer "that it is" which shines with an intimate strangeness. It happens to be without inherent necessity, and it might be called a surplus surd, but it is not absurd. The surplus givenness makes all finite intelligibilities possible, but it is presupposed by all and is not itself a finite intelligibility. Its surplus stuns us into mindfulness about what gives it to be at all, since it does not give itself to be, nor explain itself. The ontological patience of finite being makes mindfulness porous to what exceeds finite determination. To be as finite exceeds the terms of finitude itself. In being received as being, finitude is not simply thrown down in the between, but as hyperbolic and crossing the between it is thrown above itself.

Second hyperbole—*the aesthetics of happening*: astonishment becomes ontological appreciation of the incarnate glory of the manifest creation which, showing itself sensuously, exceeds finitization. Native to the material world, our nativity is saturated with rich ambiguity resistant to our soon intervening domestications. Appreciation of immanence passes a threshold of immanence into mysterious love of transience that exceeds transience. This aesthetic overdeterminacy of finitude makes us porous on the boundary of finitude, and we are transported, as if moved by a music in things, into another space of mindfulness hyperbolic to anything we can fix determinately in immanence.

Third hyperbole—*the erotics of selving*: the human being is intimately hyperbolic as both finite and yet infinitely self-surpassing. We are endowed with transcending power, but we do not endow ourselves. The immeasurable passion of our being as self-exceeding exceeds also the selving we are. It witnesses to a more primal porosity to what exceeds us. This erotics of selving is hyperbolic to a *conatus essendi* that drives itself to its own most complete self-determination in immanence. The *passio essendi* is marked by a primal porosity to what exceeds all determination and our own self-transcending.

Fourth hyperbole—*the agapeics of community*: beyond selving, our relations to others traverse the *metaxu* in receiving and in giving. The agapeics communicates a surplus generosity not only in being receptive to the gift of the other but in freeing us to give beyond ourselves to others. The giving again is the passing on of goodness itself. Giving on generously is the agapeic good of the "to be." In the finiteness of our lives together, there is the promise of a generosity beyond finite reckoning. In the agapeics of community there passes (on) a surplus good that makes itself available in an absolute porosity. Such an absolved porosity of the *passio essendi* ethically communicates itself as a *compassio essendi*. This communication takes us to the limit of ethical. In wording the between it is the incarnation of the holy.

These hyperboles, and most ultimately the hyperbole of agapeic community, offer us the richest figurations of the "to be" in finitude that also speak of the "too muchness," the overdeterminacy of being in which we participate. Wording the between, they communicate signs of the superlative overdeterminacy of God. Crossing in the between, the first hyperbole can turn us in, turn us towards a sacred intimacy, echoing the mystical side of being. The second turns us out, to the heavens and earth full of glory, and towards solidarity with the neighbor on the ethical side. The third turns us down as well as up, turns down into the clogged porosity and its purgatory, unclogging the abyss of the porosity and offering us trust to ascend again. The fourth is turned up in a transfiguring motion of readiness without demand, turned up, because what is above has come down in passage into the purged porosity. In and out, up and down intersect in the between, and confidence in the most intimate "withness" of the divine is twinned with reverence for its most superlative "aboveness." We are on an ultimate threshold, where the "withness" is so secretly nigh as to be almost incognito, the "aboveness" so surpassing as to be all but passing comprehension.

NOTES

1. See The Intimate Strangeness of Being: Metaphysics after Dialectic (Washington: Catholic University of America Press, 2012).

2. See "Between System and Poetics: On the Practices of Philosophy," in Between System and Poetics: William Desmond and Philosophy after Dialectics, ed. Thomas Kelly (Aldershot: Ashgate, 2007), 13–36.

3. It is worth remembering that Being and the Between is both a book on metaphysics and a book in metaphysics. Parts 1 and 2, on metaphysics, deal with metaphysical thinking and this fundamental fourfold sense of being; part 3, in metaphysics, deals metaxologically with origin, creation, things, intelligibilities, selves, communities, being true, being good.

4. On this, see The Intimate Strangeness of Being, chapter 6, "Metaxological Metaphysics and the Equivocity of the Everyday."

5. On this, see, The Intimate Strangeness of Being, chapter 10, "Ways of Wondering: Beyond the Barbarism of Reflection."

6. On aesthetic things, both in the inclusive sense and in the special artistic sense, see Philosophy and Its Others, chapter 2, as well as Art, Origins, Otherness.

7. See Art and the Absolute.

8. Parts I and 2 of Ethics and the Between deal with the ethos and the potencies of the ethical, as inflected and crossed by the fourfold sense of being; part 3 deals with ethical selvings, while part 4 deals more fully with ethical communities.

9. See Hegel's God, on sublationary infinitism; see also Is There a Sabbath for Thought? on postulatory finitism.

10. I can only refer here to *God and the Between* where I address our Godlessness and the resurrection for thought of a finesse for the primal ethos (part 1), our ways to God (part 2), the different ideas of God (part 3), and what God as agapeic origin means (part 4).

11. I have spoken about the intimate universal in a number of places, but see "Neither Cosmopolis nor Ghetto: Religion and the Intimate Universal," in *The Future of Political Theology: Religious and Theological Perspectives*, ed. P. Losonczi, A. Singh, and L-A Mika (Aldershot: Ashgate, 2012), chapter 7.

TWO THINKS AT A DISTANCE

An Interview with William Desmond
by Richard Kearney on 9 January 2011[1]

RK: Having just read the introduction to your *Being Between*[2] could you begin by saying a little bit for those who have not read it but would yet be interested in a personal sense of where you come from. In other words, as a fellow Irishman, I would like to start with the hermeneutical question: where do you speak from? Where does your philosophical thought originate in terms of your country, language, and creed, in addition to your intellectual influences, Irish or otherwise?

WD: I call that book my "Irish book," and it's a mixture of reflections and autobiographical pieces, plus brief essays on Irish thinkers and poets. In it I explain my sense of "being between" as a mixture of existential and more systematic/metaphysical considerations. I grew up in Ireland, where I did my BA and MA work, and then went to the U.S. to do a PhD. I might have gone to the U.K. or even to Leuven, but went to study in one of the then very few continental philosophy programs in the U.S.! I never regretted it, but going to America in the early seventies was a very different experience to nowadays when you can travel very easily between different countries and live between different countries, as you and I both do, in fact. But then when you went away a space opened up, and the possibility of mediating that space was in no way self-evident. So my experience was that the world in America was an entirely different world to the world I had experienced in Ireland, in that earlier time. And it struck me that there was no way of bringing those two worlds together into some kind of unity. Philosophically, at the same time I was thinking about the whole idea of unity and wholeness in the Hegelian sense. It struck me that this Hegelian sense finally collapsed differences in a manner that was not compatible with my own existential experience of "being between." As you know yourself, again from Irish history, being away can open up spaces that just cannot be reduced to or included in one overarching unity. That's one part of the existential background to my sense of "being between."

229

RK: You know the received wisdom, the cliché of the angry expatriate— Joyce opting for "exile, silence, and cunning" and leaving it all behind him; Beckett following Joyce to Paris, preferring "France at war to Ireland at peace," and so on . . . There's a whole history of Irish intellectual exodus. Did you have any sense of that when you first left Ireland to go to the U.S.?

WD: No, that was not on my mind. I went to do a PhD at Penn State in 1974–78.

RK: Did you stay there then, or did you come back to Ireland after the PhD?

WD: I returned to Ireland in 1979, and then went back to the U.S. in 1982. I had a teaching job in the U.S., in St. Bonaventure University in upstate New York. But we decided as a family to come back to live in Ireland. So after a year I gave up the job—a tenure-track job at that—to come back to live in Ireland. I had a number of one-year jobs, two years in Cork, and one year in Maynooth. I would have stayed in Ireland had I got a permanent job there at that particular point. My return to America was an involuntary one in that regard, though that said, my debt to America is immense.

RK: To return to James Joyce's sense of Irish paralysis, did you ever feel that Cork or Ireland was paralyzing, from the point of the church, the state, the nation? Did these things impinge on your intellectual development in any way? Or were you an exception in that regard? Did you leave because you felt cramped in your native pace?

WD: I must say I didn't feel those kinds of cramps in the same way. It may have had to do partly with the fact that I wanted to do something, and I was going to try to do it in any case. And certainly at that time you had to study abroad and get your PhD elsewhere if you wanted to get a job teaching philosophy. It wasn't an escape. I came back to Cork after five years in America as I wanted to live in Ireland. But life intervenes. I went away again, but in some sense I have always been coming back. I always liked, indeed loved Ireland, still do. Being engaged with philosophy, you're always going to be on the outside in some sense. You learn, even if you don't go away, perhaps not silence, exile, and cunning, but a certain solitude, if you're serious about these things, and that's something I felt from a very early time.

RK: You have that nice play in the introduction to your Irish book about being at home when you're not at home, and not being at home when you're at home; and the play between the inside and the outside, and the *metaxu* when you're sort of hovering. This reminds me of the early Irish monastic notion of the *circumnavigatio*, the peregrination of monks around the island of Ireland and other islands beyond. It might be a "green navigation," and they would find land; or it could be a "white" one, and they might never come home. There was a sense that spiritually and intellectually it was important to go into some kind of exile, whether voluntary or involuntary, in order to rediscover oneself. You did go into exile—is "exile" the right word? You did circumnavigate, first to America, then back to Ireland, then to Europe. So you've spent quite a bit of your philosophical life outside of Ireland. Do you think geographical displacements matter? And do you think that the experience of conflict or collision between the cultures of Ireland, America, and Belgium affected your thinking in any way?

WD: I think so. I think it's bound up with language in some ways also. People often remark on what marvelous poets Ireland has produced. The relationship between art and philosophy, between poetry and philosophy was of serious interest to me from the start. But when you go outside, you can become more existentially aware that your use of English is not the same as that of the American or the English. The academics' use of language does not have that rich, saturated character that poetic language has. I think being outside kept me attentive to the plurivocity of languages, and also away from simply assuming a univocal professorial language. I'm an academic insider in one sense, but I have a strong conviction that philosophical language, like poetic language, can test certain limits, can bring us to the sense of being on the outside. Here in Belgium, surrounded by different languages, you become more self-conscious of the English language, its roots in Germanic, Anglo-Saxon sources, as well as romance and Greek. More might be said of about the peregrination, the navigation idea, about which you yourself have extensively written in *Navigations*.[3]

RK: Ireland is a very religious nation, probably with Poland one of the most religious nations in Europe. The recent scandals in the Irish church, the suffocating association of church and state in traditional Ireland: how did you negotiate all that? How did this influence your philosophy of religion, a key concern in your thought and one we both share? To what extent do you feel part of the Catholic intellectual tradition? Or outside of it? Angry and antagonistic? Or empathic and engaged? Where do you come down on that whole issue at the moment?

WD: You have to distinguish between earlier versions of yourself and later versions. I joined the Dominicans for ten months or so when I was seventeen and spent some time in St. Mary's Priory in Pope's Quay in Cork as a novice. The experience of being a member of a religious community was very significant and formative in a way not easy to measure. This was back in the late sixties when everything was in turmoil in the West in relation to politics, religion, and culture in general. In the years of turmoil at the beginning of the seventies, I never turned my back on religion, though I was touched and troubled by the questions raised by thinkers like Marx and Nietzsche, and by the feeling that atheism was becoming the default position for many intellectuals. As a younger person, of course, the perplexities were more painful, and though they never go away, they become different. I never set out to be a religious thinker, but that triad of art, philosophy, and religion, which I later saw canonized by Hegel, supplied sources of nourishment in my thinking. In studying Hegel I had difficulty with some of the reigning powers in academic philosophy in Ireland at the time. The association was that if one is studying Hegel one is probably a Marxist, and there is a line of connection between Hegel and Lenin and Stalin, and we know where all that leads to . . . It would have been far easier to get a position in Ireland had I written on somebody like Aristotle or Aquinas. But then as the years went by there were resonances in my philosophy that came from those inherited religious sources, and decades later I find myself being clapped on the back for my timely defense of religion in this godless age . . .

RK: I want to move on to the role of art and poetry in your philosophy, but do you want to say more on the religious question before I do . . . ?

WD: The authority of institutional religion has been seriously attacked in recent years, or should I say, institutional religion has repeatedly shot itself in the foot. I find this very disturbing. It's not that horrible happenings are to be brushed under the carpet; far from it. Obviously, the institutional churches do not exhaust the sources of piety and religion in the human condition. Nevertheless, the diminishing of finesse for sacred things disturbs me quite a lot. It's a complicated issue. Religion is more than the religions, more than the institutional expressions of religion. Some of the discourse these days is not sufficiently finessed on that score. Nor is it finessed enough about the need for worthy institutions as the historical communal carriers of our ultimate pieties.

RK: We'll come back to that later in talking about your philosophy of religion and where it fits in today in the European and analytic traditions, and in the history of ideas generally. But before that I would like to press you more on the Irish hermeneutic background. There are three major coordinates in your thought: art, philosophy, and religion. As you point out in the introduction to your Irish book, the Irish poetic culture is extremely rich and acknowledged the world over. Your writing picks up on that: you write beautifully; you write very poetically. There is an aesthetic of performance in your writing. You don't just write *about* art—as you do of course in *Art and the Absolute* and in the Irish book in your essays on Yeats, Swift, and others—you also write artistically. Your thinking performs a certain poetic stance, style, and voice. Now that can be seen, I think, as very compatible with your Irish background. And indeed you quote from the Irish quite a few times in your Irish book. And the mythological figure of Oisín comes up in other books. This Irish poetic and spiritual background is not self-conscious or self-reflexive, but it does appear to inform your work in deep ways. It is a long tradition of course going back to the great pioneering saints—Patrick, Brendan, Colmcille, and later figures like John Scotus Eriugena or Bishop Berkeley. On that score, you and I have argued there is an Irish intellectual tradition of some kind. However, this as you know has been contested by a lot of people, most recently John Banville who said Ireland never produced a philosopher and never will and that Irish philosophy is a contradiction in terms. He's not the only one who thinks that. One has seen it cited again and again: we're the dreamers of dreams, the music makers, but we're not thinkers. Matthew Arnold and others in the British colonial context also said the Irish were feckless, imaginative Celts: they could stay quaint and stay put. What's your view on all that? If Irish poetry is widely acknowledged, and Irish religion is equally recognized, what about Irish thought?

WD: Irish history is marked by repeated brokenness and relative recovery, and surely this must be considered in relation to cultural and intellectual traditions. We find something many-voiced, and sometimes the voices speak violently, sometimes speak in love, sometimes the voices fall entirely silent. In that situation it is not possible to detect a one-voiced or univocal culture. That sense of a multivocal conversation, even in brokenness itself, is well communicated by your work, as well as the recent book by Tom Duddy. To someone who says that Ireland never did nor will produce a philosopher, one has to reply with the immortal words of the Rolling Stones: "Hey! You! Get off of my cloud!" The possibility of thinking is proved by its actuality or its performance. There's a certain sense in which what I'm trying to do is performatively prove not just the possibility of Irish thinking but the actuality of it.

RK: I agree that in our respective books on Irish thought, we make a pretty good case for a strong and distinctive Irish intellectual tradition running from Eriugena through Berkeley to Burke and others. We're both on the same side on this. But why do you think there is such resistance to it?

WD: There are a number of different sources. I will just voice a conjecture from the Catholic side, so to say. The Catholic Irish have emerged from peasant conditions, a hugely practical people and at the same time hugely skeptical of any fancy notions. So thinking isn't given the serious respect that it deserves. The poetic tradition in its own way has worked against it in its own self-understanding. Perhaps it is not quite the Arnoldian vision of the imagination loosed from the discipline of thinking. However, it seems to me that to suggest immense thought does not go into the production of these great works betrays a very superficial understanding of the greatness of poetry itself. And possibly a third source is the Irish Catholic religious tradition defined by a certain deference to authority and a certain scholastic initiation into a particular school manner of thinking. Thinking outside of those school parameters had a certain danger to it. The dominance of the Catholic tradition in Ireland meant that waywardness was sometimes tamed or damped down. Those are three possible reasons why the waywardness of thinking was hindered. And even in strong traditions, without a certain waywardness in thinking, the tradition will not renew itself.

RK: It is useful to recall here how much interaction there has always been between the Irish and the European minds, going back to Eriugena, who translates Dionysius for Charles the Bald at the Court of Laon and then John Toland wandering through the continent and exchanging ideas with Leibniz, Locke, and others. And then there were the Irish Colleges all over Europe, in Paris, Salamanca, Cracow, Prague, Rome. Then the great Anglo-Irish thinkers like Berkeley, Tyndall, Molyneux and Burke. All had a very keen sense of the European intellectual tradition and that Ireland was part of it. They weren't isolationist nationalists, or anything of the sort. It seems to me ironic then that there has been this resistance to the notion of an Irish philosophical tradition and capacity. This is a question we've both asked, and that you've addressed in those remarks. But taking up the idea of biography as destiny, what do you make of your ending up in Louvain where so many of the last generation of Irish philosophers, including some of our teachers, were educated? I know there is still for you the U.S. connection with Villanova, and there are Irish connections. You came from Irish universities that were very Louvain-oriented. And then you wind up yourself at Leuven. What is your sense of this—Pride? Serendipity? Irony?

WD: Yes, there is an irony in ending up in Leuven/Louvain of all places. It is interesting that we have to refer to it often in terms of its name in *two* languages—Flemish and French—a point not without relevance to the Irish theme of doubleness. Historically, the presence of the Irish in Leuven has been very significant. It was a place of refuge for the Irish—a home away from home, so to say. The Irish College in Leuven was where the first book in Irish was printed; from here Mícheál Ó Clérigh embarked on his work on the *Annals of the Four Masters*. Perhaps there is something serendipitous about my being here. Leuven is a place of the spirit for Ireland, though it's not Ireland. It's another layer of "being between" for me. Perhaps it was simpler when it was just between America and Ireland, though while here I have been hugely involved with international students from all continents. Also, in my years here I have been trying to get my head around Flemish/ Dutch to access and participate in something of this other world here. I'm still "in the midst" of all that.

RK: I also resonate very much with the idea of intimate otherness, the notion of the Irish mind as double that has so fascinated us both in our writing. And then you have the notions of heterodoxy and comedy. They're all connected. In relation to your own work I often note a deeply comic strain, and knowing you personally I can say you've got a very Irish sense of humor. Ironic, impish, wry, sometimes dark—it is not unrelated to the other side of the Irish imagination, the melancholic. I suspect this is an element that not many people pick up in your thought. And yet it is not confined to the Irish sense of contradiction. There is something universal about it too.

WD: Well, I could give a classic answer in relation to the spirit of irony that runs throughout a certain tradition of philosophy from the Socratics onwards. To my knowledge, the Greeks had a great sense of fun, which is not unlike the craziness that can take over the Irish when they start having discussions.

RK: But Aristotle is hardly a barrel of laughs . . .

WD: No, not Aristotle, no. But I find a lot of comedy in Plato. In the *Symposium* he skirts on blue, indeed touches it. I know Plato is normally presented as the dour-faced philosopher of the theory-of-ideas or the sourpuss of eros . . .

RK: Your idea of idiot wisdom is very Socratic, isn't it?

WD: Yes it is. And the spirit of dialectic itself can be turned to very comic uses. Modern dialectic in the hands of Hegel is not particularly comic, but there is a family relationship between the two. I think that one of the things about the comic in Ireland is that it's on the boundary between sense and nonsense. There are practices of philosophy that will always withdraw from that porous boundary between sense and nonsense, but I think good philosophy is always at that porous between where the nonsensical can take on a significance that doesn't fit in with standard ways of thinking. I think it's also a sense of humanity, which is often lost in some of the great thinkers, and also in the professionals—humor brings us back to the human condition, to the *humus* of our fleshed finitude. Where do you get that sense of the elemental flesh except in comedy itself? I'm convinced there's this jubilating energy in the best of comedy that refreshes your appreciation of being alive at all. And if you can get some of that into thinking, it's the thing to do.

RK: And it is very open-ended.

WD: Yes that's right.

RK: One last thing, and we'll leave the Irish connection. Why of all the figures in Celtic mythology does the figure of Oisín capture your imagination?

WD: It's probably the fact that he's a poet in the first instance and that he's half mortal, half immortal—already born as a being of the between where poetry and the sacred are twinned. I am interested less in the significance of journey to the land of youth (*Tir na nÓg*) than in the return, in the experience of a lag, in that sense of being where home is but knowing that home is no longer. Yet, having vanished, something of the mystery of home has entered into the soul. In that lag, in that opening up of a space of mindfulness, in that porosity, so to say, you outlive yourself; you've lived beyond yourself. That notion of outliving yourself is almost Lear-like in that he too outlived himself. Lear speaks of taking on the mystery of things, of becoming one of "God's spies."

RK: But you relate this to what you call in another book posthumous existence.

WD: Yes, posthumous mindfulness. There were occasions when I wanted to come back to Ireland, but things didn't work out. This was like a kind of death to me in some ways. In closing down some things, it opened up other things, not without a certain kind of suffering. From it can come a sense of being beyond, and yet from being beyond, one can be very much intimate to the here and now, though one sees the here and now quite differently, just with eyes that have gone beyond. It's not quite a hankering for the beyond in the old Platonic sense. I'm not hostile to that, and indeed the opening up of those other spaces here can make one more porous to a more radical sense of the beyond. There is an intimacy in living these porous immanent spaces of the soul. To communicate this is an extraordinarily difficult task.

RK: This ontological sense of living and thinking posthumously seems central to your own intellectual itinerary—the experience of the gap, the sundering, the loss, and the resulting metaphysical hankering.

WD: It's a kind of a double condition of being inside and outside at the same time. I probably am very lucky in having a good family life which anchors daily life in rich everyday realities. If I were a solitary, unattached person, I can't imagine what kind of creature I would be. I sometimes look at "insiders" and see that wonderful things can emerge from this "insideness." But having been to the outside, one looks at things differently. One is dissatisfied in one sense, but not bitter. It's not at all like Hegel's unhappy consciousness; it's a different kind of restlessness. At times it's a kind of restlessness, and at times it's a kind of serenity, a kind of paradoxical language; a kind of double language seems unavoidable.

RK: I find what you say very interesting. I have known you and your writing for a long time (we grew up in the same city, country, and culture after all) and have always been struck by your sense of double belonging. On the one hand, there is a very strong sense of family in your biography, a deep anchoring in your own family but also in more extended families. Spiritually, there is a sense of religious tradition in the best sense of the word, as mentioned above. And then the Platonic tradition in its various expressions seems to represent a kind of intellectual family. You've always had a skeptical eye for the fast and quick, for cheap notions of the destruction of metaphysics when not properly understood or when used as an excuse to ignore the rich complexity of the Western philosophy of Being, as if one could just sweep it aside and begin all over again from scratch, from the ground zero of our transcendental egos. And yet you do have a real fidelity to the solitary, unmoored Oisín figure or what I once described as the long-distance runner. There is that bold, pioneering, marathon side to your thinking. I sense it is the tension between the two—the family and the single one—that opens up the *metaxu*, the middle space, the between them, which so characterizes the "Desmond" mode of thinking.

WD: These are very helpful and generous remarks. I do think that these days the singular, even solitary side of philosophy is not stressed properly, not well appreciated by many. But yes, you are very right to stress family in a variety of different senses, some more intimately personal, some binding one more broadly to one's people, and to one's intellectual and spiritual heritage—all that was very well put by you and is important to me. As I get closer to retirement, I wonder where I will end up . . . it will of course be a family decision, but I find it almost impossible to get Ireland out of my mind and soul. So who knows!

RK: I would like to move on now from the more personal to a discussion of the four major coordinates of your thought: the philosophy of God, the philosophy of being, the philosophy of beauty, and philosophy of the good: what, in the metaphysical tradition, would be called the transcendentals. How would you relate to this suggestion of a certain isomorphic mapping of your thought onto the great transcendentals?

WD: When it's pointed out like that, it is very evident, but it certainly wasn't intended on my part. I didn't think of myself as remapping the transcendentals in any self-conscious way. It's just the way the cookie crumbled, the way the cards fell, when I did my thinking. I always sensed there was more to metaphysics than many of the standard criticisms of metaphysics since Kant right into our own time, the strange mystery of being called for a rethinking of what it means to be. Likewise, the devaluation of being in modernity has deeply engaged me—being has been denuded of any sense of qualitative value. So my desire to rethink some sense of the "to be" as good—this is not just an abstract transcendental doctrine but is bound up with the nihilism of modernity where given being is a valueless thereness that we exploit and appropriate as we wish. Likewise, the surplus qualitative value of the aesthetic has always been with me. The return to the elemental flesh is very important in the aesthetic. It's not just a question of art but rather of art itself growing out of that elemental flesh. In *Art and the Absolute* I wrote on beauty in relation to Hegel and idealism, but in the last year or so I've been thinking quite a lot about the gift of beauty, the strange energizing patience there is to our exposure to beauty, about the paradoxical patience that takes us outside of ourselves before we know we've been taken outside of ourselves. And the religious then, that's also been with me all the time in some sense or other. There has been a fruitful cross-fertilization between metaphysics, aesthetics, ethics, and religion all the time. But it wasn't strategic. It's illuminating to me for someone to point out that this could be fitted into something like the classical scheme of the transcendentals, but it wasn't thought out in that way in advance at all.

RK: Let's pursue this relation between questions of Being and God. As you know, much of contemporary continental thought, and even further afield, is predicated upon the idea that God is beyond being, God is without Being, otherwise than Being, *Dieu sans l'être, Dieu au délà l'être, Dieu après l'etre*. We find it in Levinas, Jean-Luc Marion, and in Derrida and Caputo, too, in the wake of the Heideggerian critique of ontotheology. How do you fit into this conversation? How do you propose to redeem or retrieve Being for a philosophy of God?

WD: I've sometimes wondered if Heidegger gives us being without the good, and Levinas gives us the good without being, and whether what we rather need is a new thinking of the hospitality of being and good. The figure of Heidegger has cast a huge shadow over those who want to break loose from him. So the Heideggerian sense of being would obviously be an issue at stake there. I agree with Heidegger about the need to reraise the so-called forgotten question of being. But how it's done is another question. And I worry about a *second* forgetfulness of being, even among the admirers of Heidegger, who comment more on Heidegger than think on being. I speak of a double sense in the "*meta*" of metaphysics. "*Meta*" can mean both "in the midst" and also "beyond." I see these two senses as joined in the between, one referring us to a more immanent ontology, the other to a transcending of thought to what exceeds immanence. I think that what I was trying to do in *Being and the Between* is to think the question of being again, in different systematic terms to Heidegger himself. I've wondered to what extent Heidegger's own turn to being is in the slipstream of the modern devaluation of being. I don't find that devaluation in the premoderns at all. The intimacy of being and good is much more operative in some way or other. Again much depends on what one means by being. I take issue with the sublationary infinitism of Hegel, as well as the postulatory finitism of Heidegger. For instance, in *God and the Between* I talk about the "hyperboles of being": happenings of immanence that exceed the terms of immanence and that bring us to the boundary where finitude becomes porous to what exceeds it. At this porous boundary one's language tends to become paradoxical, as both inside and outside, immanent and transcendent, and in a manner that it is not inhospitable to the sense of the divine as beyond being. For instance, I speak of "God beyond the whole" in *God and the Between*. How we fare on that porous boundary is at issue. One of the worries I have of a God without being is that you end up back in a kind of nihilism where you have being without God. The absence of any sense of sacred presence in the world as we live it can feed into a kind of religious nihilism once again.

RK: That's very interesting. I sense in your thought an existential, almost phenomenological (although you don't use this term very often) description of experience expressed in a poetic philosophical voice. I suspect here a positive influence of Kierkegaard and Nietzsche. You're writing with quite a sense of ontological witness: "This is the way I experience being, not as something impoverished, destitute, and derelict, but as having a deep immanent richness that opens onto something more, something else." And to pursue the hermeneutic question of how this fits into the "family conversation" with the great philosophers in the history of ideas, I would ask whether you see a certain affinity with the Aristotelian notion of being as act? Or with Spinoza's *désir d'être*—*the conatus essendi*, the desire to be? Or with aspects of Hegel?

WD: Hermeneutically in relation to the tradition of philosophy, obviously I have been most engaged with Hegel. Kant has been a huge presence also, especially in relation to the moral Kant. But there is . . .

RK: But Kant does not have a real celebration of being.

WD: Oh, no he's totally evacuated; he's anorexic from the point of view of the richness of being. He tries to make up for that then in moral terms.

RK: And then Hegel humiliates being by turning it into speculative ideas.

WD: He does. Being for him is the emptiest of categories; it's pure indeterminacy. It has no determinacy whatsoever. Systematically I talk about the overdeterminacy of being which can't be reduced to a set of determinations. And it's not mere indeterminacy. It also exceeds what is perhaps the most important thing for Hegel, the self-determination of thought. In some of my works there are engagements with the things themselves; in other works there are more dialogical interactions with a variety of different thinkers. For instance, people sometimes ask me what I think about Heidegger, to whom I make some glancing references in my more systematic works. But there is a very long engagement in *Art, Origins, Otherness*. In a sense, I've tended to keep the more systematic explorations of issues and the more extended hermeneutical engagements with diverse thinkers a little separate. I like the existential sense of the ancients, for instance, the Socratic practice of starting from where we find ourselves in the midst of things and then working out from there in a variety of more complicated intellectual moves. If you can't bring your complicated intellectual moves back to the concreteness of the human condition, there's something not true to the practice of philosophy there. I sometimes worry whether our practices of philosophy have become so anorexic that we ask less and less of thought, like conceptual hunger artists who want to prove their "radicality" in the evacuation of being. There are analytic hunger artists; there are continental ones. But sometimes less

TWO THINKS AT A DISTANCE 241

is not more; less is just less, until finally there is nothing left. We cannot eat, but the feast of life is all around us.

RK: This confirms the existential tenor of your thought. I already mentioned an affinity with Kierkegaard and Nietzsche, but there is also one with people like Gabriel Marcel, who has a very important intellectual appreciation of and attentiveness to the goodness of Being.

WD: Yes, indeed. If you remember some years ago, in your *Routledge Companion to Contemporary Continental Thought*, I did the philosophy of religion section on Jaspers, Marcel, and Levinas, so I've always admired Marcel. Again you have that triad of art, philosophy, and religion, but his attempts at a concrete ontology are often immensely suggestive. He's not a great systematic thinker, but his finessed eye for rich experiences is very worthwhile. He's understudied at the moment, probably because of his openness to the religious.

RK: A very important aspect of twentieth-century thinking I would like to broach here is psychoanalysis. Julia Kristeva says there are four ways to deal with the distressed subject in our contemporary world: art, religion, philosophy, and psychoanalysis. How would you engage with the questions raised by psychoanalytic thought—from Freud and Lacan to Kristeva and Zizek?

WD: Did Freud say something to the effect that the Irish were one race to whom psychoanalysis was of no use whatsoever? Whether he said it or not, I have always found "psychoanalytic" nourishment in great artists like Dostoevsky and Shakespeare. The erotics of being is central in my work, as also is the agapeics of being—a more ultimate and amazing grace. I think one could say that the agapeics of being are generally absent in psychoanalytic theory, though psychoanalytic practice—when it is practicing the truth with love—might be seen as a kind of agapeic metaxology—wording the between with love. Psychoanalysis, of course, is rightly engaged with the equivocity of human desire, as I am also. (Check out the fulsome kiss delivered in a footnote in *Ethics and the Between*!) Two of the thinkers with whom I've engaged very deeply are Schopenhauer and Nietzsche. Of course, the notion of the unconscious was coming to the fore in Schelling and some other thinkers around the time of the high noon of German idealistic philosophy. But especially in Schopenhauer, what strongly comes through is that sense of the dark origin on the other side of the principle of sufficient reason. I've really thought very deeply about the idea of a darker origin that lives itself in us. And similarly I think it's deeply present in Nietzsche, though he wants to affirm it in a manner that turns against the Schopenhauerian negation. In my youth I read much more of Freud. But my sense is that his underlying ontological-metaphysical presuppositions are very close to Schopenhauer and Nietzsche and their sense of the dark origin . . .

RK: As a negative, devouring force . . .

WD: Right. I call it the dark origin in a number of things I've written. It can be hugely significant in altering how we perceive being to be at bottom. If the dark origin is the most ultimate principle, it shifts the whole ethos of being. Instead of trying to get out of Plato's cave to see the sun above redeeming the ground below, we dig below the ground of the cave to a kind of second underground. It's more like going down deeper into Hades than trying to emerge onto the surface of the earth, there to face the heaven above us and the light that shines upon us. And it's for reasons like these that my primary metaphysical and ontological considerations have been focused on Schopenhauer and Nietzsche. And in both, of course, the questions of art and religion come up strongly. You already mentioned in passing the *conatus essendi*, but I've tried to talk about the *passio essendi* as more primordial than *conatus essendi*. Our endeavor to be is subtended by our being given to be. Our self-affirming will to be emerges out of a more primal being given to be. I even interpret *conatus* in the light of the co- of co-nature: conatus is a "being born with." We are birthed as ourselves but not by ourselves; we are marked by a "with," that from the origin binds us to what is more than we can produce through ourselves alone. In that sense, the conatus itself can't be just described in terms of a self-affirming will to be.

RK: This reminds me of Paul Claudel's wonderful notion of *connaisance* as *co-naissance*, a mutual birthing of being and knowing, an emerging together of self and other, and by extension, of being and God.

WD: That's a very interesting and relevant point. In relation to what I call the *passio essendi*, I talk about the porosity of being, a porosity that also defines our being. Perhaps there's something of a family resemblance to the psychoanalytic exploration of the unconscious. That resemblance is something that could be worked out more fully, but I haven't done it myself in relation to psychoanalysis. My own emphasis has been more ontological and metaphysical, in any case. I would say one of my hesitations always about Freud has been the ideological hostility that was part of his attitude to religion. This struck me as a very superficial Enlightenment hostility—even though so many of the things that surface in his own way of thinking, in fact, are saturated with mythic and religious significance. As to Žižek, I do enjoy reading him. Obviously he's complicated and at times hard to pin down, but I find him immensely enjoyable. He has brilliant insights, but he shimmies all over the place—once one reads beyond five or six pages one wonders what it all amounts to. He's the Lacanian lord of misrule. He's keeping the cultural commentariat in business these days.

RK: There is a dialectic going on there . . .

WD: Žižek *is* at times the jester of post postmodernism, so to say. Unlike Marx, whom he admires and who wanted to demystify Hegel, Žižek strikes me as in the business of a new mystification of Hegel (with the help of the "indivisible remainder" of Schelling!) . . . But to get back to psychoanalysis: I've kept a certain distance from psychoanalysis, I think because of that diffidence coming from the Freudian unwillingness to face more overtly the metaphysical implications of the Schopenhauerian horrors. I think we need to address, in more deep going *philosophical* terms, the sense that at bottom being is horror. This would also bring in the question of the hospitality of being to good. It would also mean revisiting the erotics of being—and the agapeics. These things are at the basis of some of my diffidence, in any case.

RK: . . . And in a way, maybe, an excess of the hermeneutics of suspicion.

WD: An excess of that, to be sure.

RK: We've talked about your Irish origins, your intellectual and spiritual origins . . . how you got to where you are now. So what's the next step? You've done your metaphysics. You've done your aesthetics. You've done your ethics and philosophy of religion. What's your next project? You're always writing something, being reborn again and again. So what's next?

WD: To be honest, when I finished *God and the Between*, I felt that it was like one feels after running a marathon. You don't realize how much it takes out of you. You can continue, but secretly the energy has been drained. I felt that way after finishing that book, to the point where I wondered whether I should have finished it at all. I have my energies back now. I have a number of projects. I'm working on a collection of essays (to be published before too long) entitled *The Intimate Strangeness of Being: Metaphysics after Dialectic*. I have a folder that I call "Consecrations"—you read one of the pieces called "Consecrated Love"—which I'd like to make into a book. I have a book on evil which I'm thinking of calling *Philosophical Nocturnes: On the Evil of Being*, and I have a book on what I call *The Intimate Universal* which is on religion, art, and politics in a very broad sense. I have plenty of books I could write in that more recognizable sense, but as I get older I would like to write what I simply call "Songs." At the end of *Philosophy and Its Others*, I write about this idea of "thought singing its other." I'd like to write songs which would not be simply poetic, religious, or philosophical but would be poetic-philosophical-religious. Whether I will do it or not is up to the gods. The songs would address something like the seven ages of man—for there are songs that are appropriate to earlier life, songs more fitting for adolescence and middle maturity, songs for the bitterness and ripeness of older age. If I ever do this, I would have to enter a very different space of the soul where thinking allows itself to become porous to voices and insinuations that don't come from standard academic practices. Will it ever happen? It might; it depends. Maybe I'll have to go back and live in Ireland to write those songs.

RK: I was just thinking this could be material for perambulations on the Irish beaches at Inchydoney and Owenhincha.

WD: I was thinking that myself too. That would be something entirely different, well maybe not entirely, but it would try to answer some sense of the poetic muse, or rather the religious poetic muse that has haunted me on and off over the years. I think I would have to undergo a set of spiritual exercises, to use the Ignatian term, to open myself to another space where something other might come to visit. I couldn't just produce it. I'd have to be met with or be accosted by some sources of inspiration beyond myself.

RK: Well, I look forward to further talks and walks on the west Cork coast-land as you sing the other, the stranger.

NOTES

1. The interview was done on Skype. The title is an echo of this—thinking at a distance—as "two thinks at a time" (Joyce).

2. *Being Between: Conditions of Irish Thought* (Galway, Ireland: Leabhar Breac/Center for Irish Studies, 2008)

3. Richard Kearney, *Navigations: Collected Irish Essays, 1976–2006* (Dublin: Lilliput, 2006).

INDEX

absence, 45, 48, 109, 168, 206, 239
absolute, ix–x, 10, 18, 20, 36, 42,
44–45, 47, 55, 63–65, 67, 74, 79–81,
87–89, 97, 100–101, 107–108, 110,
112, 116–17, 137–40, 142, 144,
146–47, 158, 171, 179–80, 186, 191,
197–98, 200, 202, 217, 219, 223–25;
agapeic, 88–89, 113; erotic, 88, 113;
origin(al), 45, 88–89, 107, 112, 119,
139, 147, 153
abyss, 80, 97, 104, 166, 206, 218, 221,
226
Academy, the, 26, 177
Adam, 221
Adorno, Theodor, 159
aesthetic(s), 24, 50–51, 54, 57, 69–71,
82–83, 103–105, 120–21, 123–26,
151–53, 156–63, 167, 176–77,
184–86, 188–89, 195, 204–208,
210–16, 218, 221, 224–25, 226 n. 6,
233, 238, 243; ecological, 211; Post-
Kantian, 156, 167; Western, 152. See
also beauty
agape, 19, 29, 31, 34, 44, 54, 57, 81,
83, 119, 140, 213
agapeic mind, 19–20, 22, 42, 49–50,
54–60, 87–88, 90, 125
agapeic origin(al), 71, 73–75, 88–89,
106, 119–20, 129, 139, 189, 191–92,
215, 227 n. 10. See also God, origin,
source
agapeic service, 75, 80–82, 104–105,
216; community of, 75, 82, 132–33,
216–18, 223
Ahab, Captain, 128
Alcibiades, 177

Alighieri, Dante, 201
America. 229–31, 235
analogy, viii, 112, 121, 124, 224;
doctrine of, 142; of being, viii, 67.
See also hyperbole, metaphor, symbol
analytic philosophy, ix
Ananke, 90, 139
Anaxagoras, 166
Anselm, St., 126
antinomy between autonomy and
transcendence, 6, 65, 219
Apollo, 181
Aquinas, St. Thomas, viii, xv, 66, 110,
124, 128, 136, 141, 173–74, 232
Archimedean point, 20
Argus, 162
Aristotle, 23, 26, 55, 136, 161–62, 165,
172, 174, 215–16, 232, 235
Arnold, Matthew, 233
astonishment, 4, 12, 19, 21, 25–27,
29, 31, 37, 95–96, 103, 110,
135–36, 145, 177, 189–91, 202,
204, 219, 225; agapeic, 21, 29–30,
34, 36–37, 39–40, 80; elemental,
25; first 27, 203; metaphysical, 4,
9, 172; original, 4, 25, 27–28, 117;
resurrection of, 31, 101. See also
curiosity, perplexity, wonder
atheism, x, xv, 91–92, 95, 108, 219,
232
Athens, xiv, 178
Atomism, 42–43, 47
Augustine, St., xv, 51, 216
Auschwitz, 45
autonomy, 6, 7, 57, 63–68, 75, 96,
98, 101, 104, 154, 186, 188, 190,

176–78, 180, 183, 185, 187–88,
192, 196, 202–203, 206–208, 210,
217–18, 221–22, 241

obedience, 65, 67
objectivity, 67, 125, 202
O'Clerigh, Michael, 235; *Annals of the
Four Masters*, 235
Oedipus, 169, 180
Oisin, 233, 236–37
ontology, vii–viii, 87, 170, 197, 239, 241
ontotheology, xv, 239
origin(al), 6, 10, 17, 20, 29, 33, 36–38,
47–48, 50, 56, 68, 73–74, 76, 78,
82, 88–89, 103, 106–12, 121, 124,
126–27, 129, 131, 135–42, 144–47,
151–56, 189–92, 195–96, 203,
221–22, 226 n. 3, 242–43, absolute
45, 89, 107, 112, 119, 145, 153,
167; agapeic, 71, 73–75, 88–89,
106, 119–20, 125, 127, 129, 135,
138–39, 141–42, 189, 191–92, 215,
227 n. 10; dark, 156, 175, 241–42;
Dionysian, 175; divine, 108, 111–12,
146; ultimate, 50, 175, 196, 221. *See
also* agapeic origin, God, source
Orpheus, 211
Othello, 161
otherness, vii, xiv, 3, 5, 10–11, 16, 19,
25, 27–28, 33–34, 37–39, 41–44,
49–50, 53–54, 57, 60, 64, 68, 70–73,
75, 77, 88–89, 95, 97, 99, 104,
111–12, 116, 142, 146, 151–64, 166,
174, 176, 185–87, 191–92, 198,
202, 204, 210, 212–13, 215, 218,
222; finite, 72, 215; intimate, 235;
inward, 37, 104, 128, 155, 166, 191,
199–200, 206, 218; irreducible, 146,
191; outer, 155; recalcitrant, 154;
second, 155; superior, 204, 219–20;
surplus, 69, 78, 106; tolerance of, 49,
156, 160–63
overdeterminacy/overdetermination, 4,
6, 26–27, 34–36, 47, 73, 111, 117,
122, 129, 132, 198–99, 208, 225–26,
240

Overman, the, 220
Owenhincha, 244

paganism, 223
Paley, William, 124
Paradise, 76
paradox, 49, 177, 185
Paris, 230, 234
Parmenides, 53, 143, 168, 173
participation, 6, 10, 22, 40, 75, 77, 93,
105, 113, 117, 125, 131–33, 142,
152, 155, 202, 205, 212, 216, 226,
235
particularity, 9, 49–50, 59, 161, 178,
180–81, 199
Pascal, Blaise 26, 67
passio essendi. 5, 99, 102, 105, 120,
122, 125–26, 129, 145–46, 188–89,
203, 205–206, 208, 212–14, 221,
225, 242. See also *compassio essendi,
conatus essendi,* porosity of being
patience, 11, 17, 27–28, 58–59, 60, 80,
99, 126, 128–30, 145, 157, 161, 196,
201–204, 208–10, 219–20, 223, 225,
238; paradoxical, 238; primal, 204,
206; ultimate, 120
Patrick, St., 233
perception, 123, 155, 157–59
perplexity, 3–4, 10, 12–13, 15–19,
21–22, 26–30, 36, 53–54, 69, 82–83,
103, 105, 110, 115, 126–27, 135,
169, 171, 173, 189–90, 202–203,
232; agapeic, 19; astonished,
121, 224; elemental, 15, 51, 197;
erotic/eros of, 19, 22, 29–31;
indeterminate, 26, 30–31, 37, 55,
172; metaphysical, 17–19; second,
21, 37, 55. *See also* astonishment,
curiosity, wonder
phenomenology, viii, x
Plato, xiii–xiv, xvi n. 1, 9, 30, 37,
48–50, 65–66, 87, 142, 156,
167, 171–82, 200–201, 216, 235,
242; *Phaedo*, 177, 179, 181, 182;
Platonism, 69, 211, 215; *Symposium*,
xvi n. 1, 169, 235; *Timaeus*, 174

26284666R00170

Made in the USA
Lexington, KY
21 December 2018